LONDONERS

By the same author

The Men who would be King

LONDONERS

Nicholas Shakespeare

SIDGWICK & JACKSON
LONDON

To my parents

First published in Great Britain in 1986
by Sidgwick & Jackson Limited

Copyright © Nicholas Shakespeare 1986

ISBN 0 283 99231 X (soft cover)
ISBN 0 283 99173 9 (hard cover)

Phototypeset by Falcon Graphic Art Limited
Wallington, Surrey
Printed in Great Britain by
The Garden City Press Limited,
Letchworth, Hertfordshire SG6 1JS
for Sidgwick & Jackson Limited
1 Tavistock Chambers, Bloomsbury Way
London WC1A 2SG

Contents

Acknowledgements

My greatest debt of gratitude is to those who agreed to talk to me. Sadly I was not able to include them all. The majority who do feature here are known only by their first names. It would be a breach of trust to credit them in full as they deserve. But this is their book.

However, I could not have written it without the help of others. Namely Mark Bernard, Kay Brophy, Kenneth Campbell, Francesca Cullen, Leslie Cunliffe, Peter Davalle, Patrick Disney, Antonia Douro, Justin Dowley, Krishna Dutta, Ede & Ravenscroft, Christopher Edwards, Joanna Edwards, Carlo Gebler, David Gentleman, Victoria Glendinning, Geordie Grieg, Walter Harris, Jaap Harskamp, John Hatt, John Higgins, Kerry Hood, Philip Howard, William Howard, Stephen Humphries, Simon Jenkins, Stephen Jones, Charles Knevitt, Emma Lampard, Kate Lampard, Carol Martys, John Neary, Helen O'Brien, Caryl Phillips, Dominic Prince, Christopher Shakespeare, Alexandra Shulman (not least, for her sultry tolerance), Michael Steele, Emma Tennant, Alan Titmuss, Anne Turner, Dominic Turner, Philip Ward, Peter Washington and Frances Whitaker; also British Telecom, Capital Radio, London Transport, the River Police and *Southside* magazine.

I would also like to thank *The Times* for permission to reprint material from two profiles and an article, published in August 1984, on Lonely Hearts.

Foreword

In December 1983 I was 'phoned by Nigel Newton of Sidgwick & Jackson and invited to Simpson's in the Strand. He had an idea for a book, he said, in a state of high excitement, which I would be mad to refuse. In the full knowledge that it is harder than a ship's biscuit to get a decent lunch out of a publisher, I accepted on the nail. Besides, I had never been to Simpson's. Nor, unfortunately, was I aware of its stipulation that diners must wear a jacket and tie.

Straitjacketed inside a waiter's white blazer many sizes too small and suffocated by a shirt which had not before been buttoned, I felt so embarrassed for myself – and then my host – that I signalled agreement to his proposal for a book on the subject of Londoners.

Once committed, I was relieved to discover a man who some years before had written a volume with the same title. I took him to a modest Indian restaurant in Bayswater to seek his advice. Notwithstanding his air – an air of unaccountable gloominess – I chatted about how much I was looking forward to the task. Gazing up from the menu he suddenly said, 'Don't do it!' Thus galvanised into action he continued with his warning. 'Books on London are a notorious graveyard.'

I cannot recall what we talked about after that, but the reader must forgive me if eating out does not loom large in the following pages.

I must be forgiven a lot. I was not born in London and so not marinated in the myths it likes to tell itself. In one sense this has been an advantage. In another it has meant that he who looks for the Pearly King and the theatrical queen will be disappointed. They were not discriminated against. They were merely among the six million Londoners I never got to see.

London is no longer the biggest capital in the world nor the most important; but it remains, as William Dunbar famously said, 'the Flower of Cities all'. Very soon along the way I understood the truth retailed by the writer Benny Green that, while the life of someone who lives, say, in Tokyo is the same story told 20 million times, that of a Londoner is a tale told 6,608,598 different ways.

In two and a half years, I only managed to follow the paths of some 200 Londoners. My criterion for selecting them was simple, perhaps unashamedly so. I pursued those people living in the city who caught the corner of my eye. In interviewing them, I have kept – with one exception – their real names, albeit in most instances just their first name.

Where possible I have also kept away from sentimentality. If one loves a city and its people, the fact does not need announcing at every turn.

The result is no more than one young man's journey through a landscape both familiar to everyone and claimed separately by each.

Of course it adds another tombstone to the graveyard, but I would not have missed the digging for anything.

Part One
UNREAL CITY

'Does London exist?'

M. ASH, A GUIDE TO THE STRUCTURE OF LONDON, 1972

*'A cockney in Canada was asked by a recruiting sergeant where he came
from. He replied: "London." Said the sergeant: "London what?
London, Ontario? London, N.Y.? London, Mass.?"*
*"London the b----y world!" the recruit replied with ineffable disgust.
That is how it feels to the born Londoner.'*

FORD MADOX FORD, RETURN TO YESTERDAY, 1931

*'If you look beyond it you look into fog. It sums up and includes England.
Materially England is contained in it, and the soul of England has always
inhabited it as a body. We have not had a great man who has never lived
in London.'*

ARTHUR SYMONS, LONDON, 1918

To understand a Londoner is to understand his city. Neither is easy. It is a commonplace that the six million or so who make up the capital both of England and the English-speaking world do not readily describe themselves as Londoners. Rather, they live in London. Their lack of identity with the city is partly an assertion of independence – an independence which means they carry no identity cards. It also indicates how few are born and bred here. More, though, it reveals the impossibility of defining London. In that solid word, V.S. Pritchett may hear a policeman's feet, a steam hammer, and the sound of coal. Yet, press too hard and the metropolis falls away, like water through the fingers. Grab, and it becomes a mirage.

Phlegmatically, wilfully almost, the city compounds the mirage. To stake out a border is to become tangled in several different maps: one marking the square mile of the City, another the taxi driver's six-mile circle from Charing Cross; and, in a widening ripple, those outlining the London postal and telephone areas, the London Underground and bus routes, the Metropolitan Police district and the thirty-two boroughs of the recently abolished Greater London Council. In all, anything from 677 acres to about 900 square miles.

I told a Yorkshireman I lived in London. 'So you live in the Smoke,' he said. Eliot's yellow fog no longer rubs its back against our window panes, but the view from them remains opaque – as if the mist is on the inside.

To sketch out my own boundary, I drove one still, hazy morning to Elstree airfield.

3

Every weekday, a small plane belonging to Capital Radio circles over London and reports on the 180,000 cars driving to work. The voice behind the Flying Eye is a darkly bearded man called Russ. After 9.30 a.m. Russ is a mere advertising executive. For the two hours beforehand he is, as he laboriously puts it, 'the man with the highest profile in London'.

Climbing over a wire fence in his green boiler suit, Russ strides to the hangar where John, the pilot, is wiping the windscreen. 'That's one of the things you can say about London,' says John, holding up a blackened rag. 'Only cleaned yesterday.' We climb aboard. Sitting beside the pilot in sunglasses and headphones, Russ is ready for battle. 'If you've read the papers, there's usually something to look out for. Fires,' he says, strapping himself in, 'they're nice from the air.'

John turns on the ignition, Russ the transmitter. But he knows how to fly. It was sensible to learn. 'Just in case John gets a heart attack.'

We rise up through the mist from the Elstree reservoir, over yellow rape fields and the blue swimming pools of north London. 'We'll follow the M One through Finchley up to Archway, then Leigh Valley,' Russ explains. 'They put pressure on us to find a new road, but you can't just invent a motorway. The traffic varies. Sometimes there's nothing, sometimes it's raving mad. There's no apparent reason.' Then, thinking about it, he gives a few. 'Monday morning's the worst time – about eight-thirty. People coming back from the weekend. On Jewish holidays they're not allowed to drive, which can make all the difference to north-west London. Then you have tube strikes. Yesterday there was a six-mile jam. You watch the jam growing. You tell drivers, don't go. But they do.'

John indicates his car-breaking yard below. 'I was just looking to see who was at work.' Satisfied, he opens the throttle and swings the plane towards the river and the Thames Barrier. 'It's not going to work, you know, if there's a flood.' He shakes his head gloomily. 'It's his pet theory,' Russ whispers loudly.

Over east London he delivers the first bulletin. Speaking quickly, nervously dancing his hands over a pad of scribbled notes, he tells listeners to Capital Radio of congestion at Stratford. 'It's probably due to the person I've got in the back.' Signing off, he turns and gives me a wink. Below, cars queue in colourful lines, like the strands of a bead curtain.

John suddenly spots what he thinks is a fire. He circles back, looking for the cigarette column of smoke. Not finding it, he circles again, annoyed. 'I've lost it.' Then he sees the little orange flame twinkling in the top flat of an apartment block. From a thousand feet up, it really does seem as if 'a woman might pisse it out', which is what the lord mayor said in 1666 on seeing the flames in Pudding Lane. Russ contacts the police, and within a minute fire engines have arrived. 'I think we can say we found it,' he says, chewing his green felt tip.

The Great Fire destroyed the City, but true to form Londoners resisted any plans by Christopher Wren and his contemporary John Evelyn to make it comprehensible. Like the British Constitution, unwritten, unplanned, higgledy-piggledy, it grew through networks of precedent and tradition. Today, the towers of commerce stick up from their flat surrounds, a compact cluster of toadstools between paving stones. From the air, there is only one other cluster like it – in Croydon.

From this bird's eye view, London comes into a strange focus. What impresses first is the messy enormity of the place. Yet, equally striking is the localised neatness, the order that exists within this clutter. Line after tidy line of red and grey roofs, broken by allotments, pockets of water, islands of close-cropped green – like the circuit-board of a radio set, sat on and silenced by some almighty bottom.

The final surprise is the amount of cemeteries – 103 of them.

From up here, everything takes on the same measure of importance. Chelsea looks much like Ilford. Piccadilly and Trafalgar Square are as unspectacular as Shepherd's Bush roundabout. In White City, the BBC is shaped, uncharacteristically, like a question mark.

The river doubles back on itself like an eel on a tiled floor. Trains converge on their stations. Cars wait on Putney Bridge, where John Christie, the lady killer, was arrested after a meal in the Lacy Dining Rooms. London Bridge swarms with commuters, undone by death. Like Mary Poppins, I gaze down into the gardens of Buckingham Palace. Three corgis scamper near a blue tractor. A whole Indian village, I remember, can live off what the Royal Family feeds its dogs.

John asks where I live; he likes to fly his passengers over their homes. I look but cannot see. As we make another circle Russ has to deliver his final bulletin. 'Vauxhall's bad,' he resumes with

5

dancing hands, 'and there's a mile-and-a-half tail-back on the Chelsea Embankment because of the Flower Show.'

We return to Elstree. Russ and John go off to the advertising agency and breaker's yard, and I make my way back into the city I have glimpsed.

The city: founded by Brutus in 1108 BC, and christened Troiam Novam; corrupted to Trinovantum; renamed Llyn-din or 'the Fort on the Lake' by the Celts, and then Londinium by the Romans, who had heard of the excellence of our oysters; changed to Augusta in the rule of the Emperor Gratian, and by the Saxons to Lundenwic. London: the first metropolis, the cradle of democracy, and the home of William Shakespeare, Geoffrey Chaucer, Winston Churchill, Jack the Ripper, Florence Nightingale, Sherlock Holmes, Charles Dickens, Queen Victoria, the Duke of Wellington, Henry VIII, Sid Vicious and Screaming Lord Sutch.

London.

It takes forty-two minutes, they reckon, for the average Londoner to get to work.

Some walk, some bicycle, some come by car and bus. But the majority travel by tube. Each year, the carriages of the London Underground open their silver doors to 563 million passengers. Each day 448,000 travel at least part of the 247 miles of track.

The first commuters took the Underground in 1863, from Paddington to Farringdon on the Metropolitan line. Not until 1900 was the Central line opened – 'A line for Londoners, supplying a rapid shuttlecock service between two main centres'. Connecting the West End with the City, it was known as the Twopenny Tube.

Bob has been a motorman – a driver – on the Central line for twenty-two years. Four times a day, for sixty-two hours and £157 a week, he drives from Epping or Hainault to West Ruislip. In twenty-two years he has crossed London roughly 24,000 times.

It is 3.25 p.m. and he is about to start his afternoon shift from Hainault. His morning shift had begun at 6.43 a.m. and taken three hours. 'We never do more than four at a time,' he explains, stepping into the driver's compartment. He carries a black nylon bag containing a tin teapot and two spanners. One spanner he uses to turn a bolt, releasing air pressure; the other, with which he will drive the train, he attaches to the dashboard. His hand must be on this at all times. It is ghoulishly called the 'dead-man's handle'. Should he fall down dead, the train will stop automatically.

Bob turns on the light in the cab and smooths his lustreless hair. 'There's a theory that if people see the driver, they won't jump.' People who jump are known as 'one-unders'. About fifty jump a year. The Northern line is meant to be the worst for one-unders. 'We don't get them like we used to, coming up to Christmas with the loans needing paying. There's now a suicide pit under the negative rail.'

The area manager, smoking a thin cigar and wearing a poppy, has already given his opinion of suicides. 'I'm doing me crossword an' the train jolts an' I think, Oh Christ, a one-under. Wot's up, driver, I says. I 'ad a woman jump, 'e says, shakin' an' sick. So I rushes round ter the front. A White City lady, it was. Early forties, presentable like, but she jumped too damn quick. I said to 'er, wot was goin' thro' 'er mind? I wanted ter kill meself, she said. I flew off the 'andle, I really did. You silly cow. If you'd seen the state of that driver yer wouldn't do a bloody stupid thin' like that.' He had let out a long, blue, satisfied chimney of smoke. 'You don't get a chance ter tell 'em generally.'

No one has jumped in front of Bob. He has run over one or two dogs, but they had been electrocuted already. 'They get a packet off the rail, turn round and bite it, and that's their lot.' The most common reaction he provokes, standing in his compartment with the light on, is the wave of a child. Occasionally, when running late, a man has spat through his open window.

Bob clips a tie under his collar. It is clipped, not tied, he explains, 'so we don't get strangled by the passengers.'

And off we set.

People on the streets at nine o'clock in the morning are very different to those hurrying to work fifteen minutes later. So with the tube. The first train of the day used to carry the 'fluffers', burly Irish women who cleaned the conductor rails. Bob's manager tells how, as a relief foreman at Chancery Lane, an escalator fluffer whipped open her boiler suit before him in the machine room. Thirty years on, he is visibly shaken by the memory.

Now, the first people to take the 6.43 a.m. from Epping are the postmen, office cleaners and milkmen. There is a short break before the workmen's traffic – painters, plumbers, electricians – and then at 8 a.m. the schoolchildren and office clerks get on.

'You don't get yer gentry till nine. The "nine o'clockers" we used to call them, in their bowler hats. The stationmaster would wait by the barrier, salute them and open the first-class carriage.' Today, the nine o'clockers are the ones who look slowly and grim-faced at their watches. Some embarking at Theydon Bois expect to sit in the same seat every morning.

The last group are 'the womblies', the old-age pensioners who start queuing at 9 a.m. for the cheap rate which begins half an hour later.

Travelling the complete route – the fifty-one miles from Epping to West Ruislip – takes ninety minutes, half of it underground. 'It's easy to get going and think, where am I?' admits Bob. In his mind, London does not begin until he enters the tunnel at Mile End. He is reminded where he is by the smell of urine dampening the pillar beside his window. There is a similar pillar and smell at Shepherd's Bush.

The train empties as we make our afternoon journey west-wards. In the morning, half get out at Liverpool Street; a replacement quarter – British Rail commuters – get on for Bank, where they are raucously urged by a tape recording to 'Mind the gap'. At Holborn, solicitors step off; at Chancery Lane, postmen and journalists. By the time the early train has reached Bond Street, it is more or less empty. Now, at Oxford Street, American tourists clamber aboard with their day's shopping, making for hotels in Lancaster Gate.

At Queensway, Bob says, people used to come down for the air. The purifying system made it like going to the seaside. No such system exists at Notting Hill Gate, where there is a distinct smell of cooking. Or, more necessarily, at Shepherd's Bush. At Shepherd's Bush the train is delayed. 'The Dosser gang worked here', someone has scrawled on the tunnel wall.

The delay gives one a chance to look back, past the damp pillar, at the station now smartened up with coloured tiles and murals. One or two passengers drift down the platform to the escalators. The down escalator does not work. A man called Bumper Harris was hired to travel up and down the first Underground escalator when it opened at Earl's Court in 1911. He had a wooden leg, and his perambulations were meant to boost the confidence of terrified passengers. Broken-down escalators aside, you cannot imagine London Transport hiring Bumper Harris today. Nor of anyone, like the friend of the writer Ford Madox Ford, who, when dying a long way from London, sighed queerly:

> for a sight of the gush of smoke that, on the platform of the Underground, one may see escaping in great woolly clots . . . He wanted to see it again as others have wished to see once more the Bay of Naples, the olive groves of Catania.

Bob blows his nose. 'When I started,' he says, 'and I blew my nose it would come out black.' He talks about the smog. As a child he would be let off going to school if he could not see the railings opposite. There's still black on station walls, though. People say it's dead skin.

Eventually we continue. Lights twinkle from red to green in the dark until daylight comes at White City, showing the thin, shiny rails hanging down from the tunnel's mouth like walrus teeth. At East Acton, heavy-shouldered men get off for Wormwood Scrubs. Prison officers.

Thereafter London seems to dissolve into back gardens, church-yards and allotments. The open air and green always makes Bob think of his home in Newbury Park. He would like to be walking his dog there now. At Northolt, the smell of toffee on the air reminds him he hasn't booked the Greek restaurant in Gants Hill where he has promised to take the wife. She likes the belly dancing.

At Northolt we come to a buffer. Grabbing his teapot and spanners, Bob walks back through the deserted train. Newspapers lie on the seats. In one carriage there is a paperback. People leave the weirdest things behind, he says. Wheelchairs, outboard motors, kitchen sinks. Once a stuffed gorilla was found. Once a box of glass eyes. Once a bag of human bones.

We drive back into London. Travelling under it from White City is like falling down a bottomless well, broken every now and then by bright lights. On the Underground map, the thick red rule of the Central line insists on the myth of a continuous narrative: a narrative of connected villages, strung out through the city from Ruislip to Epping. In fact, the stations, and the pockets of people lining them, give the impression of beleaguered out-posts, not linked in any way except by the dizzying tunnel.

As with the stations of the Underground map, so with each

Londoner. Any attempt to link them, like the names on the Central line, must result in this fictional narrative.

From his 24,000 trips through the city, has Bob gained a sense of how Londoners relate to each other, and the areas in which they live and work? He shakes his head. 'Most of the faces are blurred,' he says, his mind still on the belly dancers of Gants Hill. 'They're just bodies.'

Just as there is no one map for the city, so there is no single centre to it. No hierarchy or goal dominates. Therefore, everyone feels the liberty to mould London according to his own priorities. As Samuel Johnson's shadow, James Boswell, said, with the bumptious accuracy which has made him so anthologised:

> I have often amused myself with thinking how different a place London is to different people. They, whose narrow minds are contracted to the consideration of some one particular pursuit, view it only through that medium. A politician thinks of it merely as the seat of government in its different departments; a grazier, as a vast market for cattle; a mercantile man, as a place where a prodigious deal of business is done upon 'Change; a dramatick enthusiast, as the grand scene of theatrical entertainments; a man of pleasure as an assemblage of taverns, and the great emporium for ladies of easy virtue. But the intellectual man is struck with it as comprehending the whole of human life in all its variety, the contemplation of which is inexhaustible.

London's centre, the spot from which the milestones are measured, is Trafalgar Square.

Ann sits on a stone bench overlooking the sloping square and pats her dog. Sending puffs of white breath into the winter air, the labrador, which is the colour of freshly chopped wood, eyes the pigeons at her feet.

'Good girl,' Ann says. She is small, well-dressed, with gingerish hair and the thin, piping voice of a gerbil.

Ann has lived in London for twenty-five years, but she has only seen the city once. One November, as a very young Cornish girl, she came by train to Waterloo. 'It was filthy, absolutely filthy, and

my new coat was ruined by the rain.' She saw Sherlock Holmes'
Baker Street, and the waxworks at Madame Tussaud's – 'I
couldn't get away quick enough.' Thereafter she returned to
London only through her picture books, until at the age of eleven
she woke up one morning and could not see.

Today, most of her life is spent out and about in London.
Whilst raising money for guide dogs, she goes from Deptford
pubs to East End clubs to Women's Institutes in Chelsea. Her
knowledge of these places, like her knowledge of London, exists
wholly in the people she meets.

Ann's neat appearance reflects a passion for clothes. 'I enjoy
going round shops, feeling the texture of materials, the decorations. If I could see, I would love nothing more than to wander
down Oxford Street and gaze in the windows. Also, I'd go to
museums. I collect china, you see. I go to antique fairs and touch
everything. But if one allowed oneself to wish, one would never
get by. I don't bog myself down in trying to envisage what it's
like. I get about.

'I'm aware of sounds and smells, the rushing past of feet,
anonymous groups of people in a packed tube, where the doors go
swish and everyone's always in a hurry. Sometimes, not hearing
English voices, I think I'm in a foreign country. Not that I mind
hearing foreign accents, but I don't get anyone to understand
when I ask where a platform is. Some people are terribly selfish.
They walk between you and the dog.' Aware that she is under
discussion, the dog sits up. Then, not required, she continues
panting at the pigeons. 'She's a bridge-builder, aren't you? They
say Hello to her. They wouldn't talk to me if I hadn't got the dog.
She gives me independence.'

Ann's independence is such that she often goes to the ballet and
theatre. She likes to be accompanied by someone who whispers to
her what is happening on stage. 'You can follow the plot,' she tells
me. 'You can picture what people are doing when they move
around. You can understand the whole action. I only get information if I am told, or hear it. Voices tell me a lot. You can tell a
person from their voice.'

As if reminded, she tilts her face towards the square, and the
admiral on top of his fluted column of Cornish granite.

'Describe it to me,' she says.

Sitting on Ann's bench and swivelling slowly about, it is possible to take in most of London's pride. Above, on the site of the Royal Mews where Chaucer worked as clerk, is the National Gallery. Next door, in an area once known as Porridge Island, stands the Church of St Martin-in-the-Fields. Further down, South Africa House, like Canada House opposite, provides a reminder of the empire that flicked its swish over a quarter of the world. Then there is Charing Cross, which Dr Johnson thought to flow with 'the full tide of human existence', and where a plaque celebrates London's official centre. Then the Strand, walking down which the nineteenth-century French critic and historian Hippolyte Taine was possessed by the spleen and understood suicide, and where an elderly relative of Ford Madox Ford's met a lion escaped from the zoo. 'What did you do?' asked Ford. 'Do?' replied the relative. 'Why, I took a cab.'

From the Strand, in a tight, elegant arc, lie Whitehall and its statue of Charles I, Admiralty Arch and its red road to Buckingham Palace, Pall Mall and its clubs. And, at the centre, Trafalgar Square itself – the city's drawing room.

'The finest view in Europe,' the nineteenth-century statesman Robert Peel called this, the site both of London's protests and celebrations. Dominating it from the column in his name, and turning his egotistic blind eye to the scene, is Admiral Nelson. 'A rat on a stick,' wrote Taine dyspeptically. At his feet, eyeing the birds like Ann's dog, are Edwin Landseer's lions. It is said that in the ground beneath their paws were found the bones of real lions.

Before John Nash and Charles Barry levelled the slope, this was where Charles Dickens' notorious Golden Cross Hotel stood. David Copperfield stayed in a room smelling of hackney coaches. So too did Mr Pickwick. It was from its mouldy gothic doors, and in the company of Mr Jingle, that he commenced his travels.

'Are there pigeons round here?' asks Ann.

It was in Trafalgar Square, on a brilliant windswept sunny day, that Ford Madox Ford began answering his own question: What is London? Passing from the fountains, 'like haycocks of prismatic glitter', he switched his attention to a jam of baggage waggons in the City, and then to the kerosene lamps of shops. 'It will be some minute detail of the whole,' he concluded, 'we seeing things with the eye of a bird that is close to the ground . . . seeking for minute fragments of seed.'

Fifty yards away, near the edge of the square, two men in cloth caps and leather jackets sell birdseed for 15p. a plastic cup. One, young and thin, smokes the stub end of a cigarette, grimacing with each long draught. The other, fat and deaf, caresses a gold ring in which are set three diamonds. They stand side by side under a canvas, behind a tin barrow. Pigeons flutter everywhere. Three thousand of them. They come in every morning at 9.30 from St James's Park.

It is 11.15 a.m. but already the tourists are loosing their children and unstrapping their cameras. The fat man nods in the direction of the road opposite and swears at 'the Reds down there'. He is indicating the House of Commons. 'Once a bloody Red, always a bloody Red.'

An Indian girl spills her purple cup of grain and the pigeons descend. He peers through his thick black spectacles, snorts, and gives her another cup free.

'Look at Paul Johnson. He used to be Red,' he continues, contradicting himself. An American with a cigar buys four cups.

'The BBC. It's all biased. Full of lefties.'

'And poufs,' adds the thin young man, puffing.

'And poufs,' reiterates the fat man. 'Full of bloody Reds and poufters.'

I ask where they live, how long they have worked here. They shrug in unison. The fat man mumbles, Thirty years.

'See Alf. He likes to rabbit.' Alf?

'Alf the photographer. He's around somewhere. Or, what about him?' He hails a grinning tramp. 'You. Where you from?' Through his grin, the tramp mentions South Africa, then holds out his hands for seed. The fat man gives him a purple cup, pouting with generosity. The man pours it into his folded arms. The pigeons descend and he giggles.

'You can see he's South African from his tan,' says the thin man, throwing his butt away. The man is white.

Three schoolchildren come up.

'Television's rubbish. I know it's only one pound a week, but you expect to see something decent.'

A French couple buy four cups. I have stood here five minutes and the two men have sold forty cups. It is December.

'D'you see that Graham Greene last night?' the fat man says unexpectedly. He looks at me, cocking his head like a pigeon. 'D'you think Alec Guinness is a poufter?'

13

★

Londoners may regard Trafalgar Square as the capital's formal heart, but the world looks along Piccadilly. In a sense it is right to do so, for Piccadilly Circus holds a key to the unreal city.

In Rome, Paris, New York, you know where you are. The brothel announces itself. Grand avenues sweep towards each showpiece. There is no need to ask if this is the Place de la Concorde. Yet, walk east along Piccadilly for the first time and you would not know it was leading to one of the most famous landmarks on earth. Originally known as the Great Bath Road and 'the way to Reding', Piccadilly continues to draw attention away from itself.

And, when you get there, refusing to be urged on to Cambridge and Dover, what do you find? A scrappy traffic system overlooked by neon ads, and a small statue in memorial to Anthony Ashley Cooper, the seventh Earl of Shaftesbury. Today, the ads flash up images of foreign soft drinks and hi-fi, but their sentiment is fully in keeping with the once-celebrated sign for Horlicks which read, 'Do you suffer from night starvation?' Those who do have only to visit the cinema on the Circus corner, currently showing *Come Make Love With Me* and *Sweet Sexy Savage*.

As for the statue, London's most famous symbol, what do you see? A small naked boy on tiptoe representing a Victorian philanthropist. (At the moment of writing, the place where Eros stands is boarded up, and the archer removed to the South Bank. The displacement is typical.)

The same trip south, across the river, must be made to find Covent Garden, now in Nine Elms, while you need to go to the country to locate Wren's Temple Bar, famous for its severed heads, which were boiled in salt so the birds would not peck. Removed from Fleet Street in 1870, it now stands in Hertfordshire. As for Sir John Rennie's five-arched London Bridge, shipped stone by numbered stone to America, you must cross the Atlantic to Lake Havasu City, Arizona, to see that.

'A legend we have successfully sold to foreigners,' says V.S. Pritchett of London. 'Even to ourselves.'

'This aged and incorrigible deceiver,' adds the writer Jan Morris.

The London street, wrote the Czech novelist Karel Capek in 1925, is just a gulley through which life flows to get home. It is not for gossiping, nor for sitting with a drink to absorb the scene, nor for courting arm in arm. 'In short nothing, nothing, nothing.'

Arriving at this hub of empire and finding just a void, 7,000 tourists a week enter the London Information Office off Piccadilly. Their most common request, says an Irishman behind the counter, is Eros. Next is Piccadilly Circus. 'They think it's the centre of the universe,' he says with a detached smile and steady marble eyes. (Other popular requests are the ladies loo and American Express.)

'Some actually expect to find a circus. Invariably you get lost members of a family who have agreed to meet "Just near Piccadilly Circus". Yesterday I had a Peruvian lady who asked which side of the pavement she should walk on, because she kept bumping into people. Another lady said how much she liked the double-decker buses, but how did you get upstairs?'

In two years the requests have included a Swiss father who came up to the counter and began, 'I want to sleep with my son.' (He wanted to know if he was allowed to spend the night in his car.) Another man said, 'I'm looking for a tropical rain forest.' (There was an exhibition at the Museum of Mankind.) A Portuguese couple came in to get married, and a man in a pin-stripe suit wanted to know where the judicial committee of the Privy Council was meeting. 'Otherwise it's pretty much run of the mill. Americans want the way to Harrods and tickets for *Cats*. Australians want tea with the Queen. And Italians want what we call "A Life Package" – a job, a place to live and someone to teach them English in the evenings.'

'Where is Piccadilly Circus, where is Windsor Castle, where is Oxford? I get all of those,' says Donald Reeves, the Rector of St James's, Piccadilly. 'You're a soft touch in the street with a dog collar. The "Collar Bar", I call it. They either unburden themselves or avoid you like the plague. I've stopped wearing it on the tube so I can have a rest.'

He takes me to his workroom in the rectory, the last private house in Piccadilly. It overlooks the fine Wren church, a church he described on his arrival five years ago as 'the best-kept secret in London'.

In that time, he says proudly, he has come to be known as the 'Red Parson of Piccadilly'. His face is all bumps and hollows. His hair lank and grey. Over his open black shirt he wears a thick jersey. It is a colourless mufti for a modern Evangelist; one who, had he not seen the light in Lebanon, would have become an impresario.

He ushers me into a chair. It is where Mother Teresa sat, he says. His cats Mackerel and Tiger had made a beeline for her. She had asked for a glass of water and bowed her head in prayer. President Kaunda had also sat here. Instead of water he had been given honey. 'I make it from hives on the roof. London's the best place for honey because the bees can go to the parks and royal gardens, and the climate is very temperate.' For a while, he says, wiping some fluff off his jersey, his honey could be bought at Fortnum & Mason.

The son of a Chichester garage-owner, Donald Reeves passed through Sherborne public school, the Royal Sussex Regiment, Cambridge and the British Council before receiving his call. He then spent thirteen years on a council estate at the end of the Northern line. He does not appear to look back with nostalgia on his days among the flock of the St Helen's Estate in Morden. 'It was built to deal with slum clearances. There were no places to meet except the launderette. The main rival to the church was bingo; to the priest's mauve, the dinner jacket. There weren't even tupperware parties. We were a working-class community of brilliantined beer drinkers.'

The parish of St James's is more middle class. 'The people who come here can choose more about the way they live.' The corpus of 150 come from all over. One man drives from Woburn. 'There are few residents. The boundaries do not make sense. I've had to plant a church here, to make St James's a seven-days-a-week church for London and the world.'

The Reverend Reeves has done this by working seventy hours a week, and combining in his office the roles of 'manager, counsellor, impresario, ideas person'. The first thing he did on his appointment to The Best Kept Secret was to hire a public relations officer. Radio and television appearances followed. Gradually St James's came onto the map. The forecourt began to teem with street theatre, clowns, mime, music and stalls. The church started its own professional orchestra – sponsored by Lufthansa. A coffee house was opened, then a 'Peace Caravan'. Faith healing, Zen and Sufism were encouraged. So was Tony Benn.

'I like being an entrepreneur,' Reeves explains. Following the success of the 1985 Reagan–Gorbachev meeting in Geneva, he has become even more excited by the potential of his church. 'I thought, I'll do a bit of summitry myself. I'll organise some lectures on the future of the world.' When prompted, he mentions the names of Mrs Gorbachev, Winnie Mandela and Fidel Castro as possible guest speakers. 'Certainly, what I get up to here troubles people, harasses them. I had a call from the then Chairman of the Conservative Party. "John Gummer here." "Who?" I asked mischievously. "Some of us don't feel very welcome at St James's," Mr Gummer said. I think he was referring to the debate on Marxism. Or it could have been the reflexology.' Or perhaps, the holism, or the laying on of hands, or even the salvation by foot massage. 'I did have a woman at one wedding who told me she had been a little bit frightened about coming, in case she had to have her feet rubbed.'

With his eye fixed beyond Piccadilly, Donald Reeves spends little time on the streets. 'The priest and the prostitute lark,' he says, 'I'm not into that.' Nevertheless, he encourages the more traditional services, attended by a middle class that likes its religion quiet and undisturbed. 'You know, those who prefer to talk about the vicar and hats, rather than the date of Exodus.' Many go beyond mere talk. 'I've had to cope with endless letters from middle-aged women,' he says. 'I'm not very good at that. It's no good saying it's their problem. Goodness knows how pop stars cope.'

I catch a number 38 bus out of Piccadilly. The top is empty but for two men. One, in a crumpled grey suit, sits at the very front and sings tunelessly. 'I want to love you over,' he sings, and then puffs into a harmonica. 'My heart will fill with clover.' The other sits slumped at the back, also in a suit. 'No! I don't like t'at one. You sing like Lester Piggott. Can't you sing t'other way?' He speaks harshly, violently almost, as if he might not be joking. He appears to have nothing to do with the singer, who rasps in reply, 'You bastard, you fuckin' rabbit.' 'I was born an idiot,' answers the man from the back. 'What's your excuse?'

'I'm the only survivor of the *Titanic*,' says the singer morosely. He returns to his harmonica. 'As I grow older . . . I love this one,' he tells himself. 'I remember a white Christmas . . .'

From the back comes another shout. ' 'Tis a pity you can't play. What are you, a learner? I think you'd better sing downstairs.'

'All together now . . .'

'Never look in the mirror, except when you're shaving,' comes the shout, louder this time. 'You might see the devil.'

The other goes on singing. The man at the back listens silently. Then, suddenly, he joins in.

'The dewdrops in the snow,' they both sing in drunken, tuneless unison as the bus bursts out of Piccadilly, towards the park where the rector's bees make honey.

An unobvious city, and also a cosmopolitan one. For many countries, London is a foreign capital. Most countries outside Europe base their European offices here. Heathrow and Gatwick are the busiest and fourth-busiest airports in the world. Greenwich Mean Time, halfway between that of New York and Tokyo, enables the City to remain the world's pivotal financial market.

Some of the most pertinent remarks about London have been made by outsiders: Hippolyte Taine; Henry James; Russia's revolutionary thinker, Alexander Herzen; Karel Capek; the eighteenth-century German novelist, Charles Moritz; the nineteenth-century German poet, Heinrich Heine; Fyodor Dostoyevsky. Each minute of their visit, they have had to come to terms with something strange. We who live here are often blinded by familiarity.

I talk to a Frenchman, an American and a Russian.

Philippe is a French banker who tells me of Jacques Dufilho, a music hall comic famous for his sketch entitled *Suivez le guide*. 'It is a monologue to tourists, describing a visit round a country house. In a hushed voice the guide warns them of the high point. "We are now coming into the crypt," he says, "by far the most interesting part of the building. Stormed by the Saracens, rebuilt, improved, this was where the duke spent his years in captivity. From this window he looked over his lands." In minute detail the guide describes the quality of the stucco, the tracery on the ceiling. Yet, suddenly, as you raise your head, you begin to realise something is wrong. For one thing, it is raining. For another, there is no roof. "*Il n'en reste rien!*" the guide explains. Nothing remains.

'Having built up the image like mad, he then deprives you of it – just like London. Look at the guidebooks and you'll find that's exactly what they do. They carry you along in high expectation, but what you actually arrive at is pitiful. With its groves, alleys, crescents, rows, mews, parks, avenues, London is like the sur-rounds to a non-existent country house – one that is just around the corner, never down the road.

'There is this myth London is an old city. More ancient than Rome, said the twelfth-century monk, William Fitzstephen. It is not. Only bits of it are old. Yet, everywhere there are these blue plaques proclaiming such-and-such was probably somewhere near this spot; So-and-so possibly lived on a site a few yards away. Take The Globe. Most people have heard of it. They want to see it. They make their way to Southwark were there's a small notice on a derelict warehouse, in a spot where there's nothing of any interest.

'Or take the Roman baths off the Strand. You walk down a dingy alley, and what do you see? Through a semi-frosted window and a door with bars, you glimpse an abandoned bath. The door is locked. If you want to see more, you have to apply to God knows where. The thing looks poxy. Your initial enthusiasm is gone. London's a con trick. It's nowhere. People are confused. Not just the people who live here, but the people who have to make decisions about the city. They don't know what or where it is.

'In Paris, if I want to discuss my tax affairs, I go up the street to the local tax man. In London, I have to write to Salford. My car licence is sent from Swansea. Then you have institutions like the BBC and *The Times*, which are required to plug into the city and report back to it what is going on. How can they do that from Shepherd's Bush and Wapping? Why move to the middle of nowhere when you can move to Docklands, says the advert. Docklands *is* nowhere.

'In Paris you are brought up a Parisian. You are born, educated, and forced to live and work there. In London you will have been brought up in Berkshire, educated at Radley, gone to university in Oxford or Cambridge, and then gravitated to the capital, which is why Londoners are just not interested in their city. They identify themselves with an area. They're from Hackney or Chelsea or Hampstead, not London, which is a city without a heart. The War bombed out the centre, so that Mayfair looks like the shopfront in a ghost town. The centre is dead. No one lives there. The very names West End and East End communicate this idea of periphery, of the edge. Between them, supposedly, is the centre – which is the City. Yet the City is a void. Increasingly, companies from other parts of England who have meetings in London meet in The Post House at Heathrow. It's so telling. It means they think that's London, when we know it's miles away. It also shows they resent having to go into London. A German or a Frenchman looks forward to a trip to Paris or Berlin. Go into London on a Sunday evening and you see the most depressing sight in the world – a forlorn couple walking up Regent Street in the rain. Everything is shut. There is nowhere to go. The pubs are closed, and there is no one passing who speaks English.

'If people love a city they go over the top about it. They become lyrical. London's an ageing Victorian virgin like Miss Havisham, waiting in her wedding finery, and covered with cobwebs for her fiancé. In the BBC costume dramas of the old city they have colourful street life, prostitutes on every corner. Now, you walk down the street and everything's vanished. You get the feeling everyone's behind a window laughing at you.'

Gary is an American journalist working in London for NBC. Drinking Sauterne, he reiterates this sense of alienation. 'There's no sense of the city. In New York the city is made into a personality through the media. The local news comes on before the national news, not after. You feel you're fighting a battle, but at least the enemy is defined. There is a shared objective and goal. You feel in it together. In London, you don't feel you're in it with anybody. You're told nothing. If you don't know it already, you don't deserve to know. It's a club you don't belong to.

'And there is no sense that the place is boiling. New York is a cauldron. It's the hinterland in America which is calm. London is calm. But the hinterland boils.

'This means there is more civility, less anger. When you step on someone's foot, it's they who apologise. People stand for office here, they do not run for it. But there is still energy. Everyone has to have some place to go. They are busy, not relaxed – and repressed. Boy, are they repressed. They may be dying to get somewhere, but they can't break their civility. It makes for more formality. You have to book dinner weeks in advance, and reconfirm a week before. You can't call up and get together for a drink immediately. This is not because they've got something to do. It's a means of keeping you away, of distancing you. In New

York you can be best friends in twenty-four hours. Friendships in London are formed at school. People aged forty, who have known each other since they were fifteen, hang around inseparably. It's not surprising it's difficult to make new friends.

'What fascinates me is the level of interest in intellectual things. Taxi drivers in New York are murderers who can't speak English and don't know the city. Here, they discuss a play they've been to, or advise you on a restaurant, often to the extent of telling you which dishes to have. On the subways in New York, everyone reads pulp magazines and porno. In London, they read Zola and Dickens and don't say a thing.

'What I dislike is the lack of service. I'm used to people having initiative, wanting to sell things to you. Everything breaks here, and you can never get a workman. Since I've been in London, and I'm not joking, every single thing mechanical has broken. The cooker went for three months. The phone's gone three times. The dishwasher broke immediately. I finally got hold of a workman. He expected me to be here waiting from nine till one. When he came, he spent five minutes poking about. Then he said, it was too bad, it looked like an outside job, and he was an inside man. I rang again, and another man came. After five minutes he said, I'm sorry this is an inside problem. It turned out to be a couple of wires which had been spliced together without electrical tape. A friend warned me that by the time I left I would at least be on first-name terms with the man from British Telecom.'

Mikhail worked as the London correspondent for *Socialist Industry*. It was always his daughter who answered the telephone. Anastasia, she was called. Young, hesitant, curt. Once she had to cut short the conversation. The special bus had arrived, she explained in her flat vowels – as flat as a policeman's feet – to take her to school in Pembridge Villas. When, eventually, I spoke to her father, he agreed to come for a drink.

He wore a cloth cap bought in the Harrods sale, and smoked a pipe which he filled with a damp mixture of Erinmore and Three Nuns. He had a red shirt under his tweed jacket, and a face as white as powder. He was forty-three.

'I work on a daily paper which is the rough equivalent of the *FT* – minus the finance,' he added, sucking from the damp bowl. 'Yes, I suppose if you are sent to London it does mean you are a strong party worker.' He had written a thesis on the relationship between America and Cuba, and had lived in Leningrad and Moscow.

'After those classically designed cities, my first impressions of London were very colourful, very hectic and very disorganised. Russian streets are two hundred and twenty metres long by twenty-two metres wide. They are proportioned. London's buildings are much smaller. One upon the other.'

He lived in Westbourne Terrace, beneath Germaine Greer. She remembers him for all the different papers he used to order. He did not remember her. 'I instinctively escaped from there. I took my wife and daughter to the East End and Wembley and said, Would you like to live here? To me it's a low level of life. Our people wouldn't like to live in semi-detached houses, and worry all the time about their gas and central-heating bills. They only pay two pounds fifty per month for the phone, and four per cent of their salaries for a flat.

'In Russia the quality of the signs are good. There are inscriptions on every house. They say your number, then your street on a plaque, and the houses go one, two, three, four, five, six. Here they go one, three, five, sometimes without order. You could go to a street and look forever for Number nine.

'The way you mix your water is odd too. Hot and cold are separate taps, and you wash yourselves in the basin with a plug. Our tradition is to wash ourselves under running water. And we have a mixer. You have electronics to go to space, but no mixer.

'I have a feeling our aristocracy lived a little better than yours. You visit our palaces and they are so much more luscious. People don't look after themselves here. They look very funny when it's cold. It's zero and you call it Siberian weather, yet go round in shirts and leather shoes and no hats. Little kids shivering in shorts with knees as red as my shirt. Psychologically, you're not prepared for cold weather. You talk about it all the time, and yet know nothing about it. It causes many diseases, many deaths.

'My daughter is happy when it snows. She dreams of snow. Most of all she misses Russian bread. Whenever we come back from holiday, we bring six loaves and put them in the freezer. Anastasia, I say, but you have bananas. Bananas are okay, she says, but bread is essential.

'I think one of this country's best institutions, one of the things we'd like to borrow from you, is the pub and the culture of social drinking.' He laughed, twitching the triangular nose that protruded sharply from his bland face, and told how he once wandered by mistake into a gay pub in Notting Hill Gate. He admitted to liking Chinese food – there is only one such restaurant in Moscow – and making excursions into the country. He gathered mushrooms in Esher, Epping and Virginia Water, and woodruff for vodka on Hampstead Heath. Occasionally he made the trip to his ambassador's summer house ten miles from Hastings, on the A21. 'It was given by a wealthy Englishman in gratitude for the Russian sailors who saved his son on a Murmansk convoy during the war.'

Mikhail's image of London was more restricted than most, because he was not allowed to travel more than twenty-five miles from Hyde Park Corner without permission from the Foreign Office. 'It used to be thirty-five miles before Poland in 'eighty-one,' he said, unperturbed. 'You have to send two copies of your route two working days beforehand. So I have a circle reaching Hemel Hempstead, Maidenhead, Sevenoaks and Tilbury. If I cross that line without permission I might be in trouble. We first measure it on the map at home. My wife is nervous, always nervous. Don't worry, I say, it's only eighteen miles. Once we were invited to dinner in Farnborough, which was twenty-six miles away. It can be a strain, this, so that I'm happy when I'm stopped by the police. At long last, I think.'

He talked of journalism in London: how the media rejoice in juicy stories, how the average Russian is indignant at talk of rape, how there is less crime in Moscow. What Russians like to read, apparently, are happy stories. In fact, he said, tapping his pipe and coughing politely, he was wondering if he could do a profile of an English journalist for his readers. Someone like me.

On holiday a fortnight later I read the news that put paid to my profile in *Socialist Industry*. Mikhail had been expelled as one of six Soviet spymasters. The newspapers retailed stories of vodka parties he had given with his wife Nadia, a willowy, dark-haired beauty with ballet dancer's legs. 'Of course I'm a KGB agent,' he had once shouted merrily into a pot plant. 'But Nadia is more senior. She's a colonel. I'm only a major.' A blurred photograph showed the strong party worker walking across the tarmac with his wife and a ten-year-old girl. They all appeared to be smiling. None more so than the girl.

★

23

Everything being out of sight and tucked away, London works for the secret agent and the spy. Having snooped at the keyhole, he can duck his head under a cloak and lose himself in the enormity. It is just one more reason why the city is best caught in fiction, detective fiction especially; why its people prefer legends to illustrate the truth.

Enormous, enormous, that is the word which recurs all the time – to Taine, to Johnson and to Henry James, who stressed that 'the mere immensity of the place is a large part of its savour'. Because of this enormity, and because of the need to make the city manageable, all kinds of fictions flourish – from the transformations of 'Route de Roi' and 'Infanta de Castile' into 'Rotten Row' and 'Elephant and Castle', to the quaint notion of London as a string of villages.

There are over forty high streets in the *A-Z*, each one encouraging the village myth. ('If I am far away and someone whispers "London" in my ear,' wrote the journalist Nick Tomalin, 'my reaction is one of nostalgia, without real passion. But if he whispers "NW Eight", then I am caught!') Parts of London like Hampstead and Chiswick may foster this cosy self-deception successfully, professionally even, but the character of an area is established by a very small part of it, beyond which large tracts are more or less identical. Take off the blindfold behind The Sun Inn at Barnes, and it could be Neasden.

To a small, provocative extent, where a Londoner lives is a statement about himself, or his image of himself. Someone living in a Chelsea house is likely to be from a different class and income bracket to someone living in Pinner. Someone actively looking for a house in Chelsea will definitely be so.

Go into a pub, and you hear as many generalisations about villages like Pinner and Chelsea as about their villagers. Walthamstow has more old-age pensioners than anywhere else in London. Ilford more taxi drivers. Richmond more educational qualifications. Islington is characterised by lawyers and journalists, people who think of themselves as part of the governing classes. Camden by members of the alternative society and social workers, people who again want to run things. Surbiton by black magic rites and the number of calls to the Samaritans. Barnes by minor television actors, Fulham by divorcees, Paddington by prostitutes. It takes very little to libel or laud a hundred thousand people.

'Londoners', wrote the poet Hugo Williams, 'are defined not by

London at all but by their different attitudes to the different places and things that make up that non-city.' The majority of Londoners reduce this non-city to a mental village – ranging from the home to the workplace, to the bank, the club, a friend's house, a favourite restaurant. As Jonathan Raban puts it in *Soft City*, one of the best books on the capital: 'One man's London is a sum of all the routes he takes through it, a spoor as unique as a fingerprint.'

Each Londoner has a different vision of the city, each his own familiar goat-path through it. A path so well-trodden that to stray just one street away means entering a foreign land. To preserve this map he must dismiss anything off it; he must create boundaries. North of the park, south of the railway track, east of the roundabout. ('As of this moment,' A.P. Herbert said when the Chiswick flyover was built, 'Chiswick will only exist through incest.')

North of the river.

The river especially.

The Seine is an artery through Paris. It unites and waters the city. The Thames divides our city – not that you would notice, since access to the river is denied at every point. 'Battersea,' said a north-of-the-river man, 'I wouldn't let my hearse go through Battersea.' Or, as P.G. Wodehouse's Psmith said of Clapham Common: 'One has heard of it, of course, but has its existence ever been proved?'

The suburbs begin much closer south of the river. There are fewer tubes, fewer institutions, fewer aristocrats – and many more second-hand car dealers. Critics say the south is discovered at the time the first baby is due; that until that time it is regarded as a separate, almost provincial city.

South Londoners have the same disdain. 'If I cross the river, it's like going abroad', MP Bob Mellish wrote recently. 'South Londoners don't cross the river. One day I had some Jewish ladies come to me who had been given council homes in my constituency. They said, You must get us back to the East End. There are no Jewish shops round here and we don't know anybody in south London.'

East Enders have this contempt for the West End. The Worst End, they joke. West Enders lack even this contempt. Talking of Bethnal Green, the Vicar of St Philip's said that those at the West End of town knew about as little of his destitute parish as the wilds of Australia, or the islands of the South Seas. He was talking in

1844, and he was quoted by Friedrich Engels, but the sentiment still rings true.

The tradition of two centres to London – financial and political, the City and Westminster – has meant there is no single presiding hierarchy. Hand in hand with London's enormity, goes the cliché, is the freedom to be and do as you like, to step on and off the bus where you want. Londoners are not so much acclaimed for their bank balances, or the blueness of their blood, as for the extent to which they use this freedom. Without New York's pressure to be rich and successful, they can live life as fast or as slowly as they wish. The preferred pace has been likened to that of a test match. It probably matters not who is winning.

Privacy is very much part and parcel of this freedom, and it extends to the streets. Voltaire was aghast at the indifference he noted. And writing to *The Times*, an American predicted little comment if a man boarded a bus with a bloody head under his arm. Recently, an Arab kidnapped in south London broke loose from his captivity and appeared in the street shackled to a large bed. He raised few eyebrows, merely a shrugged remark from the woman opposite: 'I was a bit amazed someone was chained to a bed.'

That is one of the joys of London. There is no need to worry what the neighbours think. Pierce Egan, who devoted his literary and publishing career to the subject of London, wrote in 1821: 'The next-door neighbour of a man in London is generally as great a stranger to him as if he lived at the distance of York.'

The size, the freedom, the privacy of London account for its successful assimilation of other cultures. 'A city of refuge, the mansion house of liberty,' said John Milton, using that most London of images, the home. In exile for whatever reason, the Dutch and the Flemish, the Lombards and the Jews, the Chinese and the Indians have been able to import their traditions and religions and make London their home.

Staying with a family on the Isle of Wight, I read an unpublished diary of their ancestor, a White Russian shoemaker from Evanach, who migrated to London at the turn of the century.

I doubt very much [he wrote in his thick pencil] whether an Englishman or woman can realize the feelings of one arriving in a new country without any trouble whatsoever. It did not seem to me as if I had arrived in a strange country, but as if I were in my home town of Evanach, but only those who have had the experience will appreciate it. Coming out into the open, I felt as if someone said to me, My son, now you can go wherever you like. A new world with a new life is open before you, full of possibilities . . .

What struck the diarist most forcibly was that meetings could be held in public, and that he could walk about singing at the top of his voice.

One day during my meanderings I made up my mind to walk right through London, and get to the outskirts so that I could see the surrounding fields, which I thought must be similar to those in Evanach and Smorgon. I walked for about one and a half hours, enjoying every minute of it, until I reached a certain square in the middle of which stood a monument and a pond, and there were pigeons to be seen everywhere. These were being fed by people watching them, and one woman had them perched on her hands and arms. It was a beautiful scene and, enthralled, I stood there for some time.
I found out later that this was the famous Trafalgar Square.

The 1981 census estimated that five per cent of the population of Greater London looked to the West Indies and Africa as their country of origin, that four per cent looked to India, and six per cent looked elsewhere – to Ireland, Portugal, Italy, Hong Kong, Cyprus. The census also showed that there are as many Cypriots in London as there are in Nicosia.

Just as the Huguenots settled near their point of disembarkation, by the river, so the Pakistanis flying in to Heathrow made their homes in Southall. Coming by boat to Southampton and by train to Waterloo, the West Indians settled in south London; the Irish near Paddington Station; the Scottish, King's Cross.

'If I was going to Norway and knew nobody,' said Mr Singh, editor of the *Sikh Messenger* and one of London's 100,000 Sikhs, 'I wouldn't know where to go. But if I knew one person, I would go and see him. Which is why people huddle together, for the convenience of knowing someone in a strange country with hostility around them.'

Mr Singh has a dark beard and a black turban, and sits on a red velvet sofa. In front of him is an oval table with silver ashtrays and drink mats. On the gold wall hang pictures of snow scenes. Behind, the Wimbledon sky and trees are caught in the net curtains. 'I do consider myself a Londoner. It's a place I know more about. You can pretend to be one thing, but you are a product of your environment. You're like a snowball. You're a bit of everything you pick up. By passport I am British, by outlook neither one nor the other. I find myself saying, "these British", and then, "these Indians". If I go to a British film in India and it's a comedy, I laugh in different places from the rest of the audience. But I find it's a blessing to be brought up in two cultures. It's like seeing with two eyes rather than one.'

At school he had been teased and prodded and poked. He wore no turban over his long hair, which the boys pulled. 'The biggest difficulty for a Sikh is dress. Why do you wear a turban? they ask. Is your head hurting? That sort of remark. And there are prejudices over what we eat. I remember describing yoghurt to someone. "You mean, you really drink sour milk?" People don't understand. When England beat the West Indies at cricket, they'd say, "We've really got you this time." You try and explain you're from somewhere else. It's difficult. But in the last decade people have holidayed abroad more. The daily prejudices are fewer. Sitting on a bus, passengers are much less hesitant to sit beside one. It's put about that racism affects some people not others. I suffered the most disconcerting racism of all in India – in West Bengal. I was treated not as a foreigner, but as someone from another planet.'

Krishna is a young widowed Bengali from Arnos Grove. It is an area taken over by the Greeks who have moved north from Finsbury Park, and who will move on to detached houses in Cockfosters. In the houses opposite, the Greek women make clothes for the smart shops of Kensington. Big blue vans arrive to collect the newly sewn dresses wrapped in polythene.

Krishna has dark hair like burnt treacle and a cat called Porridge. She teaches small children on the Broadwater Farm Estate, in 1985 the scene of London's worst racial riots. She sharpens their pencils, makes angels out of doilies, and shows them pictures of what lies inside a human tummy.

Coming from a traditional Indian family, her images of

England were formed by literature and films. In *Waterloo Bridge*, she had seen Vivien Leigh cross the Thames. She had read Wordsworth on Westminster Bridge. Arriving with her husband for a course at London University, she was struck by how Victoria Station looked like the station in Bombay, only cleaner and colder.

She also noticed the loneliness of the streets. When a girl fainted in the tube, no one helped. Picking up English like a magpie, she looked for work. 'Can you spell cathedral?' said a man with a big moustache. She could, and was given a job in an income tax office. She involved herself in the old musty papers by day, and by night learnt country dancing.

Then, four years ago, her young husband died of a heart attack.

'Having depended on him, I woke up one morning and suddenly realised I had to do things on my own. All my relations said, You must go home. But I knew I would have been pampered. Everything would have been done for me. I would have been condemned to a life of widowhood. I said, I will find myself better if I stay here. I will discover what I am capable of. My loyalty to London is that it has made me a human being. It has given me both humility and independence.'

Krishna's pupils come from Cyprus, Jamaica, Scotland, Bengal. Jackie comes from Africa, but she doesn't know which country. Sean hasn't heard of Piccadilly Circus. Emma has a nice next-door neighbour called Bert. She likes London because of Bert, the Christmas lights, the shops, and the birthday party she has every year. When she thinks of London she thinks of buses, cars, trains, white people, dark brown people and light brown people. When she smells it she smells tea, burning cars, and a house on fire.

In an exclusive private school in Knightsbridge, a teacher asks her pupils – mainly the children of the immigrant rich – to write about what they like and dislike about London.

Stephan, aged ten, says he likes America better.

> I don't like London because the buildings are all stuck together and to much traffic. There only four channels on TV and the people have weird english. The house gardens are very small. And the houses are all old and the paint is uggly its also coming of. You can only see brick walls around you. Its also poluted. The food is not good at school. The cab doors open the wronge way.

Mohammed is also ten.

> The thing I like about London is the shops and airports. The
> thing that I don't like is the old science teacher, Mr Sharples.

What upsets these children are pollution, 'vandels and mugers',
the traffic, 'louts and punk rockers doing graffiti all over walls',
and rubbish.

> Nearly every step you take in a park you find the soles of your
> shoes all brown [says Janson]. But I suppose it is better than
> the country when you tred in cows and horse wotsit. In
> London there are hundreds of Embassys and big department
> stores like Harrods and there are always bomb scares and
> attemps to assasinate rich Arabs who run oil buissness.
> Outside an Embassy you always see about thirty-five Mer-
> cedes all belonging to Arab buissness men.

Andreas, aged nine, thinks London is:

> A nice place to live. maybe not the pretiest though. I like it
> because you don't have to walk very far to the nearest
> wherever you want to go. London is the centre of everything.

Which is, very roughly, what his fellow countryman Henry James
thought: 'London is indeed an epitome of the round world, the
property and even the home of the human race.'

Caryl is a writer who was brought up in the north, lives in
Shepherd's Bush, and came from St Kitts the year he was born
twenty-eight years ago. 'A scruffy pile of dirt,' he growls
affectionately towards a small map on the wall shaped like a whale
eaten by moths. His voice is the voice of a northerner raised on
Tetleys bitter, but in it you can hear the distant chew-suck-spit of
the sugar cane.

The theme of his novels is the emigration of West Indians to
Britain in the 1950s. Even his agent, he says, massaging his beard,
remembers going each weekend to Waterloo 'to watch the darkies
coming in'. Their arrival, he argues, made the greatest impact on
British social history since the Second World War. 'It sounds crass
now, after the riots, but my parents wanted to provide a better life
for me. They felt they were coming home to the cultural hub
which had provided them with a language, a religion and an
education.'

They had arrived in a fog like coconut milk, and trickled north to a council estate in Leeds. His father found work as a labourer on nights trains to Halifax. His mother, who had sat Cambridge 'O' Levels, had two more children and taught. 'She once said it was like going from a colour film to one in black and white. She had come from a society where the only white people were rich and lived in big houses on plantations. In Leeds, the conditions they found themselves in were shocking. But doubly shocking was the fact that white people had to endure them too.

'Most migrants didn't talk about what it had been like. They didn't want their children to know anything of the hardship and misery they went through. They didn't want us to have grudges against the English. They wanted us to work within the system. I knew in my heart of hearts society did not like black people, but when Enoch Powell made his "Rivers of Blood" speech, things were said which had only been understood before.'

It is a recent incident which sticks in Caryl's mind. On a vac. from Oxford, where he read English literature, he went to Lisbon and lost his passport. Calling in at the Embassy, he was made to wait. An hour later, a girl came in who had lost hers. Caryl recognised her. They shared the same bank manager in Oxford. 'She left four hours before me. "How do I know you're British?" the official said to me. "You don't even look British." '

On leaving Oxford, he became aware that half of him belonged in the Caribbean where he was born. 'I realised the clue to understanding the person who took my tube ticket at Ladbroke Grove was in the Caribbean. It was also the clue to understanding myself. There was life before Waterloo Station and Southampton, and the only way of getting to the bottom of it was to get out there.'

Since his first visit, he has returned regularly. Now, whenever he is in the one place, he misses his Sunday newspapers and football results; in the other, his grandmother's stories, a new calypso. Only in The Bush pub off Shepherd's Bush Green does he feel completely at home. 'It must be the only pub in London where you see Princess Michael of Kent stepping over a drunk. At one end of the bar is a telly and juke box, at the other, actors and television stars. I was determined to live in an area which reflected my background – West Indian, working class and media. It's an odd place. You've got the young middle classes moving in, who can't afford Notting Hill Gate. You've got the working-class

31

council houses of White City – which is exactly what it is. Even the street names reflect their attitude – South Africa Road, Bloemfontein Road, The General Smuts pub. And you've got the market, where you see the Nigerians and Arabs shopping for tropical food in their Rolls Royces.

'In Harare, people talk of Shepherd's Bush market as if it is down the road.'

'I am a Battersea boy,' says Major Pawlac, an estate agent. He lives in a white house on the edge of the common, with a wife and two bull terriers. The door bell does not work, but his nationality is obvious from the Solidarity sticker on the frosted window. He has dappled brown skin, blue eyes and a rolling voice.

'I feel completely at home in London. You are not threatened. There is total security. You cannot get bored. It can fit anybody, any age, any occupation, any education.'

But it was not always thus for Major Pawlac.

'I was a regular officer in Poland,' he says, stroking a bull terrier. 'I was five days a Russian prisoner and on the sixth of October nineteen thirty-nine I was given to the Germans. I was taken first to Oflag Two B, then to Oflag Eight B, which became the Polish contingent in Colditz. I started learning English from a German book. I must learn the language of the victors, I told my guards. Telling them that in nineteen thirty-nine was bloody cheeky. They went mad. I am a student of history, I added. It will take five years, like last time.

'I first escaped in January nineteen forty, and was caught after three days. I escaped again in May, and walked for two months across Czechoslovakia to Budapest.' He joined the Polish underground movement, saw action in Tobruk, and was in charge of the regiment that captured Bologna.

The whole of Europe was on the move. There were many Poles in Italy, including 2,000 girls of marriageable age, one of whom he married. She told him of her grandmother who used to go twice a year from St Petersburg to Paris, just for clothes; and of her grandfather, a Russian general who had committed suicide.

On Guy Fawkes night in 1946 they both arrived in England. 'We were foreigners, and we felt like foreigners because London did not have foreigners. People were not communicative. When we looked for rooms to rent, there would be notices outside shops saying, No foreigners, No catholics, No small dogs or children.

In such a situation, two or three families bought a house together. It's the reason why so many Poles are house owners. We progressed a bit when the West Indians came in. "One stage up," we joked.

'First of all I had to get a job. It was a terrific problem. There was plenty of work, but a Pole could only be employed if there was no room for an Englishman. My divisional commander was a liftman, my brigadier a barman, and at Grosvenor House about thirty majors and colonels cleaning silver were known as the Polish Silver Brigade.

'I wrote to Prudential Assurance. I asked them, please don't throw this letter into the wastepaper basket. Give me an interview. I got it. It lasted four hours in an office off Ladbroke Grove. "It's out of the question," the man said. "My company's not going to make experiments." It was unbelievable. Me, a Polish officer with a family to support. I said, I must have a job. The interview had begun at ten-thirty. At one-thirty I could see him overanxious to go to lunch. "Okay, then," he said. "But I will not take responsibility. I will have you see the deputy general manager." So I saw this man. "Alright," he said. "I will give you the area where most Poles live – Chelsea." So I went to see the area manager, who was very hostile. "Those people in head office," he said, shaking his head. "Just exactly how do you think the average Englishman's going to react when you get into his house?"

'Thinking of this interview, I got on the tram from Beaufort Street to Clapham. When a working man sat down next to me, I turned to him. "Excuse me," I said. "I know it's unknown in London to speak to a stranger without being introduced, but I have exceptional circumstances. How would an average Englishman react to me?"

' "You'll be alright, chum," he said.

'Now, the average agent at the Prudential was not expected to produce new business for six months, while he was being trained. After a week I brought in my first proposal, from the Polish hostels. The local manager made a row. "This man will cause trouble." But my boss wasn't that stupid, he called me in and said, "Don't worry about him." So I continued to go to the Polish hostels – where they spoke no English and were lost completely – sometimes getting up to twenty proposals a night. After a year, out of fourteen thousand agents I was eleventh in the country, and first in London for producing new clients.

33

'At that time, the accent when you opened your mouth was important. Quickly I realised I had to learn some cockney. When I walked into a working-class home, where I'd be offered innumerable cups of tea, I'd say, "Oh, me plates are aching." It was extremely good for business. I decided after a while if someone said, "Hey, you're not English", to say I was Welsh. That worked very well because half thought I really was, while the others gave a good hearty laugh – and a good hearty laugh is always good for business. Once, a group of London Irish came drinking and singing to a club I go to in Balham. I decided, why should I not join in? I got up and addressed them. "As the only Welshman here, I would like to sing to our Irish guests something in Welsh. As a good Catholic, I will sing what we boys sang in Cardiff to welcome Pope John Paul." I sang a happy long Polish song. When I had finished, an Irishman came up to me. "Come along, my wife wants to meet you," he said. "She is also Welsh." '

A dog barks in the next room. The milk van goes by. Major Pawlac resumes his monologue.

'Despite many experiences here because I was a foreigner, I never felt a stranger. I go outside and look around, and I feel a total satisfaction.'

The so-called 'true Londoner' is not born in St Kitts, Warsaw or Calcutta, but within the sound of Bow Bells. This traditional belief dates from the early seventeenth century, when the term 'cockney' also gained currency. Derived from *cokeney*, the Middle English for a misshapen egg, it was used by tough countrymen to describe effeminate simpletons living in town.

But the East Ender who tells you he is a proper cockney because he was born within the sound of these bells is frequently referring to the wrong Bow. Until bombs destroyed them in 1941, the original bells of St Mary-le-Bow, a church that dates back to the Middle Ages, chimed over Cheapside in the heart of the City. They did not ring in the Bow district about Stepney.

Taine had no truck with this geographical sentimentality. He judged by appearances. To him, a typical Londoner had the face of a prize cauliflower.

The true Londoner is probably neither a cockney nor a cauliflower, but the man who tells you his life story in a pub without telling you his name; a presence as solid and familiar, yet ultimately as evanescent as his city. Given London's propensity for fiction and myth, the truest Londoner of all is probably a writer. 'Shakespeare wrote nothing but doggerel lampoon before he came to London,' said Oscar Wilde. 'And never penned a line after he left.'

V.S. Pritchett goes further: 'Most literature was written in London.'

He lives off Regent's Park on what used to be the fearful no-man's-land between London and the farmlands. Historically, all the railway rubbish ended up here. Then it became renowned as the place where Dickens got rid of his wife, installing her with a large allowance in an area that was deemed out of the swim but respectable. Irish navvies and Mrs Dickens gave way to the Greeks. Finally came the intelligentsia.

Short-story writer, novelist, man of letters, critic, the author in 1962 of *London Perceived*, Sir Victor Sawdon Pritchett is a link with this past.

'I was born in nineteen hundred,' he says. He is small, tidily dressed in tweed, with a face like well-polished leather – the material of his first trade. 'You would imagine I thought the nineteenth century behind me. I don't. It lasted till the First World War. I remember, as a boy at school, my first public ride on a horse-drawn tram from London Bridge to Tower Bridge. In a glowing moment, my father would take me on a hansom cab. The streets would be packed with horse-drawn traffic. They stank of horse manure, urine and human sweat. In the smarter quarters you could smell scent.

'London was dirty, awfully dirty. It was filthy in fact. Coal smoke from the railways poisoned the sky. You had to have a bath every day, scrubbing hard to remove the grime. It was bad for chests. Coal smoke made everyone cough themselves silly. My life was despaired of when I was a child.

'The weather has greatly improved; so, with industrialisation, have the clothes. You don't see ragged children running barefoot. Yet now people wear untidy, sporty clothes on a Sunday, as opposed to their best. As for punks, a punk strikes me as someone who wants to appear as one of the needy poor. Immediately I see a shaven head, I think, Oh God, lice in the family.

'The poor were feared collectively as a domestic terror. People had a catastrophic dread of them. My fears now are quite precise. They're about being mugged or having a bag snatched. There are ten cases a day in Harrods, I was told. It's incredible that one should feel afraid to walk anywhere now. In my youth, London was a tough city, but it had very little crime. It was more characterised by fights. I remember women fighting with each other drunkenly outside a pub, watched by the crowd.

'Old London was dictated by old middle-class virtues and vices – solid respectability, a feeling you were better than your neighbours, prudency and decency, consideration to your own class, not to any outside it.

'My father, if he came back today, would like the shops enormously. But he would expect to go about and be respected and deferred to. Though his life was modest, in his own job he had a certain position.

'He would notice the vast population from Asia and India. Before the War they were an eccentricity. People were fond of the solitary black or the solitary Chinaman. Now they walk in crowds among us.

'He would notice in the little boutiques – which I find infuriating – the reproductions which hung on his wall. I remember one called *Wedded*. It had a Roman with a tiger skin walking along a castle wall with his lady. It made me laugh. Ten years ago I was given one as a present. Now it's an *objet trouvé*.

'He would notice how high London has become. Like Venice, London was a low city. When I came to this area in the fifties and walked to the top of Primrose Hill, I looked down on a flat-roofed forest because there were so many trees. The only high building was a spire. Now it's difficult to see St Paul's.

'It remains, though, a very hospitable city – a very affectionate city to strangers. A familiar city, and a very hypocritical one. I love the English hypocrisy of going to market and being called Dear and Darling and Ducks, knowing perfectly well you're not dear nor darling nor ducks. But Londoners like these customs, and the way it's always been done. If we can help it, we don't forget the past in the present.

'In their imaginations, the Victorians were never in London. Their imaginative life was outside, abroad. They wanted London to be in Rome. Now the middle classes want to be in Spain or the Bahamas, glamorously going off to places others cannot get to. Geographical heroes. East Enders are different. They're peculiar to themselves, like an extra nation. In the East End there's a hero in every street.

'That's really the secret to London, the key. It's a place where people are allowed to develop their character to a unique degree. I was in Hampstead not so long ago, rounding a corner, when I came upon two middle-aged men who had just bumped into each other. They were glad to meet again.

'"Where've you been?" said one.

'"Bosham," the other replied.

'"Bosham! Heavens, do you know Bosham?" said the other.

'"Bosham. Of course I know Bosham. I'm a well-known character there."'

'This is what a Londoner wants to be, a character. One who is known for something off-duty, something peculiar, yet something which makes him belong to a set – like people who only go to one pub. It is a conceit. We have a lot of conceit, but we are devoid of vanity.

'I don't think I'd want to live anywhere else,' he said.

Part Two
AT HOME

'*They stod without order.*'

FABIAN ON 'LONDON'S HOUSYNGE', AD 981

'*It is . . . in the multiplicity of human habitations which are crowded together that the wonderful immensity of London consists.*'

SAMUEL JOHNSON, 1763

'*Everybody here has a right to a home of their own.*'

NOTICE AT CARRINGTON HOUSE, 1986

'Manor' is thieves' slang for London. The word goes to the heart of a city where property is regarded as sacrosanct. Unlike other capitals, most people live in houses rather than apartment blocks, and, due to the vagaries of the 1957 Rent Act, most people – sixty-two per cent – choose to own what they live in.

'The London of the little houses,' says V.S. Pritchett, 'is the true London.' A Londoner's home is not only his private club and his castle – which he fortifies with crenellations, ramparts and fortress-like gates. It is his life's investment, his anchor to the city, and second in importance only to his name. More than for other city dwellers, a Londoner's address describes him, locates him, places him. Hence the insistence of the press that when X is found murdered in Muswell Hill, this news is accompanied by the price of his house.

Behind closed doors and net curtains the Londoner has his private being. One front door may conceal two spinster sisters who sit in rocking chairs looked after by their butler. They have not dusted the house in Cadogan Square since the year their fiancés died – the first falling out of a hot-air balloon; the second gored to death by a domestic pig. Another door may conceal a mother and son who have not ventured into the streets for twenty years, and who wonder if the trams still run. Behind a third may lurk Christie or Dennis Nilsen.

'The house looms large if not as a refuge, as a metaphor, live, dead and mixed,' wrote the American architect and author Bernard Rudofsky in *The Prodigious Builders*. 'It is the repository of our wishes and dreams, memories and illusions. It is, or at least ought to be, instrumental in the transition from being to well-being.'

Henry James thought fiction was a house.

★

A wet night in Spitalfields. The destination, Folgate Street, turns out to be a row of dark brick houses off the juggernaut thorough-fares around Liverpool Street. Though a gas flame putters in the lamp outside Number 18, the shutters are drawn, and the bell rings without answer.

At 8.30 p.m. prompt, the black door opens, and a small man in a collarless shirt and jeans leaps like a leprechaun into the rain. Stroking his fair beard, he introduces himself to the group – mostly fellow Americans – who are huddled in the doorway opposite. They are a captive audience. Despite their soaking, they have paid Dennis Severs £20 for the privilege of his company that night; and more importantly, of entering his house, which for six years he has painstakingly restored, decorated and stuffed in homage to its past inhabitants.

Before opening 18 Folgate Street, he treated the whole of London like a museum, giving tours through its streets in a horse-drawn carriage. Now, behind the black door, he is curator in his own home to his own fantasies of the city.

Rome was built by the Church, Paris by the State. But London, he argues, was built by the middle classes, and his is a middle-class home.

'Everything entering it is demodernised, but the house is exercised all day long. Meals are left behind. Clay pipes are smoked. Breakfast is taken in the master bedroom. It's an art form. One that is anti gloss, anti the glass-case mentality. The aim is to create a still life and break you down. I'm not showing a house to the public. I'm taking you over. I'm using your mind as a canvas. If it is smeared already with Holbein, the whole effect is ruined.'

Also, he admits, if the lodger leaves his biro out.

We hurry up the steps, over scattered straw, and into the fusty hall. Behind, the door closes. 'Has all the fussing stopped? Right.' He twists the lock and turns around. 'We are here to dream. To get the twentieth century out of our noses, out of our ears, out of our minds.'

The dream begins downstairs, in the cellar. Holding a candle, he hands round a sepia photograph of two boys, Clarence and Gervaise, who, at the turn of the century, came down here to dig, and under the cellar floor found fragments of Roman pottery and clay pipes. This, he says breathlessly, producing fragments from a bucket, is how far back we are going. Then, blowing out the candle, he leaves us in the dark. From hidden speakers, Severs' commentary resumes as a tape recording. Accompanied by flickering lights and period music, it introduces the original owners of the house – Huguenot silk weavers who fled France in 1685. Smuggled across the Channel in wine casks and holding their pet canaries, they had washed up in Spitalfields. 'Though in all our chasing we'll never quite catch up with them, we are involved in a complete and total reality. And if anyone asks at the end where I live,' the hidden voice hisses, 'I will shoot you.'

A tube train shakes the floor.

'I hope you're not claustrophobic,' says one American to another.

We filter next into a kitchen. There is a fire, the smell of cooking and herbs, and a real black cat. This is the domain of Rebecca, the cook. She is four-foot-two, says Dennis, and her voice can be heard throughout Spitalfields. Her hobby is watching the hangings. Her motto, 'Never Mind Your Own Business'. After breakfast she sweeps the floor with lavender. From outside comes the recorded sound of clopping hooves and a water seller's cry. A tap at the Dutch window is the sign for Rebecca to pass bread to the journeyman. This she scoops out and fills with the barterable commodity of tea.

'My God, that girl's a stinker.'

Also stinking is the dead rat under the table, decoyed there as a flea tormentor. From upstairs comes the sound of ladies laughing as they rise to move from dinner to the drawing room. From now on we will follow the silk weavers through several generations, and into the rooms they have just vacated. 'We are here to dream. Wake up and dream,' comes Severs' invocation. He dashes out in pursuit of Rebecca.

In the green-panelled dining room, a chair lies on its side, kicked over by Ben Truman who has been visiting. There is an overpowering aroma of roast beef. Beside the dirty plates on the table are crumpled napkins, half-empty port glasses, a porcupine quill for picking teeth. A canary hops restlessly in a wickerwork cage above a cardboard figure portraying the eldest son. He stands with his back to the fire, the flames silhouetting his shape enormously against the walls. A primitive security device, so that people outside believe someone is there.

And so, escorted by the urgent owner, his taped voice and the cat – renamed Waterloo along the way – we wander upstairs through the centuries: to an elegant drawing room, arranged about a carpet which has been swept by the ubiquitous Rebecca with damp tea leaves. 'The genius of the British drawing room is that nothing matches,' explains our host. The room smells of lavender and oranges. Festoons of walnut clusters hang on the cloth-panelled walls. A pair of tiny kid ankle boots lies discarded under a chair. Then, up more stairs to a bedroom with a four-poster and a silk flap over an ugly family portrait. And through to a dressing room, where tea is steaming on a table and the walls are lined with framed mementoes of the great. Here is the Duke of York's signature. Here the signature of Wellington, and here a lock from his horse, Copenhagen.

Waterloo marks the beginning of the end for Spitalfields' weavers. Unemployed soldiers invade the area. There are four years of court mourning and in 1825 the Free Trade Act lifts the monopoly Spitalfields enjoyed on silk. In a short time, demand for the material has given way to the rage for printed cotton and muslin – cheap and easy to wash.

It is a formidable one-man performance, and for an instant the smells, the sound effects, the faithful period detail conspire to make the house and family breathe.

Then, behind a rickety screen, are spotted a tube of Colgate toothpaste and a *Writers' & Artists' Yearbook*.

'Pay attention,' comes an anxious yell.

Too late. With the lodger's toothpaste, the dream is gone.

It was the journalist and essayist E.V. Lucas who lamented that London's chance to be a civilised city was lost forever at Waterloo. Had Wellington been defeated, the Frenchman who replanned Paris, Baron Haussmann, might have come our way, and carriages would have run four abreast down Fleet Street.

Wellington's house, standing like a Palladian packing-case on Hyde Park Corner, is a more conventional repository of the past than 18 Folgate Street. It is also known, somewhat incorrectly in fact, as the first house in London. Nevertheless, send a letter to Number 1, London, and it will drop through the door of Apsley House.

Of all London's private palaces, only this austere brown building is still inhabited. More typically, the wings lived in by the
Wellington family sandwich a museum. The superintendent, a
jolly black lady, points to a gate round the side. It leads to a door
onto a tired lawn overlooked by the Intercontinental. In the
shadow of low bushes by the fence crouch green statues. 'Come
up to the top,' says a female voice through the intercom. Beside
the door a black and white notice declares the family name. Beside
the lift, a print shows Peter and John healing the lame man at the
beautiful gate of the temple.

Apsley House was bought from the Duke of Wellington's brother
in 1816. With money voted him by the government, the Duke
paid £42,000 for the balance of his brother's lease, which he turned
into a freehold. He then spent another £66,000 facing the brick
exterior with Bath stone, and filling the inside with trophies of
battle. Twice the house was enlarged to accommodate a com-
memorative gallery and dining room, so that each year at the
Waterloo Banquet he could entertain a dwindling number of his
officers. At one gathering, Count Orloff, famous for his strength,
rolled up a silver plate. The Duke asked if he could unroll it. He
did so, but took the skin off his hands.
    In 1947 the house was given to the nation. Four years earlier, the
seventh duke had returned from Eritrea and made his way late in
the night and unannounced to Hyde Park Corner. When the
housekeeper opened the door, she was confronted by a figure
melodramatically holding a lamp against his face.
    Antonia, Lady Douro, a member of the German royal family, is
married to the present Duke of Wellington's son. Blonde hair
cascades down a white jersey to her waist. Tall, thin, and very
beautiful, she looks as if she has tumbled sleepily from a painting
by Watts. She rubs her eyes, apologising for the bags under them.
She has been up for the last two nights till five, she explains. To
prove she is not middle aged. And she had twelve to lunch
yesterday, she adds, disappearing 'to cause coffee'.
    She starts with a brisk tour, climbing up stairs that spiral round
a glass well. Below is the Wellington Museum. 'It's a great
rambling house built in a figure of eight. My father-in-law has the
ground floor. We have this level and the attic.' She pauses on the
attic landing before a drainage map. Meticulously etched by one
T. Meakin, it shows the underbutler's room, the smith's room,

the parlourmaid's room, the rooms for dust and guns, the wine cellar – 'we still use that' – and a long gallery she wants to lend to the London Library. Covering a single floor, it looks like the ground plan of a small town.

We continue through the low, dark bedrooms of her two children, squeeze past a Napoleonic chest of drawers in the narrow corridor – 'this shouldn't be here' – and plunge downstairs to her quarters. They are reached through a bathroom with a large metal bath on lion's legs and mahogany drawers which spew out clothes. Her bedroom, with its four-poster bed, overlooks the park where she rides, and the garden into which tramps occasionally climb for the night. The room is hung with nicotine-coloured paintings in elaborate gilt frames. 'I really hang them because of their frames. The furniture is all 1830s – all very masculine. I defy you to find a bow or a lace curtain. In fact, there are only three pairs of curtains in the house. I just don't like them. Because the house is floodlit till midnight, I can never turn the lights on, and have to move around in the dark.'

We pass into 'Charles' sitting room'. (Charles is her husband, the Marquess of Douro.) From there into a book-lined dining room, frescoed with a hunter riding through trees, and the green kitchen. Two women sit on stools, an open diary on each of their laps, planning the next dinner. 'This is the green colour everyone sees when they look up from Hyde Park Corner. I think we're going to paint it white.' At breakfast here on their first morning in residence, Lady Douro's husband had seen a woman in her bra in one of the Intercontinental windows. Every breakfast since, over the rim of his coffee, he has scanned the hotel front. The children turn their eyes to Marble Arch. 'A fat policeman used to hide behind a lamppost and intercept drivers turning into the bus lane.'

Circling through the nursery, we finally arrive at her study. Dark like the other rooms, it is gorged with books and paintings, and the black tin hat boxes of military forbears.

She sits, her back to the window, in a green felt chair. On the table is the coffee she has caused, and a copy of *The Hobbit*. Outside, framed in the double-glazed window, Peace lashes her four bronze horses with a wreath across Constitution Arch. Legend has it that before her unveiling, and under the horses, the sculptor, soldier and vet, Arthur Jones, gave a dinner for eight. I do not ask but suspect that Lady Douro knows.

Apart from her role as hostess, Antonia Douro is consultant

editor of the publishers Weidenfeld & Nicolson, a committee member of the London Library ('which involves serious discussion on whether there should be wooden lavatory seats in the ladies loo'), a director of Thames Valley Broadcasting, the chairman of the Guinness Housing Trust, ('which builds fifteen thousand units every year for "the deserving poor" '), and the author of *Frankenstein, the Modern Prometheus*, a ballet which has just played at Covent Garden. 'I think I'm not missing anything.' She pauses. 'I know. Reviews for *The Spectator*.' She is also at work on a doctoral thesis on Mary Shelley, and a book on the Shelleys in Italy. 'It's not a traditional biography,' she insists. 'Not, "May the first: Lady Mornington screamed her last and the baby was taken to the next room".' Her thesis is more predictable: Frustrated by Shelley's father from writing his biography, Shelley's wife found an outlet for describing her husband and his circle in fiction.

Mary Shelley's husband thought Hell was a city much like London. Antonia Douro does not agree. 'I adore London. Its pace, the fact it's a masculine city. Architecturally it's less mannered than Paris or Rome. It's elite, unforgiving. It also makes it possible for me to lead nine different lives.'

In her own ground plan of the city, she looks eastwards, down Piccadilly to her mother's family house in St James's. Very rarely does she venture west, to the shops and galleries of Chelsea, 'the tired faces of people putting on make-up at four in the afternoon'. Seminal to her life are the Piccadilly line and the number 9 bus. 'My points of call if I had to go to the loo would be the London Library, the Royal Academy, the Opera House, King's College and the British Museum.'

Apsley House, she agrees, is conveniently placed for all of them. 'Although, when I first came in nineteen seventy-six I woke at five a.m., completely rattled, as the traffic crept up like the dawn chorus. Since then I haven't been phased by the noise. The fact is, it's not noisy.' The windows used to have iron shutters, erected after fifty minutes of repeated stoning from an angry mob in October 1831 when the Reform Bill was defeated in the Lords. One stone landed in the room where the first duchess was dying. Double glazing suffices today.

'Do you know about the science of sound? Well, there's white noise, a continuous low level which you cannot hear. And black noise, like sirens. We haven't had much of that since the casualty unit closed down at St George's – although there is a police station under the arch.' She admits the garden, which backs onto Park Lane, is noisy. 'My children play football out there, but you don't feel like tearing your clothes off. We have a nice roof where we can do that – even if it is rather overlooked by the Intercontinental.'

The real worry is not noise but air pollution. 'The lead content is massive. When I tested the blood of my children, I found more in the younger than the older. And I found we had lead pipes too.' Has she changed them? 'God, you bet. And there's a special drinking tap in the kitchen.'

She lists the other disadvantages of living in the last private palace in London. 'If the lift gets stuck, you have to go right down to the basement and then up, which is a hell of a hike.' (Her notice in the lift underlines an order to close the gates firmly. Under it someone has scribbled 'Bossy Boots'.) 'And you can't drive up to to the front door – which means if you have people to lunch like we did yesterday, and it rains, you have twelve distinguished people running at this angle,' she leans forward, 'with newspapers over their heads.'

She parks in the front, beside the museum. 'Before they put the lights in, I used to whip round Hyde Park Corner in first gear. The technique was never to look right or left. I'm a very, very bad driver, so it's bad news if I meet someone who isn't thinking what they're doing. Actually, it's bad news if you meet people like that anyway.' Once, a new suitcase was pinched from her locked car in full view of the office. 'Don't you think that's gutsy?' she asks, opening her eyes wide. 'I'd love to meet the person who did it.'

She remembers another drawback, then a parallel advantage. 'You cannot walk to the corner shop, but if you run out of cigarettes you can dash out to the tube station.' Antonia Douro does not run out of anything very much. Twice a week she gives a shopping list to the estate office. The same office takes her children to school. She channels the time this leaves her into her nine lives. 'I do an absurd amount of things. That's because of living in London. One can slip in and out of one's responsibilities with total anonymity.'

This desire for anonymity extends to her home. At university she told friends she lived in a house on a roundabout. 'Technically, it's not Hyde Park Corner. It's Wellington Place, and Apsley House is one hundred and forty-nine Piccadilly. It became separated when Park Lane came through. It is pure folklore that it's Number One, London. Schoolchildren are always sending letters as an experiment, asking for a reply. And they get it.'

'Number One, London, squire? That's the old Wellington house.' Les was a postman for sixteen years on the terraced streets of Fulham where he lives. He has small blue eyes that stray insistently to the window, and a large nose that smells trouble. It takes a vest, braces and a grey cardigan to keep his stomach in.

'You wouldn't lose me in London. Sorting till nine every night, four hundred thousand letters into forty-eight cubbyholes. No, squire. You have to know there's only one Napier Avenue but umpteen Napier Roads. Only one Alderville Road, and the next one to that is called Abbeville and it's in SW Four. 'Course you get a lot of mis-sorts. There's an SW Six area in Bristol. We used to get a dozen letters regular every month from Argentina for Hurlingham. Trouble was, it was Hurlingham, Buenos Aires. They went back with a Fulham postmark.'

With 35 lbs of mail on his back, Les got to know every house on his patch. Framed by the letter box, he saw a unique slice of the community's life. 'Their lives come through to your fingers from their envelopes, and you come to know the people themselves. They tell you their worries and woes, and you automatically know what's coming up. Near enough, if they're in trouble, you can tell what type of trouble it is by the colour of the envelopes. Recorded deliveries have a pre-fixed number at the end telling you what department they're from, or what court. You see 'em have family rows. One bloke's nephew tried to blow him up with a letter bomb. Italian? Out and out British, do you mind! Or else it's husbands and wives carrying on with people, and they don't want each other to see their letters. No, it's not for you, it's for him, I'd say. People try and con mail out of yer, but the biggest offence you can do is hand someone's mail to him in the street. By law, it must go through their letter box. One time, a woman opened the door to me for a recorded delivery. When she came back with a pen, she was naked. What was I meant to do? I don't know. I wasn't going to find out either. It's there if you want it. Oh, it's there. I know some of my colleagues got a brand new car out of it an' all.'

When he retired, the street gave him a pewter mug and a large cheque. He now acts as the self-appointed caretaker of the 'turning', as he calls it, holding the keys to many properties, doing the odd bit of decorating, helping out. 'Anybody gets into trouble,' he says proudly, 'they knocks at my door.'

Les' street, which lies off the New King's Road, could not be more typical of London. Two red brick terraces of two-storey, bay-windowed houses, identical to streets in Leyton, Battersea, Shepherd's Bush, Tooting. Built at the end of the last century for the working class, such terraces still form sixty-four per cent of London's housing.

Often with a cheeseboard beside the front door announcing, in burnt black letters, Longleat or Highclere, these houses pride themselves on being miniature versions of Apsley House. The hallway may consist of a passage five feet wide with stairs running up, but it alludes confidently to its origins in the great hall of a medieval manor. The bay window, topped with crenellations, begs a comparison, sometimes odious, with castle towers.

At a glance these houses may appear the same, but a closer look at the decorations and mouldings reveals a different signature of pine leaves, parrots and poppies on each one. Inside, the differences multiply: a house may be owned by a single family, rented from the council, divided into flats, divided even into rooms. One house in Colville Road, Leyton, has six Italians squatting in a single room; one in the same road has water squirting from the doorbell; another in Bulwer Street, off Shepherd's Bush, is owned by a man who spent two years restoring the original mouldings to the capitals and plinths. Taking an electric light outside, he performed a *son et lumière* on the façade. 'That's where I rebuilt the ledges. That's where I cut the stones in and pinned them. That's where I carved a face of a gargoyle.' As a matter of fact, he said disarmingly, it was when carving the gargoyle that he had his nervous breakdown.

In their sociological study, *Family and Class in a London Suburb*, Willmott and Young analyse the Londoner's preoccupation with his home. The most obvious explanation is the pride of owning a small estate. Improving it, he not only adds to his own stature, he develops his talents as a craftsman who can plaster, garden, plumb and paint. Furthermore, he is able to treat his home as a business, saving money by owning rather than renting it, and doing his own odd jobs instead of getting workmen in. In 1919 ninety per cent of London homes were rented. Today, the figure is less than fourteen per cent, but it includes Les.

Les' house was bought by his wife's family when it was first built in 1896. It cost about £200. It was sold when his wife still lived there, and the freeholder is now a Palestinian, who in the last nine years has upped the rent from £6 a month to £160. 'He's even tried to thump me for more.' Eleven years ago, the house next door went for £38,000. This year, Number 46 has gone for £150,000. 'What makes me smile,' says Les, not smiling, 'is how do they pay their mortgages?' He stands up, stares through the netted window, and jangles the coins in his pocket. 'Makes me think I've been a silly, lazy, blind old sod all me life.'

Bred on the Fulham Road, the son of a lab technician and a school cleaner, Les' first income was the two bob he was paid by the North End Road costermongers for shouting 'Copper!' when they played 'Pieman'. 'Heads and Tails,' he translates. He remembers when the small park at the end was The Hurlingham Club's number two polo pitch, and when Hurlingham Road was 'Snob Alley', to the extent that coalmen and totters were not allowed to rumble down it.

'This was just a working man's turning – nothing but policemen and cabbies. You got a different class of people living here now. You name it, you got it. Snobs and all that caper.'

Peering down the street, he rattles out names at random. 'Over there's a nice coloured chap called Bob, who works at London Transport. Then there's Nita, who lives at Number Seventeen, which is a council house divided into two flats. She pays thirty-two pounds a week. At Number Twenty-Nine there's an independent lady of private means, who's an artist. We all look the same from the front, but some have cellars, some don't. Some have lofts you can get into, some haven't. Some have back additions that slant, some ones that go flat. Some houses in the street haven't even got central heating. The old couple in Number Seven haven't got a bath. They cross the road each night to bath at Number Six. We've done this house up all modern,' he says, turning back into the room, and grabbing the turkey flap under his chin. 'You've got to keep up with the Joneses.' Which reminds him of Mrs Jones in Number 3. She was born in a back room where the family of four slept in the same bed.

The prettification has had its drawbacks. The influx of different classes has not contributed to the community spirit Les remembers. 'It used to be a village.' He sighs. He cannot avoid the cliché. 'With a chemist, a greengrocer, a butcher. Now they've become estate agents and antique shops. The Co-op has turned into John D. Wood, the butcher's into Friend & Falcke, United Dairies into a cycle shop. There's no life in the turning. You used to see kids play. Now they've put ramps down to stop the petrol lorries, and there's just one little boy – at Number Seventeen. Everyone used to be in and out of each other's houses. Now they don't want to know you, except when they want something done. "Mr B., can you put a brass number on our door? We've blocked our drains, Mr B. Mr B., can we borrow a ladder, we've locked ourselves out."'

There is no doubt in his mind who symbolises the change. The young man in Number 18.

'Lord Henry. He's not a lord, but I call him that. He's a Rodney in the banking business.' He says it with unconcealed disgust. 'He gives barbeques. You've got these three young ladies and a gentleman hired to pour drinks for them, their glasses going clackle, clackle, clackle. What a bit of fun, what a bit of fun. Then the girls throw a bucket of water over our Rodney and leave. There was one night, his neighbour was in a state because water was coming in through the back of her outside toilet. Turned out the sewage was all messed up – from his end. The plumber did it for free, but the old lady wouldn't have it. She paid him five pound for his trouble. I told Henry Hiawatha this. "Oh, I must remember to reimburse the good woman," he says. Sod's never even knocked. I was picked up by him after he'd been burgled. Pulls me up. "Did you hear I got burgled? When you had my keys, you didn't have a duplicate cut?" You saucy bugger, I thought. My, when I say I hold 'em, I hold 'em! I could have kicked the sod in the bloody street.' Les wipes his nose. 'No squire, you don't see anybody talk to him.'

Jack up Les' terrace into the sky and no one talks to anyone. London's first high-rise was Queen Anne's Mansions off Victoria Street. Queen Victoria objected to the ruination of her view, and ten years later, in 1888, the height of buildings like it was restricted to the length of a fireman's ladder, or the width of the street. In 1954 building licences were abolished, and the sky became the limit.

In 1978, at an address to The Royal Institute of British

Architects, George Tremlett, chairman of the GLC Housing Committee, outlined the results of this abolition. 'Has it ever occurred to you how miserable it must be never to hear the song of a bird or see the waving of leaves on a tree because here, twenty storeys high, no birds sing and no trees reach . . . *Yours was the hand that signed the paper that felled a city.*'

Kenneth Campbell was chief housing architect at the GLC from 1959 to 1974, and oversaw the fiasco of the high-rise block. 'Do you want to cast me in the role of villain, hero or impartial observer?' he asks on the telephone.

'All three,' I say.

He gives directions to his house in Sydenham, at the entrance of the Hogarth Court Estate. 'It is very difficult to see,' he warns. 'It's a wilderness.'

'All my homes work extremely well,' he says, when I have found the low brick bungalow. 'But they're a bit dull. The nicest thing my daughter said about this one was, "It's cool."'

Campbell is tall and white with a grey moustache and hairs that sprout from his nose. Amiable, candid, talkative, he has the air – in his green cardigan and slippers – of a military man who has been too long from the battle. 'The damn thing,' he swears, taking the wrong glass of gin. 'I do that more and more often now.' His father was in the leather trade. He was brought up in a Victorian house in Crofton Park with frost on the inside windowpane, and a carpet that rose and fell with every draught. When he married, at twenty-three, he moved to Welwyn Garden City – 'As far from south London as you could get and yet still live in London. It had a cultural image. Bernard Shaw was nearby, and old gents in Norfolk jackets and knickerbockers cycled solemnly round its streets.'

Campbell served his apprenticeship in his uncle's firm of architects a quarter of a mile from Big Ben. His uncle was a great draughtsman. He could take a burnt match, draw a line on brown paper, and it would be beautiful. He ran an old-fashioned firm of twelve people, and he showed no favouritism to his nephew. 'If you took too long to sharpen your pencil, he would scream you had reduced the firm's profits,' Campbell remembers. On his first day at work he was told to colour up the copy of a large transparent drawing. Taking the wrong sheet, he spent one day laboriously colouring the original, and two days taking the colour off. It is possible to see in this the shape of things to come.

The firm's work centred on the building of offices, country houses and hospitals – Woolwich War Memorial Hospital, Sutton General Hospital, Carshalton Cottage Hospital. 'I'm fascinated by hospitals. Their smell, their atmosphere. Yet, I've never had cause to go to one,' he adds, perhaps significantly.

Soon he tired of imitating the past. 'If the Governors were keen for their hospital to look like a large country house, we did it neo-Georgian. If a client wanted Tudor magnate, we did it half-timbered. If he thought he would really shine as a Spanish grandee, we gave him white large curly gables and ironwork. It was all pastiche. Our generation began to get very very tired of playing games. There had to be a better way than just making a poor, or even a good copy of what had been done before. Though we never lost our admiration for Georgian and Caroline, we thought we were insulting Wren and his followers by trying to apply their architecture to office blocks.'

So he was ripe for Corbusier. 'It was like a great light,' he remembers, rising to pour another drink. 'We had no doubts. The doubts only come now.'

A house, thought this young Swiss architect and city planner, was a machine for living in. 'Industry on the grand scale must occupy itself with building,' he proposed in *Vers une Architecture*, published in 1923 . . . And bring to the home the beauties of mass production. First came Le Corbusier's 'Domino House'; then his vertical city, the *ville radieuse* bathed in light and air. 'A great new epoch has begun,' he wrote.

'We shape our buildings,' observed Churchill. 'But afterwards our buildings shape us.' In some quarters, Le Corbusier is now equated with Hitler.

'If there hadn't been a war,' Campbell resumes, 'the modern movement would have missed its opportunity for large-scale development and worked itself out. As it was, the modern movement was suddenly given the task of rebuilding whole chunks of the city. When we came to build, it wasn't what people wanted. Building a house in the same way as building a factory just didn't work.'

The Blitz destroyed 200,000 homes and made as many more uninhabitable. In a blue tin hat, and clutching a Canadian P17 rifle, Campbell worked as an Air Raid Precautions engineer in the City. Its streets were still paved with wooden blocks. Often when they caught fire, blue flames would lick the surface like those on a Christmas pudding. By day, he prevented single-minded London businessmen from entering their damaged offices. Work continued in the unscathed buildings. It was like a wildlife film, he says. The animals running like mad till one was caught. Then standing quietly grazing while it was eaten.

The buildings that could not be propped up were demolished. Campbell manned a bulldozer. 'I felt like a small boy with a very large catapult. Heavy buildings came down easier than light. When I think of the buildings that were gone . . . The last medieval buildings in the alleys around St Paul's. I saw St Paul's ringed with fire – absolutely ringed with it. I felt, this is the end.'

But one morning at the close of 1940, Campbell was rung up by a former colleague and told to report to County Hall. When he arrived, he was greeted by the shy, Edwardian figure in charge of rebuilding London – Patrick Abercrombie. 'I've been looking for you,' said Abercrombie. 'Will you help us? Probably the housing department is the best thing.' So Campbell was made responsible for housing, given a desk in the corner of the drawing office, and told to get on with it.

That was his brief? 'That was my brief,' he nods. 'To see how the city demolished by Hitler could be turned into a city of light and green and air.' He gets up to fetch a book. 'There was no damn reason why I should have been asked to do it.'

The researches undertaken by Abercrombie's team resulted in *The County of London Plan*, published in 1943. 'No one's ever read the thing, but it's damn good,' Campbell complains, flicking through the bulky grey volume. Like the large-scale plans of Wren and Evelyn, Nash and Barry, this came to little. The plan for doing away with Charing Cross was never put into action. The inner ring road joining Wandsworth to Rotherhithe was never built; the tunnels under Hyde Park and the City never dug. 'I suppose the one thing that happened was the Plan for Housing. It was the bible for the housing branch of the London County Council.' He closes the book and prods it sadly away down the sofa. 'My God, we were so starry-eyed and naive.'

The term 'concrete jungle' was first coined to describe the Alton West Estate at Roehampton. It was one of the first estates in Britain to be inspired by Le Corbusier. Overlooking the deer and golfers on Richmond Park, 1,850 homes were raised in eleven-storey rectangular or 'slab' blocks, twelve-storey tower blocks, four-storey maisonettes, and two-storey family houses. 'When it was built in nineteen fifty-one, we thought, "This is it,"' says Kenneth Campbell.

The following Sunday morning, he shows me round the Roehampton estate. It is a day such as might have been envisaged for the estate by its creators: with sunlight slanting through the blocks, trees in bud, and rolling expanses of grass. Had the men who built it returned like us today, ignorant of the intervening years, they too would probably maintain that *this is it* – despite tiers of white-net curtains streaming into one another like a single dirty waterfall, and the stains where acid rain has sweated salt from the concrete.

Kenneth Campbell makes a half-hearted stab as an apologist. 'One of those flats overlooking the park would suit me very well. They'd go like hot cakes on the open market.' He knows that this is irrelevant, but continues in the same vein, indicating a house with a varnished period door, a smart garden, and a wall with the surface of a dry mud lake. 'Where people have bought, they have promptly stone-cladded. The point about that house is that it's well looked after. The others are not, and it stands out a mile. Everybody's property is nobody's property.' Or, as the Chinese say, no one sweeps a common hall.

The last time Kenneth Campbell ventured back was for the estate's twenty-fifth anniversary. 'Reading the press reports that Roehampton had turned everyone into murderers, I thought we would need armoured cars.' He looks up at a tower block and shakes his head. 'Here we're in the heart of Corbusier. The worst part of his ethos, as translated by young men after the War, was that ornament could only arise from the structure itself. There's no tracery in the windows. The austerity is pathological. They even wanted black brick.'

He nods at a modern sculpture of a bull, daubed with paint, brooding over uncleared rubbish. 'We really thought that by putting families into this environment, they would change into ordinary middle-class people. The Scots, the French, the Americans all lived in high-rises. They were not mad.'

The final argument in favour of mammoth projects like this was political. By 1964 Harold Wilson was promising the electorate 500,000 new homes a year – and telling the local authorities to construct them at maximum speed. By 1965 the GLC, for which Kenneth Campbell worked as chief housing architect, had become the biggest landlord in Europe. The city was required to have 160 people per acre, and that meant building up rather than out. 'If you wanted to keep Londoners in London, near where they worked, it was tall buildings, chum. Full stop.' Not that the government minded. There could be no more visible proof that it was fulfilling its electoral pledge.

Campbell compares the climb upwards to a Greek tragedy. It is a troubled tale that started with the lifts. Until 1960, twelve storeys, as at Roehampton, was the limit for a slow lift. Then an estate was built in Kennington with sixteen storeys. Faster, more expensive, lifts had to be installed. As other estates were planned, it was decided the limit could be raised to twenty storeys – to reduce the extra cost per flat. This, however, was beyond the gravity feed for water. So pumps and spare pumps had to be introduced. At which point, it was argued, Why stop at twenty?

We enter one of two lifts to a tower block. 'There should have been three,' Campbell concedes. 'They need frequent servicing. And there's the milkman problem. Understandably, when delivering to each floor, he jams his crate in the door. But it's just at the time most people go to work. If the other lift is out of order, what do you do? Later, we had the coffin problem. This lift is only four foot square. Granddad had to be stood on end. The families didn't like it. So, to keep within costs, we built lifts seven foot by three – which means, when full, it's a struggle to get out.'

We step out at the top floor. There are four doors. One is extravagantly fitted in mahogany. 'The idea of only having four families per floor was that they would be jolly good chums. They would talk to each other at the front door instead of at the garden fence. In fact, the only middle-class characteristic the tenants gained instantaneously was non–neighbourliness.'

Later, I met a woman from the Citizens Advice Bureau in Wandsworth. She said: 'I'm always saying to people, haven't you got a friend to help out, and they're living in a block of two thousand people, and they say, I don't know anybody. That happens again and again.'

Surveying the deserted estate, Campbell admits to other failures. Roehampton was planned with one car space to every twenty families. Today the landscaped lawns are fringed with impenetrable ranks of Ford Capris, DER vans and black cabs. The naive segregation of young families and childless couples was equally absurd. 'If you put a childless couple into a tower block, two things would happen – they would buy new curtains, and they would have a baby. Similarly, after ten years the kids of parents in maisonettes would grow up and leave. We thought the families could simply swap over, but the idea completely floundered. Within fifteen years, the whole thing began to creak badly. It was hell on earth.'

The most obvious manifestation of this was vandalism. Less obvious was the collapse of management. Before and after the War, caretakers had been largely recruited from the navy. They were petty officers who were used to looking after men cooped up in iron boxes, and could handle both the tenants and the boilers. By the mid-sixties, the supply had dried up. 'Caretakers became chaps who went from estate to estate in a van.'

The watershed was 16 May 1968. At 5.45 that morning a lady put her match to a badly fitted oven on the eighteenth floor of Ronan Point in Canning Town. 'When the phone rang, I thought at first it was one of ours. It was a horrible sight.' Five people had died in the explosion. Seventeen had been injured. And the knell had sounded for the tower block.

'The best thing that ever happened to British architecture was the collapse of Ronan Point,' the architect and author Theo Crosby wrote in *How to Play the Environment Game*.

> The building of tall blocks without any intrinsic message . . . devalues the identity of a city and robs it of meaningful symbols. In a mass society, the identity of the individual is a precious responsibility, to be reinforced at every stage.

Estates like Roehampton did not reinforce this identity, but Kenneth Campbell maintains that the decisions surrounding their construction were made neither by fools nor rogues. They were made by people like him, who acted in the belief that people would learn to love their surrounds.

It is still hard to judge, as he walks out of the downstairs lift, through the smell of disinfectant and into the blue morning, whether he remains a believer in human perfectibility.

'People like Theo Crosby and Alice Coleman,' he adds as an afterthought, 'think such decisions were made both by fools and rogues.'

★

In 1985 Alice Coleman, a reader in geography at King's College London, published the fruits of four years' research into 4,099 tower blocks. The blocks were mainly situated in the London boroughs of Southwark and Tower Hamlets. The book was called *Utopia on Trial*. Before a half-filled hall at RIBA, and under the title of 'Design Disadvantagement in Housing', she gave a lecture on her findings.

She turned out to be a middle-aged woman in brown, with hair the colour and shape of a thunderstorm. Holding a cane like a gigantic billiard cue, tripping over the microphone cables, she poked at a screen on which flashed spidery, incomprehensible graphs. Shaped like the slab blocks she was criticising, they purported to document the results of what happens when humanity turns termite. A grimy catalogue of litter, theft, sexual assault, faecal pollution, graffiti and murder.

Broadly, Coleman's thesis is that bad design increases the odds against which people struggle to preserve civilised standards; and that, the higher the building, the greater its associated social malaise. Conceived in compassion, born in authoritarianism, bred in profligacy, the plans of men like Kenneth Campbell had 'aspired to beautify the urban environment, but had been transmogrified into the epitome of ugliness'. Utopia's designers had effectively placed before law-abiding citizens the temptation to be criminal. In the blocks represented by Alice Coleman's graphs, there existed no community structure, merely isolation, anonymity, loneliness. In these barbarous barracks, vandals thrived unseen and unchallenged. Self policing had ceased to operate. Children had nowhere they wanted to play.

Halfway through her lecture, which was laced with expressions like 'space syntax', and did not isolate the experiences of a single person, Alice Coleman announced that she was deaf. I left and went to read her book. Its main burden was that 'reasoning in the abstract can be very misleading'.

In a shop on the Roehampton Estate, I bought a bar of bitter chocolate from a rotund Irish lady. She was uprooted from Fulham nineteen years ago to a maisonette across the road. The shadow of a slab block falls across her door. In nineteen years she has never once been up its stairs. She complains about the smallness of her kitchen. Five of them have to eat in the drawing room. Not like in Fulham. At night she is kept awake by the kids on their bikes. She grimaces at her modern environment – 'It's not modern anymore.' At the weekend, she says, they smash your windows if the metal isn't down. The baker's was done before Christmas. Da Costa's last week. It is early January.

Pat and her pale, chubby daughter Leslie live on the Aylesbury Estate in south London. It is the biggest estate in the world. Every Tuesday, they make their one weekly foray – to the pub where they play darts. They are so scared, says Pat, they take a taxi there and back. Behind them, at the sink of the club where they work, a Greek Cypriot woman is in tears. Small, unremarkable, with a face the colour of her dishwater, Maria has lived here for thirty-seven years. She has little mastery of the language, and less confidence in herself. A few months ago, her husband tried to throw himself out of their flat on the fourteenth floor. He couldn't stand living there any more. Three days ago, without a word, he took his coat and walked out. She had waited till today to ask the council for help in finding him. 'They didn't care,' she sobs. 'They didn't care.' Last night, two groups of blacks had pounded at her door.

I took a tube to Bow and walked to an estate in Tower Hamlets – 'the meths capital of the world'. There was no sound of bells, nor anyone about. No figure moved in the unwinking windows. No airguns cracked. But graffiti, as Alice Coleman warned, was everywhere.

The lift doors hung inert, so I walked to the seventh floor. The steps smelt acidly of urine – on every level. The defecation was not just an aesthetic reaction to the surroundings. It seemed also a statement of possession – like the tigers at London Zoo, marking out their territory with excrement.

Emerging onto an open-air balcony, with the wind swirling bitterly, I thought first of space syntax, then of Le Corbusier.

Sun in the house.

Sky through their windows.

Trees to look at as they step outside.

Doris lives behind a chained yellow door at the end. 'The approach is dreadful,' she apologises, withdrawing the chain. 'I'm ashamed of it. It's a strange world where man can reach the moon and we can't use the lift.' Next door is a boarded-up flat known as a 'void', the damp plywood like a modern sign of the plague. It is used by meths drinkers who shout frighteningly. She apologises again – for not knowing the names of her neighbours.

We sit in the kitchen, where she offers tea with Carnation milk. A television obscures the view over the estate. 'You used to be able to see St Paul's,' she says. She laughs. 'Do you know what Christopher Wren said when asked what he wanted as an epitaph? He said, "Look around." '

Doris attends evening classes for an Open University course – 'so as not to be a prisoner'. It is odd, she says, feeling like that in an area where you were born.

She is the daughter of a Stepney lighterman, who painted names on barges and drowned in a fog one November morning in 1922. His disfigured body was not found for months, and only recognised as his by a war wound and a tattoo.

'Mum was left with no widow's pension and five children. She went up the steps of the town hall with me, and stood on the carpet holding her new baby, sad and unhappy, while a man fired questions. The baby you can keep, he said. That one – pointing at me – can work. The others can go to an orphanage. All they gave us were a few food tickets. I left school and worked in a jam factory, putting little doves and cupids on cakes for five shillings a week. Mum scrubbed. After four years, she married another lighterman and moved to West Ham.'

Because of the factories, West Ham was one of the first boroughs to receive electricity. 'We were afraid to use it, and the council had to give us classes every Wednesday afternoon to show us how. People used it wrongly. There were explosions when they put their trays of water into the oven, like they always did to catch the gas fumes. To this day I know women who won't use electric irons.'

Doris worked as a nippy in a Lyons tea room for £2 10s. a week and married a van driver. They paid 12s. rent for a two-roomed house in East Ham, then at the end of the War bought a house in Stepney for £700. 'I've tasted the good life,' she says, licking her lips and looking at the blank television screen. 'I stayed in a hotel in Harrogate for two weeks. The Majestic, do you know it?' It reminds her of how things have changed. 'I never get off the bus now without somethings in my hands. See what I got in my pocket?' She produces a bunch of keys. 'If someone attacks me, that's what they get in their side. It's terrible to get to that pitch.

Elderly people were respected and thought a lot of. Now they are an easy target.'

The result is that they do not go out. 'My GP complains his patients are boring themselves to death. And they are not allowed dogs. I had a beautiful one, but when I moved in it had to be put down. Now young people break the rules and have two or three. They do just as they like.'

Doris returns once more to the past. 'When I was a kid we didn't have an indoor toilet, a wireless, a television. They've got all that now, but I doubt if they're happier. We relied on each other for entertainment, and made our own enjoyment. We loved to go to the West End, which we knew as the "Worst End". We loved to watch the debs line up along The Mall. We knew who they all were because we'd read about them in the papers. It was a taste of something we'd never had. As they went by, you could smell their perfume. It was gorgeous, absolutely gorgeous. It was the highlight of the Londoner's day.'

Emma Tennant's latest novel, *The Adventures of Robina*, carries as its subtitle, 'The Memoirs of a Debutante at the Court of Queen Elizabeth II'.

Tall, blonde, her nails full of the pheasant she has just plucked, Emma Tennant stands at her Elgin Crescent window in North Kensington and remembers the day she was presented at Court. A Lenare portrait taken at the time, in 1956, shows her in an afternoon dress, dark gloves, and a choker of pearls. 'Artificial,' she says triumphantly.

'That green dress looked like a crushed lettuce leaf by the time we reached the Palace. Everyone had hired Daimlers, and we sat in this queue which edged slowly, slowly forward. It must have taken twenty minutes to get down The Mall, and it was terribly embarrassing because, of course, you felt a twit.'

Bobbing a flustered curtsey before the queen, who sat 'drumming her fingers like a waxwork' – had she lost an innocence by being shown to the sovereign in this way? Emma Tennant thinks possibly she had.

She replaces the portrait in its brown paper bundle under a drinks table, and goes on to talk about moving house.

★

In Kensington, more people – sixty-eight per cent – own their homes than in any other part of London. (Tower Hamlets, not surprisingly, comes at the bottom of the league with less than three per cent.) Emma Tennant is moving round the corner because she needs the money she will make from buying a smaller house. And because, ironically, the area has become too smart.

'This area used to have the highest density of writers in London. Now it's like the smart Paris suburb of Passy. Full of French and Belgian bankers and heads of BBC departments. Last year, I watched two compete in the parents egg-and-spoon race. They both held their eggs with their thumbs, which made me suspect that was how they'd got to the top.' She gestures through the window at the communal gardens. 'I'm the bane of the Garden Committee. Twice a year the bell rings, and everyone rushes out to plant crocuses and sweep leaves. It's just like a village, they say. We've got a squirrel and two owls here now,' she adds with mock pride, in mimicry of this inner-city rural fantasy. 'One male that goes toowit-to-woo. One female that goes goo-wit, goo-wit.'

She turns back into the shambolic, crumbling room and continues excitedly. 'Actually, there's a really bad taste story about the owls. I overheard a neighbour saying, "Isn't it wonderful, we've got the owls back." I told Hilary Bailey, who's lived here for ages in a flat that costs her five pounds a week or something. She said, apparently it isn't the owls at all. It's the call the Notting Hill Gate rapist makes every time he plunges into an au pair's basement.'

Comic, grotesque, outrageous, it is the kind of story that appeals to the author of fantasies like *The Crack* – an apocalyptic tale of what happens when the Thames splits open. 'But I'd never have written my books here had it not been for the communal gardens, and the fact my children could run out and play without me worrying they were wandering into the road. Sadly, you no longer hear the shriek of children. It's complete silence because they're all at Eton.'

Emma Tennant's mid-Victorian Italianate home, like the home she is buying, lies on the Ladbroke Estate. Conceived as a great circus, with villas rising from the fields and quarries west of Notting Hill, it was a speculative development that signally failed. The collapse of the estate in the 1850s made the word 'Ladbroke' synonymous with the risks attached to property – 'a graveyard of buried hopes', according to an 1861 edition of *Building News*.

The houses built for the gentry became rookeries. Whole families lived in a single room, dividing where they slept from where they ate with a curtain down the middle. Then the gentry began moving into the mews houses previously occupied by their servants.

Recently, albeit over a century later than intended, they have started to inhabit the villas in the way originally planned by developers like Cith Blake, Samuel Walker and Thomas Allom. Today, many of the houses around Elgin Crescent have been restored to the status of single homes, and their honeycomb conversions removed. 'The money about,' said one estate agent, 'never ceases to amaze me.'

It takes some doing to amaze an estate agent.

In 1985 the value of property in London went up nineteen per cent. Andy, who is a partner in Emma Tennant's local estate agent, Faron Sutaria, reckons the telephone rings, on average, every ten seconds. Last year he only went out to lunch twice: once with a cousin who had come back from abroad, and once with another estate agent. They went next door for half an hour and had a pizza. That, says Andy, is how hard he works.

Andy is an unlikely young man to find in property. A graduate in Russian studies, he decided that the only way to secure himself a job was to advertise. Offering £1,000 for the most interesting job opportunity, and with the catchline *I Want To Move With The Times*, he placed an advertisement in that paper. He could not have foreseen the result. The newspaper stole his phrase. More importantly, other newspapers reported the ad.

The London *Standard* ran their story the following day. The headline changed with each edition. 'There were two reasons why it was taken up,' Andy says. 'My offer coincided with the latest record unemployment figures. And no one till then had accepted the idea that a graduate would find it difficult to get a job. After the first few 'phone calls, I realised I wouldn't have to pay a thing.'

He spent three days at the BBC, being interviewed on various radio programmes as to what had prompted him. Offers of job interviews came in their hundreds. 'I'll give you five grand in cash,' said one insurance executive, 'if you say you are going to join my company. Because of the publicity I'll get.'

Totting it all up, Capital Radio reckoned Andy had earned himself £700,000 worth of international publicity. He had calls from Australia, Vancouver and Switzerland. The most persistent was from a man who said urgently he had to meet him at the Skyline Hotel. 'He wouldn't give a name, just said that he had to meet me. He would be wearing such and such. It was so bizarre, I felt I had to go through with it. Not even then did he tell me what he wanted. Then he called from Canada to arrange lunch. We met in Mayfair. It turned out he wanted me to sell gas stoves to north-east England.'

In the midst of this, Andy met Faron Sutaria, and Indian Parsee who, calling himself the 'Real Estate Agent', had started up his business in a basement flat off Baker Street. Andy was impressed. 'Most estate agents are complete nurds. They don't need any qualifications. Often they are as thick as the bricks they are selling. And they spend most of the time with the purchasers, when they should be acting for the vendors. In America, you pay for both services. You use an agent to both buy and find.'

Each day, Andy shows four or five people round the properties on his books. *Immaculate* is not an adjective he eschews to describe a lavatorially bricked terraced house. Nor is *superb*. But then, what he is offering for £150,000 is the fantasy to make it so.

Most people coming to Andy want to live in the Notting Hill Gate area because of the Central line. It is therefore an ideal location for, say, the bankers and broadcasters so disliked by Emma Tennant. Andy finds it easy to divide the city like this. Mention Bayswater, and to him the word conjures up the first-time flat buyer and Arabs overlooking the park. Mention Barnes, and out come epithets like snob, arty-farty, minor television actors. Mention Richmond, and he tells you, with a dreamy, faraway look in his eye, of wealthy, liberal middle classes with the highest educational standards of any borough in the country.

'As in jobs, everyone upgrades themselves.' He tells of the 'Sloan-ies' – 'only ten minutes from Sloane Square'. Of those who talk of 'St Ockwell' and 'Clarm'; who describe Queen's Park as 'North North Kensington', and Battersea as 'South South Chelsea'. And of those constitutionally unable to say even Battercia, who describe it as 'SW One One'.

'People don't live in West Eight or West Two. They live in Kensington or Bayswater. They mention the area because of the connotations that go with it. Also, because some postal codes cover a multitude of sins. West Eleven includes parts of both

Westbourne Grove and Holland Park – overlaying a gulf wider than any you can imagine. South-West One embraces both Belgravia and Pimlico. No doubt in certain areas of Belgravia they say Eaton Square and not Belgravia.'

He jokes. I smile, recalling Lady Douro on the subject of living in Belgravia.

'Perish the thought,' had been her words.

The notion of London as a series of interconnecting villages is a strong one in the Londoner's mind. It is a marketable one in Andy's. Kenway Village in Earl's Court is a term created by estate agents, but for some it helps make Earl's Court inhabitable. Similarly, Hillgate Village, behind Notting Hill, will not be found on any map.

While Andy has been steadily forging north, planting his £30 signs in the stony reaches of Kensal Green, Maida Vale and Queen's Park, Michael of Ashton, Steele & Day has been going west.

'The acceptable centre of London increases year by year,' he says, citing *The Good Food Guide* of 1964, which dealt first with Central London, then Kensington and Chelsea. 'In 1986, Central London is Kensington and Chelsea. In the last decade London has moved westwards. From Kensington to Holland Park and Brook Green, and from Hammersmith to Shepherd's Bush.'

A lover of antiquarian books, Michael worked for Christie's on leaving Cambridge. He lost the will to auctioneer when he realised that he could not afford to buy what he was selling. So he plumped for property, and for a time masterminded the operations of Marsh & Parsons in Brook Green and Shepherd's Bush.

To illustrate the boom, he tells of a contemporary who for £25,000 seven years before had bought a one-bedroom flat in Ladbroke Square (known colloquially after the property collapse in 1847 as 'Coffin-Row'). Selling this for £40,000, he moved to a house in North Kensington, which he sold after a year for £90,000. Three transactions later, he has ended up in a seven-bedroom house back on Ladbroke Square worth £800,000.

A solemn sum, considering the £747,954 2s. 9d. it cost for Wren's cathedral.

Michael has not yet developed this magic touch. His own house in Kensington, passed by a trusted surveyor, had to be completely gutted. 'Dry rot, damp, rotten foundations . . . you name it.'

Three days before our conversation, the water pipes had burst and flooded his kitchen floor to a depth of two feet. Nor was this the first time, he adds dustily.

Nevertheless, property is 'in'. Parents are much more likely to help out with capital, realising, with the present tax advantages, that they can fund a mortgage with what they might pay on rent. 'Before, they would have had kittens at the prospect of Fiona living outside Kensington and Chelsea. Now they boast about how she's brought this darling little house in Africa Road – "Where, dear?" "Shepherd's Bush, you know. Melissa de Previously lives there."' You can also bet that living in Fiona's house, paying low cash-in-hand rent and sharing her bills, will be one or two of Fiona's friends.

'A street "comes up" because of the people in it,' Michael continues, tapping his tortoise-shell glasses and pointing a thin finger at a large-scale map on the wall. 'And one street can be very different from the next.

'Take this small circle – an area of about two miles in diameter. The epicentre is Shepherd's Bush roundabout. If you divide the map into four quarters, you'll find each has its own characteristics and ambience.'

'The first quarter is bounded on the west by Holland Road, and on the north by Holland Park Avenue. It comprises much of the old Ilchester Estate, centred on Holland House, which was reduced to rubble in the Blitz. The large double-fronted houses on Holland Villas Road and Addison Road are inhabited by very rich foreigners. The Marcos family, for instance, own four. And there is a smattering of slightly trendy types like Anouska Hempel and the Marquis of Dufferin and Ava. Here, one does not drop in for a cuppa, but for a glass of vintage Bollinger.

'Immediately south of Holland Park are roads like Melbury Road and Holland Park Road – in high-Victorian times the haunts of fashionable artists such as Lord Leighton. Their modern-day equivalents are film directors like Michael Winner.

'Moving north, you get large blocks such as Campden Hill Court, until recently occupied by older residents of the Royal Borough – retired district officers and Indian Army colonels. Nowadays, they're more likely to be found in the Distressed Gentlefolks Aid Association Nursing Home in Palace Gardens Terrace. The flats of one's great-aunts and -uncles are fast being

The Environs of Shepherd's Bush Roundabout

gobbled up by the developer with an eye for gold-plated taps and video entryphones, who sells them to foreign businessmen and their companies.

'Running east off the top end of Campden Hill Road are little streets of multi-coloured flat-fronted terraced houses, known to one and all as Hillgate Village, and owned by Young Upwardly Mobile Professionals and a few older people who like pink gins at eleven. Once they were the houses of the lowliest servants at Kensington Palace.'

'Going anti-clockwise we come to the second quarter, separated from the first by Holland Park Avenue, and bounded on the west by the West Cross Route.

'Until ten years ago Holland Park Avenue was known as "the Great Divide" – dividing West Eight and the Kensington part of West Fourteen from West Eleven and oblivion. The increase in demand for smart Kensington-style houses, and the attractive architecture of mansion blocks backing onto private garden squares, have contributed to the meteoric rise in value and popularity of Notting Hill.

'Roads such as Kensington Park Gardens, Lansdowne Road and Crescent, Ladbroke Square and Elgin Crescent were in the fifties and sixties run-down and peopled by Irishmen, foreigners and others just able to afford the squalid letting rooms rented out by the notorious Mr Rachman and his cronies. A rapid change in public opinion and the introduction of the nineteen sixty-five Rent Bill then made letting a less attractive proposition, and a few hardy souls moved across the Great Divide and pioneered the conversion of such buildings.

'In eighty-three I attempted to buy a large double-fronted house in Chepstow Villas. It consisted of sixteen letting rooms, and was owned by a mousey little man who was a night waiter at the Westbury Hotel off Bond Street. He had arrived in Notting Hill in the fifties, and with less than a hundred pounds had acquired a part-tenanted house. Gradually, as tenants died, left of their own volition, or were weeded out, he would buy another house, and so the process continued. By nineteen eighty-three he owned property to the value of one and half million pounds in West Eleven and was still working as a waiter at the Westbury. The tips must have been good.

'The process by which the area around Notting Hill acquired status and value is fairly typical. Several houses in roads such as Elgin Crescent were smartened up, encouraging friends of friends to follow suit and move in. Perhaps the area was "not so bad after all". The boundaries grew, the shops changed. The local corner store became an art gallery dealing in the sort of pictures appealing to the new inhabitants – nineteenth-century prints and primitives, or earthenware "specially" imported from Mexico and Nicaragua.

Wine bars sprouted: places like Julie's in Clarendon Road, and One Nine Two in Kensington Park Road, attracting hordes of media people, many of whom live in Notting Hill – the smarter streets of which are described as "Holland Park" by newcomers.

'And now, where Kentucky Fried Chicken was sold, Cullens advertise Sevruga Caviar. The Irish have long since departed from their letting rooms in Kensington Park Gardens, to live in the council development fifty yards west of St James's Gardens – home of Tim Rice – or the more congenial climes of Kilburn and the Harrow Road. The only Irish to be seen in the vicinity of Ladbroke Square are builders doing up the last unconverted houses.'

'The third quarter lies to the west, just five minutes distant by car, but an age away in every other sense. The feature binding together these two disparate regions is the megalithic BBC Television Centre at White City – shortly to be augmented by new studios. Jobs will be provided for an extra six thousand employees, some of whom will wish to live nearby.

'Already the pioneers, the nineteen eighties equivalent of the sixties Notting Hill trekkers, are exploring the possibilities. Up-and-coming young bankers and accountants with a certain amount of courage, families needing to release cash to educate children, and country dwellers who want a London pad are moving in. And the Pakistanis and Poles are moving out, taking their icons and their pictures of the pope to Ealing.'

Peter Jones drawing rooms may have spread to Shepherd's Bush, and family portraits overhang the mantelpieces along the Uxbridge Road, but as Michael warns, it would be unwise to treat the area as comfortably middle class. 'A young couple with two black labradors moved into Godolphin Road. On the first morning, the husband, bleary-eyed, looked out of his window to see what he thought was water streaming down the front of the house opposite. He rubbed his eyes, and saw a man peeing from the top window. When he attempted to remonstrate, his neighbour turned round and defecated.

'It goes without saying that the astute estate agent selling such houses to the parents of prospective buyers, will approach via the scenic route, and not by the Uxbridge Road, Queen's Park Rangers' football ground or the nether regions by the old White City Stadium.'

At Home

*

★

'We now move south, across the Goldhawk Road and into the final quarter. This runs down to West Kensington and comprises parts of Hammersmith, and the part of West Fourteen known to old-established locals as Shepherd's Bush, but to newcomers as Brook Green. This last section is a particularly good illustration of how a peripheral area can improve.

'A small common, and originally London's vineyard area, Brook Green is surrounded by a number of quite attractive Georgian, Victorian and Edwardian houses, which are not built in ubiquitous Fulham red brick. It runs off Hammersmith Road, in itself the continuation of Kensington High Street, and for over a hundred years St Paul's Girls School has been located here. With easy access to Heathrow and the west, it is a perfect place for nurturing.

'Like a bush fire, in the seventies, the roads running off the green were fast improved. Then those parallel with it. The properties converted well into five-bedroom, two-bathroom family houses, the roads were fairly quiet, and there were no parking restrictions. Hammersmith's King Street was given a new look and the Lyric Theatre reopened. "Villages" such as Brackenbury were created.

'Two years ago, I went at about eight-thirty a.m. to look at a house in Iffley Road, West Six. It belonged to a rather florid, pompous young stockbroker. Dressed in his city suit, he bade me goodbye on his way to work. At the same time, his neighbour opened his front door. Wearing typical labourer's clothes, he doffed his cloth cap to my client, saying, "Morning, sir." "Morning, Jones," the stockbroker replied. The labourer no longer lives in that road, having realised sixty grand by selling to an accountant desperate to live in his house.

'In nearby Carthew Road, peers' daughters jostle with Kensington Palace kitchenmaids, prostitutes and used-car dealers. Again, the wine bars and delicatessens have mushroomed. At the southern end of this quarter, smart new blocks of flats have been built on the Cadby Hall site of J. Lyons. Two- and three-bedroom flats in these complexes have been selling for hundreds of thousands of pounds – figures unthinkable even eighteen months ago. The old five-bedroom Lyons caretaker's house on Brook Green is presently undergoing improvement, and will soon be sold for an anticipated three hundred thous-

71

and.

'And all this,' Michael says, tapping the map again with a knuckle, 'is within a two-mile circle.'

On the outer rim of the city, estate agents are also busy making all sorts of properties palatable.

Nothing can be more unappetising than the timbered mock-Edwardian villas bordering every dual carriageway out of London.

'I'd no more live there than fly in the sky,' says a bearded Jewish estate agent, indicating Woodford Avenue outside the window. The six-lane thoroughfare near Gants Hill is the only way to reach Cambridge and East Anglia. Yellow Ford Capris slope up the short drives. Lorries pass like tired thunderbolts.

'Yet we have people who specifically want to live on that road.' He shows me one on his books with a swimming pool. 'A hundred and forty thousand pounds. And we'll get it.' He grins. 'Interested?'

Bill is a car mechanic who lives in a three-bedroom house on the A3, leaving London. The turning off is difficult to find, but if you miss it you have to drive on for several miles.

'I used to live on the other side,' Bill says. 'That's definitely the side for first-time buyers. Funnily enough, it was quieter there, except in the mornings. Then the noise would start like turning a tap on. You'd know it was seven-thirty because of the cars just sitting outside your window in a jam.'

When he went across the road to see his present house, there were twelve prospective buyers outside. 'I had the Ferrari then,' he says, prompted by the memory.

The previous occupant had been a keen gardener, but Bill admits that it is not particularly comfortable sitting out there on a Sunday afternoon – what with the smell and the noise. 'The noise was really bad until I put the double glazing in. Now you just hear the really meaty stuff burning down, and the motor bikes as they rev up from the Robin Hood roundabout. Sometimes you hear cars coming along the road on their roofs. They make a really bad scraping noise. I've actually got to the stage now when I don't get out of bed for crashes.'

The telephone rings. 'Ah, Kevin. Glad you called. I'm a little bit concerned about the wheels on the Porsche,' he says.

'Well, they're cracked.'

In Downing Road, Dagenham, I meet a man in a blue boilersuit who also lives beside a motorway. He has elfin eyes, a black beard, and a face sprayed with blackheads. He earns his keep by roadsweeping, but he too is a car fanatic. I suppose you have to be.

He lives on Scrattons Terrace on the A13, in a council house for which he pays a score. His parents live nine doors down. 'I grew up there, and what better place to come back to than the place where you grew up.' He can also walk to work.

'I don't find anything in these roads. In Barking you'd find the odd quid. I collected tin cans for an old boy who'd give me two quid a load for scrap.'

He used to be a high-pressure water jetter, but it involved too much travel, and he never got to see his wife and four kids. The last job he had done was in Anglesey. That finished him, so he applied to the council and got this present job. Really, he'd like to go back to drainage and sewage. Meanwhile, he makes do, rising as seven and working till four. He likes the open air, and people stop and talk to him. 'You'll never have everything you want, but you'll get by, and to me it's better than being on the dole. Even though there's only a couple of quid in it, it's better.'

A car draws up, and a young man saunters over. They chat about cars. The roadie lets out he has a Capri to sell for 'a oner in cash'. The other looks surprised. 'I know someone who'll 'ave that.' 'Well, tell him to come over at four-thirty.' When the man drives off, he explains how he'd noticed the car in question on his rounds. It hadn't been moved for two weeks, so he went round and asked if it was for sale.

He keeps his cars beside the six-lane highway. The traffic dies down by 11 p.m., he says. The biggest problem is careless driving. 'If anything comes off that A Thirteen, it's straight across! Once, a few doors down, a tanker had slewn through a garden wall and embedded itself in the house's front. And last night I was under a nineteen thirty-six Triumph Vitesse when an Escort van came off, hit a bump, hit my neighbour's car, hit the Triumph, and smashed into my own car.'

No doubt the Ford Capri.

★

I walked on through the Dagenham estate: four square miles of white houses – 27,000 of them, each identical. Construction on the Becontree Estate had started in 1927, on what had been one of the earliest Saxon settlements in the land. There had been 9,000 inhabitants of Dagenham in 1921. Ten years later there were 115,000, rehoused from the East End slums in a dormitory town which never woke up. Plans for a town centre came to nothing. Nor did proposals for a shopping centre. In a borough of some 150,000, there are only fifty-seven pubs.

A lot of people in Dagenham consider themselves to be living in Essex.

So far, about 8,000 houses have been bought from the council. Average prices are £35,000, and the majority go to couples in their early twenties who have decided on a mortgage rather than a baby. When they want to improve themselves, they move to Hornchurch or Romford. When they want to improve their houses, to show they own them, they pebble-dash the walls. 'Like sore thumbs,' says Lill, who first came in 1935, from Battersea. 'They even carpet the doors.'

At least it makes them different, I suggest. 'If you look, they *are* different.' She draws the curtains and points to the variously coloured doors, the cat statues in the front gardens. She admits, though, it had become an old people's town. 'A lot of these houses have only one person.' And the cinemas had shut down. 'We came down here because we thought this place was a palace.'

She was born in Livingstone Road, SW 11, under the smell of the candle factory. Her father, a navvy, was ill all her life, so she supported the family by working as a wood chopper, selling penny bundles of chips to start a fire. It was a seasonal job.

'Battersea was a very poor place. Many's the time we never had a meal. My sister and I used to scrounge. Sometimes we'd get threepence for washing the doorsteps of those la-di-da houses round about Clapham Common.'

If she had all the money in the world, where would she live? She thinks for a second, adjusts her red slippers, then points decisively to the whorls of brown on her carpet.

I tell her Battersea has become very smart now. 'I take your word for it,' she sniffs disbelievingly, her nose still acrid with the smell of candles.

★

Aboukir Bay is a bright blue houseboat tethered on the embankment near Battersea Bridge. An old coal barge once harnessed to a horse, it is virtually the biggest boat on the reach.

It has five bedrooms and cost £50,000 – in cash. You may mortgage yourself to the hilt for a house on a roundabout, a motorway, a no-go estate. But you will never get a mortgage on a boat. The Post Office refuses to deliver mail to *Aboukir Bay* because the gangplanks are considered dangerous. Letters are left in a bin addressed 'opposite 106 Cheyne Walk'.

Unreal City . . .

'You don't feel you're in London,' says Lady R., who works in a publishing firm over the river. She is young and sensuous and speaks with a drawl. 'You have this feeling of light and space,' she enthuses, waving her hand at the windows. The lush interior lurches gently. The wooden walls are hung with prints. There is even a mantelpiece, white with the invitations known by Lady R. as 'stiffies'.

The first thing one notices, after the light and the space, is the rub and lap and squeak. 'You also hear the rain on the roof,' she says, trying hard to think of other peculiarities. 'I know. The pipes are always freezing. There was someone living here who had a job interview, and there was no water for him to shave in. So he shaved in milk.' She snickers. 'As the day went on, he smelled increasingly like bad yoghurt.'

Some adjustment in balance has to be made when stepping on dry land, she says, then jokes about being a floating voter who rubs along with her neighbours – lawyers, merchant bankers and an ex-member of the Sex Pistols. The truth is, she is tied to them with hooks and lines and sinkers. Only two boats are seaworthy. One went off to Oxford recently, but the associated hullaballo of disconnecting the water, electricity and telephone lines did not suggest mobility.

There is plenty of other movement, however. 'It can get very rough. At weekends, the party boats go past blaring Donna Summer and leaving a great wake.'

At low tide the barge sits on the mud. The moment when it refloats is always a little unexpected. 'You suddenly hear the suction of water, then the bottom comes off with a jolt. It's hell if you are running a bath. And if it takes off in the middle of a dinner party, people think they've had too much to drink.' She once returned to a scene of 'total devastation' after two local lads had tightened the warps against a rising tide. The plants had fallen down, the video was on its side, her invitations littered the floor. 'I opened the kitchen cupboard and all the glasses fell out, smashed.'

Lady R. entertains a lot. She has even thrown a drinks party for a hundred. 'Everyone has a preconception that houseboats are small, poky, damp and insanitary. It's nonsense.'

On sunny days, she has breakfast outside, looking out towards the Hovis factory, and down the river which Turner painted. Every day something different sticks up from the river bed – a fridge door, a wheel, a pram.

Once, at one of her parties, she dropped a champagne glass overboard. Next morning, there it was, sitting upright in the mud.

'None of my friends have ever fallen in. The only person I've seen go off the boat is the Water Board Inspector. He came snooping round the back in the middle of the day and lost his balance. I just heard this terrible plop.'

Some make an effort to fall in, especially the tramps on the Embankment, sloppy with cider. She tells of an Irishman who had climbed over the railings on Battersea Bridge, and yelled through the night how he was going to throw himself off. 'I've had enough of life. Of the world in general,' he shouted relentlessly. Eventually a cry came from the adjoining boat, 'If you're going to jump, get on with it!'

Some do get on with it. At two one mid-winter morning she was woken by the tramp of feet on the roof. Twenty policemen were looking for someone who had plummeted from Chelsea Bridge. Their lights finally found the spinning figure. 'They threw a lifejacket. It never reached him. He came floating down to here, then his little arms went up and he went right under.'

According to the law, Orwell wrote in *Down and Out in Paris and London*, you may sit down for the night in London, but the police must move you on if they see you asleep. The Embankment is a special exception.

'De whole 'ting wid de Embankment is gettin' to sleep early,' says Orwell's Paddy, wrapped in newspaper and blocking his ears from 'dem bloody trams'. ' 'Tis too cold to sleep much after twelve o'clock, an' de police turns you off at four in de mornin'.' What with the sky signs flicking on and off across the river, 'you'd be bloody lucky if you got t'ree hours sleep'.

The number of homeless in London is estimated at anything between 30,000 and 50,000. The figure is rough, but it is growing. 'The shortage of housing is chronic and frightening,' says a thin, spiky, angular girl who works at the Citizens Advice Bureau in Wandsworth. She is dressed in a violet top and skirt which flap loose from her, like towels on a clothes line.

Each day, she attends patiently to five or six different families who come in from their bed and breakfast hotels and want a more permanent roof. Some have had to stay nine months in these lodgings. Recently, the government slashed their full board and lodging allowance from £77 to £48.30. That makes it easier, in the summer, for hoteliers to turf them out and make way for tourists.

The girl translates their paperwork, clearing up confusions over entitlements, explaining council possession orders. It would be a foolish person, she says, who claimed to understand the regulations, and cites the case of a woman on supplementary benefit – or 'sup ben' as she calls it. To survive, she relies on abbreviations.

The woman in question had received £40 a week, out of which she paid £25 rent and looked after an invalid son. In fact she was receiving the wrong amount. For a time she survived fatalistically on £15 a week. Then, at her wits' end, she had meekly complained that she could not cope.

'I'm constantly amazed how people can live on what for you and me is just a week's spending money. I've come to the conclusion that a substantial number of people in this area cannot afford to have fuel or electricity.' Last year a woman and child were found frozen to death. 'Sup ben was never intended to support people on a long-term basis,' she says hoarsely. For many it's now their only prospect of income – and they're no longer able to manage.

From the Embankment, I took a train to New Cross and walked. Deptford High Street, where Peter the Great had worshipped, was boarded up and caged. Only The Bear, where Marlowe was murdered, had any life. There I learnt that Ronald Reagan's grandfather had lived in the district. The son of a soap-maker from Ireland, he had fled here during the potato famine.

A young man with an earring sipped his soapy lager. 'Today Deptford', read his T-shirt, 'Tomorrow the world.'

They fight dogs under the railway bridge crossing the high street, I was told. Train them all night on wheels, like hamsters. The man who has British Rail's concession on the arches has a £150,000 house in Blackheath, and a pool. He walks about with wads of money bumping his back pocket. A little bit is rent from Lenny, known as 'Pickles'. In the shadow of his arch, he makes brandy butter, paprika and condiments for Fortnum & Mason.

They are not so streetwise, the men who congregate on corners further down. Grouped in twos and threes, they do not seem to talk or listen. They just sway, holding their bottles. Puddles run from doorways to the street. There is a smell of drink and urine on the cold air.

I follow one man down Brookmill Road. He wears a tweed jacket, shabby dark trousers, and gym shoes without heels. He shakes his head in conversation with himself, and draws a sleeve under a beard tangled with spittle and drink. Hunching his shoulders, and letting his hand out to hit the lampposts, he drifts in an aimless way.

In fact he is going home.

I follow him up the steps and into Carrington House.

The Liberal Lord Carrington built this vast twin-towered hostel at the turn of the century. It was intended for working men at a time when Deptford was a community thriving on the Surrey Docks. The 834 inmates were charged sixpence a night. Inside, they had the use of a barber and shops.

When Carrington House opened, local church dignitaries complained it was too grand. It would influence men to leave their wives, they said.

'Have a squat,' said Brian, the manager, and went to boil some tea. In a tray on his desk a letter referred to dermatitis contracted by a woman in the laundry department. A door opened opposite onto a room piled high with towels. On the wall was a chart listing various forms of sup ben.

Brian returns with a mug, closing the door with his foot. He has grey sideburns, a thinly triangled mouth, and a featureless voice. He has been at Carrington House for four years, with a year off at a home for the elderly. Before that he worked in Lambeth – 'where the people are poor and there are a lot of rag shops', according to Orwell. Brian never went north. 'Is there a north?' he says with what passes for a smile.

He asks me for my perception of those at Carrington House. I describe the scene outside, but avoid words like tramp and dosser. 'I see red when people call them dossers,' he says, his podgy fingers whitening around his mug. 'When you talk to them, they are gentlemen. They lack dignity because society doesn't allow for it. To society they represent a threat. But it's they who are in danger.' Only a few weeks back, he says, one was knifed to death by youths as he stood sheltering in the door of a bank.

He talks about the 'circuit of homelessness'. In most cases, it begins simply with a man's arrival in London. He has come from Ireland, perhaps, as part of a road gang, and has drifted south, with no fixed abode because he has always slept where he worked. Reaching London he has shared a small bedsit in Leyton with six others, and then fallen out with the ganger. He has moved into a cheap hotel; from there to the shelter of a railway station or the Embankment; and then to Arlington Lodge in Camden, Bruce House in Westminster, and over the river to Deptford.

There are about 400 today in Carrington House. They are known as Carringtonians. About 250 have been there for years. 'It's their home, it's all they can remember, and they wouldn't give a thank you or tuppence for any other. Old John, for instance, not yet seventy, and a former sports writer on the *Orkney Herald*, could move into a council house tomorrow. But he doesn't want to. He drinks, yes, a couple of pints. But it's a couple of pints of sterilised milk. The majority are from Ireland and Scotland. But they're Londoners now,' says Brian, picking his ear.

There are also many ex–servicemen: army officers, merchant seamen, even squadron leaders; institutionalised men from bedsits who never made arrangements. He is not boasting, merely trying to dissipate a preconceived image; to show there are as many reasons for ending up here as there are people who do so. 'The only thing they have in common is that they're homeless. One,' he says, 'a commercial traveller, was sitting in his hotel watching television when the news flashed up that his son had been killed in Northern Ireland. He took to drink and never went back home.

Or you've got marital breakdowns. The woman gets the home, and the man has no friends or relatives.' Or, and this is a more disturbing trend, there are mental breakdowns.

Brian worries about the growing number of post-psychiatric cases at Carrington House, the most distinguished of whom was a brain surgeon from the Royal College in Dublin. 'No one ever comes to enquire how they are getting on.'

Once you enter Carrington House, you are not only forgotten by the authorities. In Brian's first week as manager, a Carringtonian died. He put on a suit and went to the funeral. In the corner of the cemetery, there was one other man – the priest.

He rises to show me round.

'If you're a human being, a rational human being, you'll get very angry,' he says.

Brian's first act on his appointment was to remove the iron turnstile by the entrance. Anyone wanting to spend the night checks in at the office. A bed is £32 a week, up front, which leaves £40 from social security for food and drink. (Orwell reckoned 8s. – 40p. – would last him three days and four nights in 1933.) Drink is not allowed in the house.

'You can tell if a man's going on a bender. He stops cleaning his shoes.' A man usually saves the weekend for his bender.

We go through swing doors into the snooker room. There are about twenty men in suits, in anoraks, in smart-casual dress. They range in age from thirty to seventy, each wrapped in his evening paper, his crossword puzzle, his pipe. No one looks up. There is silence except for the sound of balls clicking on felt.

We pass down a grey-tiled corridor. On one side are lockers where for 50p. for three months a man can store his possessions. On the same side is a door leading to a dark room with two television sets, one for ITV, one for BBC. Further down, in a room reserved for those over sixty-five, they are watching a programme called *Treasure Hunt*. The screen is fixed to a wall and, too far away for most of them to see, Anneka Rice giggles from a helicopter. 'It's a distraction, a nice bit of noise.'

Most are asleep, lolling in coats and under cloth caps against mock-Edwardian chairs. These chairs are covered in bright green and red, and have wings at head height to prevent their occupants falling out. By the door is a bookcase of remaindered novels, from which someone has half pulled a coverless copy of *Reader's Digest*.

The tiredness of life is palpable. It is the most melancholic sight I have ever seen.

The room stinks of *ennui*. The phrase again is Orwell's, but looking round it is impossible to forget his familiar descriptions of lodging-house life, and its squalid, eventless, crushing boredom:

> In childhood we have been taught that tramps are blackguards and consequently there exists in our minds a sort of ideal or typical tramp – a repulsive, dangerous creature who would rather die than work and wants nothing but to bed, drink and rob hen-houses. This tramp monster is no truer to life than the sinister Chinaman of the magazine stories . . . Indeed, if one remembers that a tramp is only an Englishman out of work, forced by law to live like a vagabond, then the tramp monster vanishes.

Opposite is the entrance to the eating area, where a three-course lunch costs £1.55 and porridge 17p. Many prefer to cook for themselves. Over naked flames, a man dries his saucepan. Again, no one looks up. 'Part of the attraction of the place is the privacy, the anonymity,' says Brian. 'They are loners who don't want to be social-worked. They never make deep friendships – just the friendship to share a meal. Men who have been buddies for four or five months can up and depart without a Hello. The responsibility of taking on an intimate relationship is too much.'

A man walks past the de-lousing room. Under his long coat he wears a corduroy jacket. The plastic bag he swings is full of newspaper. When it comes, the explanation – 'post-psychiatric' – carries the force of despair.

Round the corner we bump into a large, jolly Irishman called Steve. He is smartly turned out in a green tweed jacket, a fawn cloth cap and neat white neckerchief. His eyes are like forget-me-nots which have been in water too long. Steve has been in Carrington House since 1932. He first came when he was eighteen and cheated to do so – pretending he was twenty in order to get a working man's benefit. He came from Ireland as a navvy, and worked in Yorkshire and South Wales before returning here.

'D'yer noo Horseferry Magistrates Court?' he prods me proudly. He spent a year building it, he did.

Eight years ago he returned there, to answer a charge of 'skippering' (sleeping in an empty house).

Steve looks forward to four or five pints a night at the John

Evelyn pub. His sisters here tried to take him back to Ireland, but he won't have it. This is his home – 'Near enough'.

On a notice board by the exit is pinned a piece of paper outlining the Homemaker's Scheme, for those who want to move out. 'Everyone here has the right to a home of their own,' it begins. Pacing beside the board is one of Carrington House's youngest inmates. His hands are thrust deep into the pockets of his lavender cardigan. When he removes them, it remains stretched and attenuated over his grey cords. He speaks with a whistling lisp through a gap in his teeth. He has been here ten months. Not long enough for the manager to remember his name.

'I don't know how I've made it,' he says, nervously fiddling with what looks like two bottle tops screwed together. 'I feel like one of those elephants crossing the desert in Africa.' His father is a decorator who lives in Pimlico. His young brother has grown up to be a stranger. It's a long story how he's come to be here, he keeps saying. It's a spiral. He used to go out every day to look for work. He couldn't even find casual work. So one day he stopped bothering. What he really wants to do is catering or hotel work. But when they ask where you live and you say Carrington House, it's hopeless. He's started putting 1, Brookmill Road, instead.

He says he's not afraid, then qualifies this by admitting to an underlying fear. 'I wanted to watch *Tuesday, Tuesday* on telly, but I wasn't allowed. I've been beaten up too, by guys on the hard stuff. But I haven't helped myself. I've said some stupid things.' A court case pends for what he said to his girlfriend in the park when she chucked him out. He trails off.

I ask if I can get him anything. He tenses away. A book, perhaps? He looks more interested. He confesses he had been half way through Tolkien's *Hobbit*, but the library wouldn't let him in again. Galvanised now, he talks of Tolkien's life at Oxford in the 1940s, of the royalties he must earn on the paperbacks, and eventually of the goblin kingdom. I promise to get him a copy, remembering it had been the book on Lady Douro's coffee table.

Waiting for the train at New Cross, I have a take-away in a kebab house that had once been a pie shop. The owner claims Aphrodite came from his native Cyprus. I tell him it is unlikely she followed him to Deptford.

At Home

★

There used to be two statues outside the Bethlehem Royal Hospital in Lambeth. Both were by seventeenth-century sculptor Caius Cibber, in painted Portland stone. One was called *Melancholy*. The other, said to be modelled on Oliver Cromwell's porter – an inmate – was entitled *Raving Madness*.

'It is generally accepted that England is the country with the greatest number of insane,' wrote Flora Tristan★ in her *London Journal* of 1840 on her visit to Bedlam. 'It is also the home of the greatest excesses of every type.'

In its early days, to the taunting of visitors, Bedlam's miserable and 'distracted' patients would be chained to the walls, or dunked in water. One of the sights of London, and at one time quartered in a building which resembled the Tuileries, the lunatic asylum became doubly popular when George III went mad. The tuppence charged for entry must have seemed an oblique and cheap way of feeling superior to royalty.

For a small extra charge, and accepting the risks, it was possible to take tea with inmates like James Hadfield, who had thrown a rock at George IV; a Frenchman who considered himself the Messiah; and a bull-necked man who claimed to be the Queen's lover. For a time it was even possible to have tea with the Gothic decorator of the Houses of Parliament, Augustus Pugin.

There are no statues at the entrance of the Puginesque psychiatric hospital I visit in south London. Instead, two steel gates swing open mechanically and lead to a drive bumpy with sleeping policemen. Opened six years before the Palace of Westminster, with a capacity for 940 patients, it spreads its long red wings like a vulture settling on the ground. We drive to the furthest tip. Out of that window, I am told, a 34-year-old woman called Janice has on two occasions stood holding hands with a man, before watching each tumble to his death.

In her bouts of sanity, Janice works as a prostitute. In her madness, she falls in love with the patients. She had made a pact

---

★A descendant of Montezuma, and the grandmother of Gauguin, this French Peruvian lady had left her violent husband and taken a position in England as a lady's maid. In September 1838, her spouse, an inveterate gambler, shot her in the street. Flora survived, but the bullet stayed under her left breast for the remaining six years of her life.

with both lovers. 'We adore each other,' she had said. 'But you know we're mad. You know there's no future for us here. Let's die together.' Then, hand in hand, they had walked the stairs.

We go through locked doors into a ward named after a flower. An elderly woman sits scratching a slipper frilled with red fluff. She is called Violet. 'What's going on? How did you get in here?' she asks, her face puckered with anger. 'They wouldn't let me out. It's bloody ridiculous,' she says, indicating an iron door at the end of the corridor. 'Which ward are you in?' And then, without waiting for an answer, and nodding at the way I had come in, 'Where's that door go to then?' I tell her the kitchen, and she relaxes. How long has she been here? 'Not long. This afternoon. When the ambulance came, as bloody usual.' In fact, she has been here four months.

'Londoner? Yes, I'm a Londoner. From Southfields. I know all London. The East End . . . Southfields. They're different, Londoners. They talk hoity-toity – a bit like you.'

Does she ever go out there? I nod at the iron door. 'Yes,' she says sulkily. 'When I want. All the time.'

What is it like?

'Lonely.'

The nurse upstairs is from Trinidad, where she was taught by the novelist V.S. Naipaul's sister. She cannot wait to go back. Recently a man burst into the office where she was reading, furiously turned out the light, and slapped her for wasting electricity. He thought he was paying the bill.

'I've bought you a man,' she tells Hilda, who is 102. Hilda lies blinking in bed, her face drawn long and tight like Edward Munch's *Scream*. 'That's nice,' she says.

The ward is named after a precious stone.

'That's Anita who keeps wanting me to sing Polish lullabies with her. That's Mabel,' says the nurse of another sleeping figure. 'She's the maddest. She's very working class, and is always having a go at Nancy who likes to talk posh.'

The week before, she had pulled up her nightie and twisted her back towards Nancy. 'Here's arse,' she had said, mimicking Nancy's exaggerated drawl. 'Yes ma'am, no ma'am, three bags full ma'am.' The following night, slumped in a chair opposite, she had drawn up her nightie again.

'Look at Fanny. Come and talk to her.'

'Too awful. It's too awful,' Nancy had said, wiping her brow theatrically.

Nancy, who has been moved to the next room, is proud of her theatrical background. 'I'm a singer, but my father was the real one. He knew everyone. We always got free theatre tickets because of him.' Beside her bed is a black-bound book. It is called *The Butler's Revenge*. She has been reading it for ten years. There is a crease on every page.

'I love reading so much, don't you?' she says, scratching her leg under a red nightie. She has been passed on from home to home because of her habit of scratching nurses. She loves it here in the country, she tells me, near Canterbury. 'But I used to go up to London the whole time, to the theatre.' She stops scratching and raises herself on an elbow. There is a glitter in her eye. 'Maybe it's because I'm a Londoner,' she warbles, her posh voice curdling into cockney and rising, 'that I love London so.' From the next ward comes an answering chant. In Polish.

The Greater London Boroughs

A Selection of Blue Plaques and Modern Contenders by Borough

BLUE PLAQUES	MODERN CONTENDERS	BLUE PLAQUES	MODERN CONTENDERS
Barnet		**Croydon**	
William Blake		Sir Arthur Conan Doyle	
		Alfred Russel Wallace	
Bromley			
W.G. Grace		**Ealing**	
			Peter Jay
Camden			Neil Kinnock
Sir Edward Burne-Jones	Kingsley Amis		
Thomas Carlyle	Lindsey Anderson	**Enfield**	
John Constable	Tom Conti		Nigel Hawthorne
Charles Dickens	Peter Cook		
Benjamin Disraeli	Judi Dench	**Greenwich**	
Friedrich Engels	Lesley-Anne Down	Nathaniel Hawthorne	Michael Frayn
Sigmund Freud	Margaret Drabble	Herbert Morrison	Libby Purves
John Galsworthy	Michael Foot		
Kate Greenaway	Terry Gilliam	**Hackney**	
John Keats	Nigel Kennedy	Daniel Defoe	
John Maynard Keynes	Diana Quick	Philip and Edmund Gosse	
D.H. Lawrence	Peter York	Joseph Priestley	
Katherine Mansfield			
Henry Mayhew		**Hammersmith**	
Giuseppe Mazzini		Samuel Taylor Coleridge	William Boyd
George Orwell		Edward Elgar	Anita Brookner
Dante Gabriel Rossetti		Lucien Pissarro	Billy Connolly/ Pamela Stephenson
George Bernard Shaw			Henry Root
Lytton Strachey			
Dylan Thomas		**Haringey**	
Virginia Woolf		A.E. Housman	
William Butler Yeats			
City of London			
	Clive James		
	Arthur Scargill		

L-4

BLUE PLAQUES	MODERN CONTENDERS	BLUE PLAQUES	MODERN CONTENDERS

Harrow

W.S. Gilbert
W. Heath Robinson

Hounslow

E.M. Forster
Johann Zoffany

Michael Billington
Mark Boxer/
  Anna Ford
Jo Grimond
Duke of
  Northumberland
Esther Rantzen/
  Desmond Wilcox
Vanessa Redgrave

Kensington

Robert Baden
  Powell
Hilaire Belloc
Arnold Bennett
Charles Booth
G.K. Chesterton
Sir Winston
  Churchill
George Eliot
Ford Madox Ford
Elizabeth Gaskell
George Gissing
W.H. Hudson
Henry James
Augustus John
Lillie Langtry
Frederick Leighton
Percy Wyndham
  Lewis
John Stuart Mill
John Everett Millais
A.A. Milne
Sylvia Pankhurst
Dante Gabriel
  Rossetti
Tobias Smollett
Philip Wilson Steer
Leslie Stephen
William Makepeace
  Thackeray
Herbert Beerbohm
  Tree
Mark Twain
James Whistler
Oscar Wilde

Peter Ackroyd
Maria Aitken
Martin Amis
Adam Ant
Jane Asher
Tony Benn
Hugh Casson
John Cleese
Clare Francis
Antonia Fraser/
  Harold Pinter
Bob Geldof/
  Paula Yates
Michael Holroyd
David Jacobs
Bianca Jagger
Miles Kington
George Melly
George Michael
Laurence Olivier
David Puttnam
Christopher Reeve
Tim Rice
Rolling Stones office
Gerald Scarfe
Lord Snowdon
Emma Tennant
Laurens van der Post
Charles Wilson

Lambeth

Charles Barry
William Bligh
Jack Hobbs
John Ruskin
Vincent van Gogh
Violet Szabo

Jim Callaghan
Angela Carter
Michael Fish
Michael Gough
Simon Le Bon
Cynthia Payne
The Thompson
  Twins

Lewisham

Ernest Shackleton
Samuel Smiles

Merton

      Anthony Andrews

Richmond-upon-Thames

Henry Fielding
David Garrick
Cardinal Newman
Leonard and Virginia
  Woolf
J.M.W. Turner

David Attenborough
Simon Dee
Bamber Gascoigne
Sue Lawley
Elaine Paige
Dorothy Tutin
Jimmy Young

Southwark

John Logie Baird
Joseph Chamberlain

Faith Brown
Anna Cartwright
Harriet Harman
Terry Jones
Eric Morley
Margaret Thatcher

Tower Hamlets

Dr Thomas Barnado
Isambard Kingdom
  Brunel
Captain James Cook
Mahatma Gandhi
Israel Zangwill

David Lean
David Owen
Reginald and Ronnie
  Kray

At Home

Part Three
AT WORK

'In England money dominates everything.'

FLORA TRISTAN'S LONDON JOURNAL, 1840

'The possession of money is of course immensely an advantage, but that is a very different thing from a disqualification at the lack of it.'

HENRY JAMES, ENGLISH HOURS, 1905

According to a United Nations table, compiled from a survey on the cost of living for UN officials round the world, London ranks eleventh on a level with Port au Prince, Haiti, and behind Conkary in Guinea, Tokyo, Copenhagen and New York.

TAKEN FROM THE LONDONER'S ALMANAC, 1985

In 1985, before leaving his post as Minister of the Arts and joining the auctioneers Sotheby's as chairman, Lord Gowrie fired a parting shot that went deep into the Tory party's political foot. It was impossible to finance life in London, he claimed, for the £33,260 he was paid a year.

At £200.60, the average weekly income per household in London is less than a third of that.

Chris is a young man trying to earn a living at the bottom end of the art market. A former estate agent, he has decided to deal in antiques, concentrating on the Arts and Crafts movement. In the last four weeks he has driven 1,200 miles and bought four pieces at country auctions. He takes them to a shop in Kensington which buys them for double what he paid. The most he has ever paid for an item is £400. In the country he had some trouble with runners from the big warehouses, under contract to supply so much per month to America. They spotted the type of items he was after and bid him up. He had to pay them off. Though he has a habit of underlying what he says with 'for sure', he is still very much feeling his way.

Long before the first tube leaves Hainault, Chris takes me to the market he visits every Friday in Southall.

We arrive shortly before five. Several lorries are already being unloaded into the stalls which by day form part of a cattle market. One truck is covered by a green tarpaulin, starched with frost. Lifting its stiff flaps, three men with torches peer and poke.

In a stall to the rear, I find a cheery man who works as a caretaker in Richmond. Made redundant from a meat firm in the East End, he has moved to the outskirts. He moved, he says, openly admitting his racism, because he hated the blacks taking over the centre. In the same breath, he praises the Indians of Southall. 'They're very gentle. The know a bargain, and whatever they do, they do to each other at home. It's the old white ladies with bags who are the worst for shoplifting,' he says, cackling at his own prejudices.

He unloads a van packed with the fruits of an auction on the Sussex coast. 'Pretty crappy, but I'll try it twice, and then if it doesn't sell I'll put it on the skip.' The best stuff he keeps for a stall in Richmond.

'Pretty crappy' describes a moth-eaten stag's head, some chairs, a damp cardboard box of books, an electric oven – 'Two quid, but it works' – a white wardrobe, and a basket of trinkets; old binoculars, older bottles, and a memento from Cornwall which doubled as an egg timer. Nothing from the Arts and Crafts period. Sadly, he began unpacking a suitcase of children's clothes. 'It breaks my heart to do this,' he says, hanging the little gloves and jerseys on the line. They belonged to his own children.

Two stalls away, a man with wayward hair and spectacles sellotaped round the nose is uncertainly holding a box of tatty books. Among them is Kenneth Clark's autobiography, which he lets me have for 25p. He turns out to be a chartered accountant in his mid-forties. Five weeks before, he had given up his job in north London. 'I was just fed up. The only people I ever saw were other accountants and tax men. I much prefer this.' His mate gruffly bawls at him to keep unloading. Sucking the last of a home-rolled cigarette, he turns sheepishly to receive an armful of dresses.

Steadily, imperceptibly, the market fills with noise. An impeccable English accent announces, 'This is London', and a radio blares out the familiar signature tune of the BBC's World Service News. From a reel-to-reel tape recorder, in a truck full of fruit machines, comes the sound of opera.

In a corner near the market entrance I come across a corpulent Caribbean with a beer belly and a goatee beard shiny with saliva. The back of his van is down, and he stands on it like a stage. 'I tell you, I got the cream today!' he shouts. 'C.R.E.M.E. Cream.' Beneath him on a trestle table spreads a rusty, dirty tangle of broken tools, spare parts, sewer valves, nuts, bolts and spanners. They have taken two hours to unpack.

'You can come back if you change your mind,' he promises.

'That's the thing about England. You can change your mind.'

He came to England thirty years ago and lives in Shepherd's Bush. When he talks about himself rather than his wares, his ebullience fades away. 'I tell you, I work so hard for a few bob for my wife. I just don't know why I do it. It's so difficult, no wonder people turn to crime. If I didn't work, I'd wear a tie and look smart, and do nothing.' He strokes his fat front distractedly and jerks his head. 'I get depressed when the weather's like this. You know,' he says, catching sight of his stall, 'I'd like to sell all this and save to buy something decent to sell. Everything will end up on the skip today.'

An Indian comes up and asks the price of the single-bar fire perched on the fridge. 'Three-fifty I want for that. Not a penny below three pound fifty. You know how much it costs in the shops? I tell you. Seven quid, that's how much.' He pauses. 'Okay, since you're so cute, three pounds.'

The Indian puts the fire down. 'But there's one over there for seventy-five pence,' he says.

'Look man, this fire's here and that fire's there. It's a different fire . . . Okay. Fifty p.'

The Indian looks up. 'You don't mean fifty p.'

'Yea, give me fifty p.'

The man looks baffled. 'No, I'll give you a quid.'

Chris materialises with a Cheshire-cat smile. He has found a line of false book covers made in wood. He caresses the artificial spines. 'The Americans will lap it up,' he promises. 'For sure.'

Another Christopher has an art gallery in Bond Street – at the other end of the market. The case of false books against his wall is glass-fronted, panelled and tall. The red and ochre shelves boast volumes of Picard's *Religious Ceremonies* and *Memoirs des Chinois*. The spines are not wood but leather, the titles embossed with gold. The cheapest item in Christopher's gallery is £300. The most expensive, £400,000.

His showrooms are tucked away down a corridor, past another glass panel protecting photographs of his greatest sales.

Typeset in Polyphilus and printed on Artlaid paper, the blue-bound catalogue begins with a quotation from the seventh-century saint, Maximus of Tyre, talking of God the Father and Fashioner of all that is:

> But we being unable to apprehend His Essence use the help of sounds and names and pictures, of beaten gold and ivory and silver, of plants and rivers, mountain peaks and torrents, yearning for the knowledge of Him and in our weakness naming all that is beautiful in this world after His name – just as happens to earthly lovers.

The foreword carries the information that Christopher's treasures are open to the public between 9.30 a.m. and 5.30 p.m., except in August; and the promise, 'We try to show here the rarest and the most beautiful things we can find'.

His office is a small room connecting two large galleries. In the corner, a tiny black-and-white television screen gives a blurred picture of the main room. The secretary, a girl in a T-shirt which bears the legend 'Kent', has stopped looking at it. 'You can only see people coming in, not leaving,' she complains, collecting her things for the night. Christopher raises his eyes behind her back. A cup of tea, he asks – camomile, Lapsan? – and disappears up a spiral staircase hidden in a cupboard. He remains there for some time.

When he returns the tea is very brown. The 'phone had rung, he apologises, sitting back into a red-and-white upholstered chair. He wears a black sweater, a black-and-white barrister's tie, and lavender socks. Straw hair sweeps neatly across a good-looking forehead. The chair, he says, is part of Giovanni Boldini's studio furniture. Drawings exist of society ladies sitting where he sits, running long fingers along its wooden arms.

'Have I sold anything today? Well, I haven't bought anything, and I don't think I've sold anything.' He reaches out to a book. 'Maybe I have. Oh, yes, a marble bust to a French dealer.' In the last six months he has sold a total of ninety-seven works of art. 'You may take a hundred and fifty thousand pounds in a few days,' he says sipping his lukewarm brew. 'Or eighteen pounds for the next four weeks.'

Christopher is a character who swung in the sixties. He mixed with society from Cheyne Row to Southwark, when it was smart to know the Krays – 'Coarse people,' he says now, 'in bright suits, with good-looking chauffeurs, talking rubbish late into the night.' He drifted into the art world after a few months in the army, and a short time in a building society 'fleecing the small investor in an alley off St Martin's Lane.' The building society opened his eyes: 'Let's say, it broadened my outlook on how business should be conducted.'

The first business he conducted was from a shop in Camden Passage. 'Those were the good old days,' he purrs. 'You just needed taste, nerve, and a tiny bit of money' – which he had, coming as he does from a long line of merchant bankers.

'There was an enormous volume of distinguished stuff on the market. The great houses were being broken up by absurd trustees, who told the owners they couldn't possibly go on living there and should move into a bungalow on the estate. If I'd had a few thousand and bought the right things, I could have gone and lived in Marrakesh for twenty years, and come back a rich man.' Notwithstanding Maximus of Tyre, 'things' is the word Christopher uses most to describe his *objets d'art*. Often he has bought the wrong things. 'I paid fifteen thousand pounds for a wonderful picture by the nineteenth-century Irish artist Daniel Maclise. I spent a few thousand more on cleaning it. A few thousand more on advertising it. No one was interested. Four years later, I let it go at auction for three thousand. Colnaghi's, the Bond Street art dealers, immediately sold it to the House of Lords for twenty.'

His clients go back to the days of Camden Passage. They are people who have things and like things, and get rid of the things they don't like so much to the man who first sold them. He buys for their London house, and when they move to the country he helps buy for that too.

The gallery has an atmosphere approaching that of a country house – 'Relaxed, yet scholarly. It's my vision, my rather mixed vision of the things I like, all of which are an extension of some huge vanity or other. I'm interested in everything. That is to say,' he says, putting down his half-drunk mug, 'I'm interested in hardly anything at all.'

We wander into the larger of the two rooms. In the spring, he says, there are snowdrops in the flowerpots from his garden in the country. He spends an increasing amount of time there. 'You have to be committed to the hustle, and I'm not. Pampering the clients to death, going round the auction rooms . . . I used to do a hundred shops a day. Now I go to Christie's and Sotheby's once a week.' What still gives him pleasure is researching a provenance. In a glass case are two large, whiskered birds. 'Mid-nineteenth-century. The last great bustards to be shot in England – on Salisbury Plain. Yours for six thousand pounds.' There is no price tag, merely a label with the figures X2254.

He indicates what appear to be two moorings for a gondola: 'The Duke of Westminster's curtain poles.'

The room is delicately jumbled with marble console tables, carved gilt mirrors, and a selection of portraits. 'That's George, the fairy Earl of Kildare,' he says of a bearded man in pink. 'He was three foot eight.'

Another canvas shows a grey country house in a valley, with a sleeping cow in the foreground. It is the house of Sir Thomas Phillips, a fanatic book-lover who kept his precious volumes in coffins, so that if there was a fire he could easily haul them to safety. In the tower of his home a press printed lists of the medieval manuscripts in his collection. Eventually the coffins took over the house, and the family had to move out. The oil painting is the work of the butler. 'He was never paid. The only way he earned anything was by selling his paintings to visitors.'

One wall is occupied entirely by a dark wooden screen, shaped and engraved like the front of a temple. Designed, like Somerset House and the Kew Gardens pagoda, by Sir William Chambers, it is Christopher's most expensive thing. He bought it from Lord Iveagh. 'It used to be in his dressing room at Elvedon. It's a medal and coin cabinet built in 1767 for the first Earl of Charlemont's house in Dublin. Lord Charlemont was a very cultivated man. The very rabble approaching his person became civilised, according to Edmund Burke.' He opens a panel, revealing Chambers' neo-classical designs and drawers: one side for Greek coins, one side for Roman.

Will he get the £400,000? 'Oh, yes. It's completely documented. It's a great show-stopper. It will go to an institution which can teach people how important coins are.'

In a heap beneath the Duke of Westminster's curtain poles is the cheapest item in Christopher's gallery. When assembled, the green cast-iron pieces, shaped like twigs, will make a garden bench. There seem better things to do with £300.

Switching off the lights and setting the burglar alarm, Christopher mumbles about the problems of having to deal in dollars, the difficulties of getting back-up from girls who stop unfailingly at 5.24 p.m. and the market in general.

'London must still be the centre of the world art market.

There's more good art in private hands here than anywhere else. The trouble now is that if people want to buy a combine harvester they have to get rid of their bronze ancestors.' Certainly, it is difficult to envisage one aristocrat rushing to spend millions on a painting offered for sale by another.

'It's the spirit that's changed vastly. London's become a coarser place. Sotheby's is now owned by the Americans. Before, there was a hierarchy of excellence. The room was divided between what was important and what was not. Now, there's the idea that everything is important. This highly important fountain pen, they gush. People will hype anything today, and modern art dealers are the most hypeful of all.'

Will Christopher survive? He splutters charmingly from the dark. 'God, yes. I know what things are. I know what's good, what's bad. I know where things are.'

For exactly fifty years, since he arrived here from Poland in 1935, the artist Feliks Topolski has earned his living from drawing and painting Londoners: sometimes in the streets, in movement, unaware; sometimes posed in his studio, nursing a glass of sweet red Polish vodka.

'That Impressionist in black and white,' Bernard Shaw called him, referring to his vibrant portraits of Evelyn Waugh, Cyril Connolly, Ivy Compton-Burnett. Even our Royal Family has clasped him to its purple heart, commissioning the long Buckingham Palace mural of the Trooping of the Colour.

'It's a matter-of-fact city,' he says, lying on a bed on a brown rug, and running a finger back and forth over it like a windscreen wiper. Above him rises the cavernous ceiling of his tower flat, at the top of a mansion block near Whitehall. He was first attracted here when he visited Bernard Shaw. His balcony overlooks the city. Outside, through the night, the lights from Hungerford Bridge shine orange on the Thames, as if they have rusted into the dark water. In two arches under the bridge, a short walk across the river, is his studio and gallery. The trains rumble over frequently, prompting the unkind quip that all he has to do is put pencil to paper. In tall canvases around the gallery walls snakes his *Memoir of the Century*. It is a compound work, depicting his life and travels, and will not be completed until he dies.

He wears a key round his neck, suggestively, and a green army battledress, as if he exists in some permanent state of confrontation. He does not like to be attached to anything, to belong anywhere, he insists. His art relies on him floating detached. His conversation can also seem unhitched. 'This will amuse you,' he says seriously, but you never know where his stories are leading. Sometimes his sentences, like the lines in his drawings, are scribbles whirling into smudged blank spaces.

Feliks first came to London for a fortnight in 1933, on a cheap excursion from Paris. 'For European males' – and Feliks is a very European male – 'London was a paradisical promise. We knew all about English snobberies. I'd been moving in Poland in smartish bohemian circles, peopled mainly by homosexuals, who, as rich aristocrats, were schooled in England and anglicised in apparel. They were vigorous poets in Locke hats, umbrellas and navy-blue overcoats. There was even an "Old English" shop in Warsaw. So there was no surprise. I was prepared. And being fond of nineteenth-century draughtsmanship, I found the England of 1933 extremely and vigorously nineteenth-century – even exotic. People divided into classes in costume and behaviour. And because they lived within their class, their neighbourhood and their profession they were exciting to an artist.'

He returned for George V's jubilee in 1935, crossing on a Polish boat which eventually moored at Tower Bridge. He remembers coming up the Thames 'through the monumentality of industrial maritime glory – soaring, roaring warehouses, busy, black and high, which offered the complete vision of nineteenth-century Britain. It was ugly, but it had extreme beauty, and it made a contrast with Tony, the count who met me on the quayside. Everything he wore was in the right place, placed there with dandyish elegance. A hanky in his sleeve, a hat on his nose.'

From his balcony, it is just possible to see where he landed. 'I didn't mean to stay. I had what the Germans call *Reisefieber* – a fever for journeying. But, but, but . . . because of friendliness, of jolly chaps crying out my glory, and organising an exhibition for me in Mayfair, and publishing a book, and engagements in *Vogue* and *News Chronicle* – because of all this I stayed.'

He was held also by London's traditions, embodied in the cavalier hats of the street cleaners, the Edwardian suits of Savile Row, the uniforms of soldiers trooping the colour – 'these were real soldiers, not like in Denmark or Poland'; and he could not leave because of the fascination with the life that moved beneath the ceremony, with its extraordinary, cockneyish gestures and shapes.

'Only in London did I understand the reality of Shaw's *Pygmalion*. In Poland, the division between the buxom girls of peasant stock and the educated classes was a division that could not be overcome. The fantastic thing about London was that a perky-nosed girl from the outskirts could become Eliza Doolittle. And I fancied lots of English girls, particularly common girls, with their leggy quality as they moved against the wind in the street.'

Even today their magic has not gone entirely. Recently he has been painting two tiny punks with pale, glaring faces. He prides himself on the way he keeps up, ever since he was invaded 'by hippydom'.

In the sixties, Feliks' arch became a watering hole for thirsty young men and women. 'There was a terrific, orgiastic promiscuity.' Complete strangers dropped in for LSD sessions and at parties, where bands like Hawkwind played, there would be everyone from Snowdon to Stephen Ward. 'One dawn, newspaper boys entered a party that was still going on. On the front page of the first edition was a photograph of Milford Haven making his peace with a Hungarian film star earlier in the evening.'

He talks about the faces of Londoners today: the Indians, the blacks with their ghetto-blasters, the policemen with their shields, the shaven heads of the National Front. But, for him, the quintessential Londoner remains the middle-class elderly lady. 'Everything she does and wears and says is right. She's the one who votes for Mrs Thatcher.'

Yet Feliks has tired of Thatcher's London. 'It used to be mechanical to say this is the best place in the world to live, the safest. But things change rapidly. The liberal democratic tolerance which has made London the central point in Western knowledge and Western minds was based on meekness. Today, with the shrinkage of the empire, and this new Victorianism, I notice a closing of ranks, a hostility towards outsiders. And because my name ends in "-ski" and not "-smith", I feel less accepted now.'

We walk through Trafalgar Square, and up Shaftesbury Avenue to the Groucho Club. Inspired by Groucho Marx's riposte that he would not join any club that would have him as a member, this club in Dean Street had recently opened as a haven for young writers, publishers and artists. Feliks has not yet been there. As we walk, he talks about London's artistic meeting place before the War – the Café Royale.

'It was much more than La Coupole in Paris' – where Hemingway and his friends met in the 1930s. 'It had an immense, ugly, ochre interior divided into two halves by seats back to back. The part where we sat was for coffee and beer. The other was the top restaurant in London, with the so-called best people going for pompous dinners – Augustus John, Jacob Epstein, Nye Bevan . . . And there was a vast number of well-bred girls who went bohemian then, who used to meet us there. Entirely beautiful, with elegant bodies, but deliberately messy. Penniless too, but living in flats which their parents had given them. Usually I had a partner,' he adds superfluously.

He pauses by the car park at the edge of Dean Street, walks on, stops, and then returns. 'Astonishing,' he says, fingering his key. 'But this is where I was bombed during the Blitz, this very spot. And that,' he points at a doorway one down from the Groucho Club, 'was the shoe shop where I sat in my smart overcoat, streaked in blood and powder.' He seems genuinely moved by the recollection. 'I sat here thinking, I must get my tin hat, I must get my tin hat, and I staggered back to the rubbish heap. Finally, I was picked up in Warren Street and bandaged up. I still wasn't in pain, but through the bandages I heard this woman's voice, a very cultivated Chelsea voice. And I said to her through my bandages, Can you help me? Do you know the Honourable Such-and-such. I have a lunch engagement with her tomorrow. And the woman, who was loading me onto the ARP ambulance, said, "Yes I know her. Don't worry, I'll tell her you won't be able to make lunch." '

'Social life's a job,' says Lady M., who drove an ambulance during the Blitz. 'I don't think I paid for anything in public till I was fifty-five. I sang for my supper.'

At seventy-two, she retains the gipsy beauty which Topolski's drawing catches on the wall behind. She sits in red trousers and redder lipstick beside the electric fire. Outside her small flat on the Earl's Court Road, the traffic hums. Every now and then, when a particularly noisy lorry passes, she puts down her gold-glazed tea cup and runs a thin hand through a tumble of black hair. She has just returned from a two-mile walk on which she spotted some policemen. 'I found myself saying *pigs*! They were attaching clamps to someone's car and spoiling a lovely snowy day.'

At first she thought I had come to mend the roof.

Lady M. is the daughter of an earl. On either side of the fire hang two small prints, reminders of the country house in Surrey where she was brought up.

'I was to Discover', confesses Emma Tennant's Robina, 'the Nobility have no Care for their younger Sons or Daughters and will treat them Lower than servants or throw them out altogether to Starve'. The way Lady M. has earned her living is not conventional, but it is valid. When she describes social life as a job, she means just that. And she has worked hard at it: both in the milieu to which she was born, and in the very different world she has come to espouse. Singing for your supper with a silver spoon in your mouth could produce an ugly noise. In Lady M.'s case, the sound has been beguiling.

'Parents were very strict with their daughters till eighteen. Then suddenly you'd be told, I'm writing to Jo-Jo and she'll invite you to a party. Then it was okay for you to be picked up in an MG by a man who was perfectly drunk and a terrible driver to boot. I would be allowed to come up from Guildford on the train, which cost three shillings and ninepence, and stay in my grandma's club in Grosvenor Street. It was called the Sesame, and I used to sleep in a little room with no proper window.

'I made my own clothes. I was absolutely penniless. It was not done to mention money or titles. My brother, who was very good-looking, I thought, called me "Lump", with that ghastly understatement of the upper classes. I didn't know I was pretty. Now, looking at photos, I realise how pretty I was. Men were writing poems about my shoulders at sixteen, but I didn't take any notice. Men have always made passes at me – from fourteen till yesterday. I felt like a coloured boy must feel who's never been told he's coloured till he came to Brixton. Bob Geldof said to me, "Do you regret losing your looks?" I said, No, but I regret not catching a millionaire when I had them. Oh, I was so green. So, so green.'

She married, but not well. 'A penniless, glamorous, amusing boy. We lived in a flat over a shop by Selfridges. We spent the marriage in nightclubs. In four years, I didn't spend a single night

in. There would be two cocktail parties, two or three nightclubs –
The Embassy, The Café de Paris, The Four Hundred – and you'd
never know which club you were in, or who was paying.' It is
now that she confesses to not paying anything till she was
fifty-five. 'I ran away with another penniless catch, an actor this
time, and we lived in a bedsit in Orange Street off Leicester
Square. I modelled to keep him.' She nods at the framed black-
and-white photographs on the wall. 'Beaton, Parkinson, Mac-
bean. There were pictures in the paper of me twice a week. I did
the famous cigarette ad for Baron. He said he never took a bad
photo of me. All I thought was, Well, I've helped Baron and I've
got a guinea.' She speaks placidly, without vanity.

She talks of the Blitz, reminded of it by a gas explosion in
Putney which has killed eight people. 'I fell in love with Londoners in the Blitz. When it started I was living in London, and I was
determined to stay in London. It was where I belonged. I drove an
ambulance in the St Paul's district . . . Those wonderful firemen.
The smell of gas, the waiting for people to be dug out, policemen
asking me for dates on my night off. In war everyone goes
through great danger together. You get to know types you
couldn't know otherwise. You sleep on the floor with thirteen to a
room. It's like being on stage – what my son calls scathingly,
"Mother's Love Affair with Working Man".'

She became a pub wanderer in 1941 when all her friends were
killed. After the War she went to run a bar in Cornwall. In the
sixties she came back – 'missing the bottles and the men, I
suppose' – and wandered again through London. By day she
worked at Harrods as a query clerk. In the evenings she learnt
Chinese and Spanish, and visited the pubs. 'I remember Finch's, a
drunks' pub in Chelsea, The Colony Room in Soho. I lived for
four pounds a week in a bedsit on Coleherne Road, with two
hundred pounds a year in alimony, and unlimited petrol. I had no
money. I remember one day taping Richard Burton reading Dylan
Thomas on the radio. I had to hold a screwdriver in the tape
recorder to keep it going whilst the rent man hammered on the
door.' She smiles dreamily. 'I got it all. The whole one-and-a-half
hours.'

We return to her favourite subject. 'London offers you a little
island of privacy, then you go into the street and it immediately
offers you social life. I feel the same about London as the Scots
who wander about their moors. I love Londoners and their speed

of thought, their sense of humour, their immense courage. Londoners understand me. When I speak to a lorry driver, he understands what I mean. Most of my friends don't. I find talking to my friends and family one long misunderstanding. All my family are Etonians. My mother said she'd never marry a man who wasn't an Etonian. She married two. My grandson's the most awful Etonian I've ever seen. He's a little horror. I can't bear to be in the same room as him. You know exactly the borderline of these people, even when you get into bed with them.

'As for the women . . . My daughter has a lot of friends all called Venetia and Miranda – rich divorcees and widows, who sit around in their houses watching videos. In London a lot of women live alone, and they're all so depressed. Much better to go and talk to some drunken Irishman. I can go to the smartest dinner parties in the world and talk and be amusing, but it's not real to me.

'What's a title? You're born with a silly little name that means nothing. I think my husbands married me because I had a name, but you're always married because of something. My children point it out, but they seem more aware of it than I am. A title's only useful if you want to take a handbag back to Harrods, or if you are making a fantastic fuss about residents' parking. Much of the time it stops you from being able to make friends. People use me because of it. I know quite a lot of drunks, and after I'd appeared once on TV they liked me more. One at Finch's asked if I'd be a reference, and a friend I had at the Chelsea Arts Club started calling me "Lady". I got so bored. He took me to a snug at the Denmark and was shocked when he found we were sitting next to a milkman and he and I started singing "Maybe it's because I'm a Londoner".'

'Singing with the milkman,' Lady M. concludes. 'That's what I call reality.'

I go and look for a milkman and find a young man called Steve. He lives in the first-floor flat of a terraced house in Battersea overlooking a council estate. The mirror over the fireplace incorporates a picture of Big Ben. The walls are varnished brick. It is midday and he has just returned from work, hence the slippers and the white ribbed jersey. The earring and the gold cross around his neck are more permanent fixtures.

He works as a milkman in Richmond. Before that he ran an off-licence in Lavender Hill. You could set your watch by some of them, he says. Especially the Guinness drinkers. When they delivered their empties after a month, there would be beer flies in the bottom.

He was born in Wimbledon, the son of a builder, and though he lives only a couple of hundred yards from the Thames, he has stayed south. 'If I go over that bridge I'm lost. It's all quick and rushy-rushy. Occasionally we've gone over there. What 'ave we gone over there for, love?' He turns to his wife. They cannot think.

His day begins at 4.00 a.m. 'I used to hate it,' his wife says. 'I can sleep through the alarm now.' The drive to Richmond takes ten minutes. He is already dressed in overalls. Sometimes he wears a bodywarmer. 'The earlier you start, the earlier you finish. If you don't get in by four-thirty, you go to the back of the loading queue.'

He pulls his float out and leaves it in the queue. Then he goes upstairs to the depot, for pool and darts, and plenty of tea. At 5.30 a.m. he starts loading up: 1,000 bottles of milk, and then the rest – orange juice, apples, eggs, potatoes, cheese and cereal. It takes ten minutes, and a quarter of an hour more for him to reach the Upper Richmond Road and the first of his 426 calls.

Steve's round takes in both the council estates along Woodlands Road and the large houses in Roehampton Lane. 'I reckon sixty per cent of them 'ave swimming pools. One Arab proudly showed me the bath 'e 'ad put in. It was pure bronze, and shaped like an oyster shell. In the lid there was an infra-red lamp and a shower.' Of his 426 customers, there is only one he has not met. 'I can knock 'em off in three hours,' he boasts, in the course of which he sees everyone from the boys at the bottom to them at the top – like John Entwhistle of The Who. 'I serve Roy Kinnear, the fat comedian. 'E's so boring. But if you don't want to talk, you don't. You're your own guv'nor.'

Within limits. The dairy encourages its milkmen never to extend more than £840 total credit. 'I've never got it below twelve hundred pounds, so I go without twenty-five quid a month commission,' Steve admits. When collecting payment for the milk bill, he is often walking around with £1,500 in his pocket. 'It's something you don't think about.' Working six days a week, he takes home £130. Tips account for a further £10 to £20. At Christmas, it can be as much as £700.

Steve is amused at the way his customers categorise themselves by their choice of milk. 'The council 'ouses 'ave silver top. They're not bothered by fat-free milk. The upper class want semi-skimmed and homogenised. Stripey is a favourite too. It's the stuff they used to throw away or feed to the pigs. Now they sell it as fat-free milk for twenty-one pence, and people think it's lovely. People will think anything. People think their milk is fresh on their doorstep, but it isn't. It could be up to a week old.'

Midway through his morning, at 9.30, Steve drives his cart to the Richmond Golf Club, where he is given a free breakfast of eggs, bacon, sausage and beans. By 11.30 a.m. he is finished for the day. He unloads his empties, puts the battery on the charger, and goes home. If it's a Thursday or Friday he will do his books. Otherwise, he'll watch the video.

'All the milkman wants to do is deliver 'is milk and get 'ome as soon as possible. It's such a boring job, really. At the weekend I do it the other way round, just to make it different.'

He dismisses the so-called temptations of the job as myth. 'People think that naughty stuff is part and parcel of a milkman's round,' he says, fingering his earring. 'I only know two blokes who actually 'ad anyone on their rounds. Big Clive was supposed to 'ave 'ad a couple, and Les Thatcher ended up married to one. It started with a note in the milk bottle, which said, *My dear Les, Would you come out for dinner tonight?* In four weeks 'e'd moved in and got 'er pregnant. They were married a fortnight ago.'

Steve removes the finger from his ear. 'I got propositioned by a pouf once. It was a real bad winter, and I'm like a frozen turd, creeping about on the ice. This chap I'd just taken onto my books, 'e said, "I'm John," so I automatically said, "I'm Steve."

' "Steve," 'e said, "would you like a cup of tea?"

' "Terrific idea, John. Put the kettle on. I'll just do these two, and I'll be in."

'Well, there we were, sipping our tea, and looking over the snow at some 'orses which were being rounded up.

' "Do you ride, Steve? That's a pity. I'd have thought you'd look good in riding gear."

' 'E thought a bit, then a minute later, 'e said, "Do you ride a motor bike?"

'I thought of the leather bit, swallowed me tea, and dashed out. It turned out later we 'ad the same birthday.

' "I knew we had something in common," 'e said.

'About f— all! I don't go round for tea, now. That's all.'

The Indesit engineer who comes to mend the washing machine says, yes, he is often propositioned by gays. He is bearded and friendly and comes from Jamaica. They demand he comes back the following day because there is something wrong with the machine. There is never anything wrong.

He came to England when he was three. He does not know why. He went back to Jamaica once, but found it too hot. He couldn't sleep at night. He studied engineering for five years at the City and Guilds, worked in a television company that made him redundant, and has been eight years with Indesit.

Once he was met at the door by a naked woman, wet from the shower. She sat at the table in her towel as he worked. Another time there was a woman dressed only in her knickers; another, a French woman in a smart flat in Stanmore Court, behind Kensington Square. She asked what he was doing later, then rang up the office to say she was his girlfriend.

He is married. He wouldn't sleep with them because he 'would not know what they had'.

'If they'd sleep with me, they'd sleep with anybody,' he says.

Next day, when the washing machine breaks down, I decide not to complain.

Lucy also spends her life in other people's houses. Her family is named after the town in northern Portugal where she came from ten years ago. She came to earn more money than her dead father could ever make as a builder.

'What are you here for? To work,' she says, sipping coffee from a mug. And London offered her the opportunity to work far harder than at home.

She sits in purple cords, her collar up, in her drawing room on the topmost level of a council block. She has a cheerful face and brown curly hair, like the top of a breaking wave. Photographs of three children smile with her smile from embossed gold frames on the television set. Outside on the empty washing line, clothes pegs dip in the wind like thin birds. Above Ladbroke Grove, there is a sky full of rain.

'Our first thought was to earn for a house in Portugal.' She smiles at her husband, a young man who served in the Portuguese navy and today works as a waiter in a Clapham restaurant. 'Funny, in'it?'

He also laughs at the ambition. Now he has to be content with serving Cecil Parkinson and Gloria Hunniford. Once he served Sarah Ferguson. "Fergie," he explains through his moustache. He would give it all up, though, to run a shop. How he would love a shop.

'I was in high school,' says Lucy, coming down to earth. 'But I knew when I came here I didn't have a chance to do anything other than to clean. "Mummy," my children ask, "if you are at college, why are you a cleaning lady?" But the Portuguese, that's their position, cleaning, as everybody knows. Most of the Portuguese women I know are cleaners, and the men waiters. And they are wanted because they are good workers, honest, trustworthy.'

In ten years, Lucy has cleaned for fifteen households. The majority have been British. 'English people are more dirty, that's the truth. I couldn't say why, either. But cleaning suits me fine. If you work so many hours, so many days, they tend to like you. You are part of their lives. "Some friends are coming, Lucy," they say. "They don't know we are separated, so it might be better to say nothing."

'But I work not as a detective, I like to think. If I know a person wouldn't trust me I'd leave. Also if I think they are too bossy or fussy without reason, I wouldn't take that. This gentleman I work for, my God, is he a gentleman. I once cleaned his bath and left the cleaner on the side, and he left a note saying, "This doesn't belong here." I was mad, really mad. But then I thought, he pays me. Only if he carry on leaving notes I would do something.'

She works now just for this man, shopping, washing up, polishing his shoes. "Everything." For £4 per hour, five hours per day. (When she first came, the rate was £1.)

'I have not broken anything, except glasses, but once I spoilt a grand piano worth thousands. There was a lovely picture of his daughter on a frame for the music. I didn't know the glass was loose, and it fell and smashed and chipped the lid. I was very upset. I left a note saying I would pay for the damage. He said, No, also because it could not be repaired.'

Does Lucy ever clean her husband's shoes. 'Never,' he grumbles. 'He'd be lucky,' she laughs, rubbing her flat face, like that of a young woman pressed to the window. 'That's what makes me very angry. So much time in these houses, and you come home and you're fed up with it.'

What does she *feel* when she works in these houses? Putting down her mug, she looks out at the empty clotheslines. 'I wish,' she says at last. 'I don't feel jealous, but I wish I could share some of it.' Then looking at her watch she realises with a leap how late it is and her children will be waiting to be collected from school.

'You're your own guv'nor,' said Steve the milkman of his job. Being your own guv'nor is what much of living and working in London is about. Typically, a Londoner will judge his job less by the money than by the independence it brings; the fewer people he answers to, the better. Which is why the image of the London cabby dangles like a talisman in the mind. A London cabby answers to no one. Or, as one of them put it: 'Show me a cabby and I'll show you an argumentative sod.'

The satirical magazine *Private Eye* runs an irregular column entitled 'A Cab-driver Writes'. Never particularly reticent before, cabbies have been impossible ever since one of their number, Fred Housego, won BBC TV's *Mastermind*. There can be no more cocksure repository of racism, conservatism, blarney, and sheer articulate bloodymindedness. Try stopping a driver in mid-prejudice, and you will see why only tourists have successfully invaded Britain in the last millennium.

What attracts a man to the wheel of a taxi is the freedom to work when he likes. Also, the freedom to have other work. Or, the freedom to claim he has no work at all. 'At least fifty per cent of our drivers are sign-drawers,' exaggerates a cabby called Lawrence. In the parlance of cabbies, a 'sign-drawer' is one collecting the dole.

Lawrence is fairly typical of a breed that likes to consider itself unique. An East Ender from Hackney, he has moved out to Hertfordshire. He says it is cheaper. In Hackney, he paid the council £38 a month for a two-bedroom flat. Where he lives now, he pays £31 for a three-bedroom house. But Lawrence does not have to worry about the money. When, finally, I needle him into confessing how much he earns a week – by telling him the salary of a journalist – he guardedly bites his lip. 'I could earn that in three days,' he mumbles. 'Any cab driver could earn more than you could.' It is quite a thought.

London begins at a different place for Lawrence every day – 'Where I pick up my first job.' He was chuffed when we met, after his last job of the day. He had just picked up a girl who asked him when she was going to see him again. He had arranged the following Wednesday. He would take a suit, put it in the boot, take her out to a restaurant in Knightsbridge, drive back to her flat and, later, dip his hands in oil and tell his wife he had broken down.

He met his wife when he worked on the buses from Liverpool Street to Hammersmith. 'The number one-one-five, known as the banana route because we never came along, and when we did it was in bunches. Why? Because we didn't like picking people up.' His wife was the conductress, he the driver. 'When I got fed up, I'd break an injector pipe or something. I ran up on the kerb in the King's Road once. That meant two hours in the garage. Crashes could take four or five hours. You'd never look in the mirror, just indicate and pull out. They'd either pull up or hit you. If they hit, you'd get time off. Sometimes we had three or four mechanicals a week.'

After nine months as a driving instructor – 'A good life, as it happens, but not if you're married' – he got a job 'on the dust' as a driver and loader.

'The day started officially at seven-thirty, but we'd get there at ten to eight, and have tea and toast and jam.' (George Orwell wrote in *Down and Out* of 'the tea and two slices which the Londoner swallows every day'.) The main job consisted of collecting the big round bins at the bottom of tower block shutes. 'For one estate there would be ten bins, say. We were supposed to clear them three times a week. Instead, we'd go twice and pick up more bins. We could empty ten or twelve in twenty minutes' work. Then we'd have breakfast.

'Smell? I could go to work in a suit. All you had to wear was a pair of gloves. But you were supplied with two pairs of boots, four pairs of jeans, and summer and winter jackets. My wife smokes, so she wouldn't get worried. No, you didn't smell, but you smelled some horrible things . . . People would get rid of their dogs in the bins. We'd find rabbits and birds. Sometimes the rubbish would set alight.

'The older blokes looked at the rubbish. They built their homes on it. My boy has the biggest Scalectrix in the street – a five-hundred-yard track and twenty-eight cars. I didn't buy any of it. I bought two triggers.

'Barley twirl tables, televisions. People used to throw them out. They were so easy to fix it was untrue. You could guarantee two or three tellies a week, take them to the shop and get fifteen pounds. And then there were house clearances. I suppose I was supplementing my income by another half with second-hand furniture that would never reach the tip.'

The sale of televisions and furniture took place en route to the incinerator, where the morning would finish about midday. The afternoon was for moonlighting. 'Between forty-five and sixty blokes were moonlighting. One fellow was doing another two jobs. I just helped my brother. He had a car-cleaning firm at the time.'

Then there were tips. 'At Christmas they were colossal. And most people paid. If they didn't, we wouldn't not collect – just spill a bit.'

Tips are the staple of his present job. 'A legal', I learn, is a fare without a tip. Once he was offered 5p. from the airport. 'You need that more than me, guv',' he had said, refusing. 'I could tell you virtually what area anyone is going to as soon as they open their mouth. Jewish cowboy and its Stamford Hill, Irish and its Willesden. Someone with a plum in their mouth, it's usually Richmond. Someone without so much plum and it's Chelsea or Kensington.' He will not take anyone to Brixton, Balham or Tottenham.

'What attracted me to it? I had relations in it. What don't I like about it? Well, the social side's out. And people tell you stories. They don't ask, they tell you. They tell you *anything*.'

The London borough of Redbridge contains the largest Jewish community in Europe. It also contains the largest number of licensed taxi drivers in England. At the time of writing there are 18,421 licensed drivers in London, and about 8,000 live near Gants Hill.

I took a cab to meet a cabby in 'Gantville', as it is known. Bored, the driver slid the glass partition open – like a confessional.

'My dad lived in King's Cross,' his monologue began, unprompted. ' . . . A clever bastard. He looked after the shire horses. Not like his son. I lived in Bethnal Green. You heard of it? I ain't got no education, no house of my own, no money. I ain't got a pot to piss in. I live in a council house. Nice flowers on the lawn. A place to park my cab. And I've built a fishpond, a little one. Do you know, there are more anglers than football fans. Ain't that a shaker? And it's an art. Tell me, why do the government put millions into philharmonic orchestras and yet nothing into the rivers? We were brought up to work, not to ponce about. When my son was twelve, I sent him to the market on Sunday. I ain't done so bad though. I'm a member of the Royal Chapter, freeman of the City of London. Dodgy lot of bastards, Masons. Read that book? It's an education. No different from the secret service, the judges, the police. They're all a dodgy lot of bastards . . . '

My destination is the house of a cabby called Arnold. In the drawing room a man mounts loudspeakers to brackets on the wall, whistling tunelessly. On the wall, the plaster has been put on, deliberately, in circles.

I sit waiting for Arnold on a toad-green plastic settee, studded with gold tacks. Later I discover he once merchandised upholstery. On the television is a copper flask and an onyx ashtray. The television is where the fireplace would have been . . . Previous occupants, gazing silently at the coals, would have conjured up images from the flames. Today they are bombarded with images not of their own making. Different coals fall out and ignite – violence, fleshly temptations, material promise . . . Arnold, in a grey suit and thick black-framed glasses, interrupts my reverie.

Arnold was born in Christian Road in 1930, the son of a Polish Jew who had escaped to England the previous year. He spoke Polish before he spoke Yiddish, Yiddish before English. Now he also speaks Spanish, which he learns on Thursday afternoons. When he was five his father, a master builder, moved to Hackney. They were the first family in the street to have a car. It added to the anti-Semitism. 'I can remember standing, my back to the school wall, fighting off two or three at a time.'

In 1939 he visited his granny in Poland. She wanted him to stay an extra week. His father declined. They were the last British-passport-holders to leave. Of his family left behind when the Germans invaded, seventy were sent to the gas chamber. It is an emigré past common to many Londoners. Arnold just happens to be a particularly good example of the exile who becomes the native.

He summarises the cab trade for me. Of the aforementioned 18,421 licensed cabs, about 15,000 are Green Badges, meaning they can go anywhere in the Metropolitan District. (By law, cabbies are expected to show their badge above the waist.) The remainder are Yellow Badge holders, who can only operate in the suburbs. These drivers have not yet passed The Knowledge – the traumatic test of a driver's familiarity with 438 well-used routes within six miles of Charing Cross. A Yellow Badge holder may take a passenger into the centre of London, from Ilford to Victoria, say, but he may not pick up there. Under threat of a heavy fine, he must switch his light off and come all the way back to the suburbs. Not surprisingly, most Yellows are keen to become Green. Any weekend, they can be seen revising their routes, mounted unsteadily on mopeds, and peering at clipboards.

There are several ways a driver can pay for his cab. He can rent it: either 'half-flat', an arrangement under which he has the days, someone else the nights; or 'full-flat', whereby he pays so much per mile, or a percentage of the take. Or he can buy it outright from Mann and Overton in Wandsworth, who have the monopoly. The meter is rented separately for about £80 a year.

Three times a year the vehicle is subject to an inspection from the Carriage Office. 'If they don't like what they see, a little notice comes through the door which says *Stop.*' Every twelve months the white number plate is removed and returned to the Carriage Office, and the cab is sent to the garage. After a thorough service and steam-cleaning, it is inspected again, and the driver is issued with a new plate. A 'butterboy' is a new cabby who has not yet had to change his plate.

'The real money's in town,' Arnold says, 'but your day's take is sheer luck. You can be as low as five pounds, as high as one hundred and fifty.' He prefers days to nights because there are more 'reasonable excuses' not to pick someone up – 'reasonable excuse' being the discretion, officially given, for cabbies to ignore or refuse passengers if they wish. Despite notices, smoking does not constitute such an excuse. A cabby *must* take you only when the 'For Hire' light is lit and the vehicle stationary.

Arnold reckons you can tell a person simply by the way he hails a cab: if he keeps his arm up confidently; or if he raises it at the last minute. Nevertheless, he is sometimes wrong. 'I once had four drunks trying to turn the cab over. Another time, a drunk didn't like the extras, so he smashed his way through the glass partition. Luckily,' Arnold smiles, 'I had a heavy duty spanner.'

Security was the reason he had his two-way radio installed. 'I had a couple of guys. They wanted to go to Belsize Park. They didn't tell me it was Belsize Park *Gardens* they wanted. They went berserk and started threatening me. I pushed the emergency button. In two minutes there were six cabs round me, rapidly followed by the police.'

The increase in the two-way system has also meant an increase in business. 'One day I heard someone needed a Spanish-speaker. I was five minutes away, but another cabby radioed he was nearer. I dropped by, just to see. It was a couple who'd left their bag in a cab. No one could understand what they were saying. This other bloke spoke beautifully. It wasn't surprising, he said. He was born in Barcelona.

'That's the thing about cabbies, they are not stereotypes,' he says. 'They're independent. One cabby I know had a bee in his bonnet about something and qualified as a barrister. One is a landscape gardener.' Others have a hobby or a trade. The biggest section of part-timers are printers and dockers. 'I became a cabby because it's something you can pick up and put down. Very few people in this life can allocate their time. Cabbies can.'

As with many cabbies, Arnold has another source of income. After working as a clerk in the coalfields, a linen buyer, and a watch and clock repairer, he acquired some flats, which he now rents out for a total of £60 a week.

What principally distinguishes him, however, is his interest in politics – an interest which has led him to become a member of the GLC and, as chairman of the Covent Garden Committee, to be among those responsible for what he unequivocally calls 'one of the best things London has ever seen'.

In the late 1960s Covent Garden's fruit and vegetable market was moved south of the river to Nine Elms. It left a space in the heart of London which sent planners at the GLC into an ecstatic spin. They proposed to demolish the former site and Charles Fowler's 1830 building in favour of a six-lane motorway and conference centre.

The outcry that followed resulted in the slogan 'Covent Garden belongs to the people'. With it Londoners created their first 'Action Area'. Instead of consigning the site to a hole in the ground, the fate that befell Les Halles in Paris, the GLC spent £28 million on the purchase and restoration of the market and its surrounding buildings. The old flower market was transformed into the London Transport Museum, cafés and clothes shops were opened, and the buskers and artists who had once tickled Pepys were encouraged to do the same for the four million visitors now drawn there every year.

Arnold's involvement in politics began in 1972 with a local issue. 'I live near the tube and there's a massive parking problem.' With neighbours he fought for restrictions. Successfully, he says. A lorry reversing outside brings him to his feet. 'If a copper sees him, he'll get blistered.'

Elected as a Conservative to Redbridge Borough Council in 1974, Arnold became the GLC's representative for Ilford South and vice-chairman of planning for south of the river three years later. He was at County Hall for four years, and spent his proudest moments there on the Covent Garden project. And, he says, in opposing Ken Livingstone.

'When he was the Labour transport spokesman, he wanted the GLC to take over the licensed cab trade. I threatened a repeat of the 1976 cab strike. Then Labour had wanted to introduce a speedbus, which would stop the access of licensed cabs to places like Oxford Street where a lot of our living comes from. The gateman at County Hall was bribed and, at seven in the morning, after an agreed codeword on the radio, a thousand cabbies turned up. They parked their cabs so that every space was taken, locked their doors and went to breakfast.

'When I threatened to repeat that, Ken Livingstone didn't even reply.'

There is little forgiveness in the mind of the cabby who takes me to County Hall. What would he like to know about Ken Livingstone, I enquire.

'Ask him what he's doing still alive.'

It was some months before the abolition of the Greater London Council on April Fools' Day, 1986. Rumour had it that the GLC offices were to become a luxury hotel. Green and white, like a chunk of veal that has been left too long in the air, it will take a magician to turn County Hall into the Cipriani. What it needs, one cannot help feeling, is for a GLC planner to exercise his last wish on the site – and build a six-lane motorway.

The boy at the reception desk has to look up the Livingstone office number. 'F staircase,' he points eventually. 'Up those steps to the first floor, then right and right again.' I follow his instructions and get lost down the shiny floored corridors. I am reminded of my first day at school. I wander into the kitchens and suppose I have gone too far. Not far enough, in fact.

'Fire Zone' proclaims the red sticker outside his office. He comes out with a shy black girl, to fix a date in the diary.

'Wednesday's the strike, so it'll have to be Thursday. How about Thursday?' he says, looking up, in his flat familiar nasal drawl. She bites her lip uncertainly, he enters the date, she starts mumbling, he smiles and says, 'It'll have to be Thursday. Look, I've written it in.' It is not hard to see why he is held in great affection by his staff. Seeing me, he yawns.

Few people in local government become household names. One such was Herbert Morrison, the Labour leader, between the wars, of what was then the London County Council. Another is Kenneth Robert Livingstone, a forty-year-old once described by *The Sun* as 'the most odious man in Britain', and once voted by listeners to BBC Radio 4 as the most popular man in the world after the pope.

As leader of the Greater London Council, he has for five years been responsible for more people than any other local authority official in Europe – even if, as his critics point out, his responsibilities make up for only eleven per cent of London's local government functions. Despite his imminent abolition at the time of writing, Ken Livingstone is still very much alive. As John Carvel writes in *Citizen Ken*, 'Livingstone is one of only a handful from his generation who can be marked down as possible contenders for power around the turn of the century'. Reading this biography, one cannot fail to be struck by the achievements of charm, confidence, and that very un-English quality – lack of embarrassment.

He was born opposite the police station in Streatham, at 21B, Shrubbery Road. His father, Bob, was a trawler fisherman who had spent his early years in Argentina, returned to Scotland, become a merchant seaman and been torpedoed on a run to Murmansk. His mother, Ethel, was an acrobatic dancer who balanced on elephants and back-flipped her way about the country in a three-woman team called the Kenleigh Sisters. They met after a feat of illusionism at a music hall in Worthington. Bob sat in the front row, while on stage Ethel helped the Great Lyle saw someone in half.

In 1957 the Livingstones bought their own home in Norwood. For the deposit on the mortgage, Bob worked as a window cleaner. Sometimes he shifted scenery at the local theatre. The family went to the cinema twice a week and holidayed on the Isle of Wight. On election days Bob manned the polling station, supporting the Conservatives. Both he and Ethel were card-carrying Tories. 'Thatcher was the final straw for my mother,' laughs their son. 'She became a Bennite.'

Twenty-five years later, their first child, living in a Maida Vale bedsit for £20 a week, had become the most vilified and the most loved Londoner of his time. While it took seven pet salamanders to turn him into the equivalent of a music hall joke, his espousal of homosexuals, blacks, and Sinn Fein whipped the establishment into indignant anger. Dubbed 'Red Ken', he was hounded ceaselessly by the press. One of the more memorable Livingstone cartoons depicts Mickey Mouse at a newspaper's editorial conference. The search is on for a headline. 'I've got it,' exclaims Mickey Mouse. 'RED KEN IN GAY IRA SALAMANDER SEX-CHANGE STORM.' Photographers hid behind his dustbins to see who he took home. To secure an interview following his refusal to attend the Royal Wedding, a female television researcher offered to go to bed with him.

Given that, for the outside world, his diary is booked up four months in advance, I could see her point.

Slumped in a green velvet sofa, he yawns again. 'It's because I'm tired, not because I'm talking to you.' It is difficult to know if he is telling the truth. He wears an open-neck cream shirt which appears to be synthetic, blue leather moccasins, short blue socks and grey terylene trousers. Fortunately, despite the yawns, his conversation turns out to be more dapper than his dress sense.

'I like San Francisco, and I like Paris, but London is wonderful.

A pigeon's eye view of Trafalgar Square. At ground level, according to Robert Peel, it is 'the finest view in Europe' (*Camera Press*)

What is London? asked Ford Madox Ford standing in Trafalgar Square in 1905, and
then answered his own question. We can understand it through 'some minute detail
of the whole, we seeing things with the eye of a bird that is close to the ground . . .
seeking for minute fragments of seed' (*Dominic Turner*)

Londoners drawn by children at the Risley Avenue Infant School, Broadwater Farm

Behind closed doors (*James Abelson*)

(A) Les the postman's home in a terraced street in Fulham
(B) 18 Folgate Street, Spitalfields, where Dennis Severs is curator to his own
fantasies of the city
(C) Carrington House, Deptford, 'the circuit of homelessness'
(D) Doris' front door, and a 'void' next door, Tower Hamlets
(E) 23 - 24 Leinster Gardens, a door that does not open
(F) Apsley House, 'Number 1, London', open to the public

A Londoner's home is his private club and his castle

The writer, V. S. Pritchett. 'I don't think I'd live anywhere else'
(*Tara Heinemann, Camera Press*)

The novelist Emma Tennant, now and (insert – a portrait by Lenare) on the day she was presented at court as a debutante. 'The green dress looked like a crushed lettuce leaf by the time we reached the Palace' (*Suresh Karadia*, The Times)

Lady Antonia Douro, who lives in Apsley House on Hyde Park Corner. 'The fact is, it's not noisy' (*Christopher Simon Sykes*)

Kenneth Campbell, who oversaw the rise of the tower block. 'My God, we were so starry-eyed and naive' (*The Architect's Journal*)

Terrace into Tower
by John Walters

Inner City by Louis
Hellman. 'Yours was the
hand that signed the
paper that felled a city.'
So George Tremlett told
a gathering of architects
in 1978

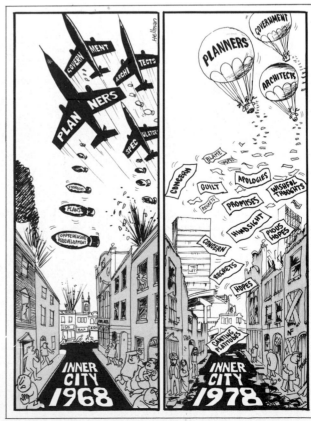

One of London's homeless. '"You'd be bloody lucky if you got t'ree hours' sleep,"' a
down-and-out called Paddy told George Orwell (*Dominic Turner*)

In his studio in an arch under Hungerford Bridge, the artist Feliks Topolski, who has spent fifty years drawing and painting Londoners (*Associated Press Photo*)

Two of London's best-known figures, Kenneth Robert Livingstone and Eros
(*Peter Francis, Camera Press*)

Reggie Kray – professional of violence. 'I wouldn't like to live in London now,' he says. 'You can't walk down the street without being mugged' (*Popperfoto*)

William Howard and son, ratcatchers to Harrods and the Bank of England. The
tradition carries on. 'I killed my first rat when I was less than six,' says the present
William Howard. What with? 'My hands' (*Photopress*)

The Serpentine Swimming Club in 1923. Come rain, shine or ice, members of the club have plunged in every day since 1864 . . . until the summer of 1986, when the pool was closed for health reasons

'To be a Londoner, you've got to be first intelligent. And second good-looking.' At
least according to one of the speakers proclaiming at Hyde Park Corner, a location
described by George Orwell as 'one of the minor wonders of the world'
(*Dominic Turner*)

It has so much. Nothing rivals it.'

Outside, on the other side of the river, the traffic passes silently along the Embankment. Eavesdropping. Or chuffing over the prospect of a six-lane motorway.

'The next-largest city in the UK has a population of nine hundred and fifty thousand. That's less than a sixth the size of London. There is no conceivable future where London will not be the cultural and financial centre of influence. London is always on the winning side. It supported the Roundheads against the Crown, and it usually backs the winner in terms of struggle and power. Whoever wins the most seats in London wins nationally.

'I was born and grew up here and always lived in the core, rather than the suburbs. Here change is quicker, the problems are greater, and the strength of identity is stronger. It keeps you active and thinking and alive.

'During the War the inner Londoner was the true stereotype. Now there are a dozen types. It's almost a federal city. Six million people, a million blacks, half a million lesbians and gays . . . ' He reels off statistics. 'What makes London beautiful is a combination of all these different groups, with all their separate qualities.

'People travelling abroad who live in Hounslow or Tulse Hill, when asked where they live, say London. They could say Essex or Kent or Middlesex. In the last twenty years seventy per cent of Londoners have come in from outside. Half the city is made up of migrants, so there's always movement. A city has to be dynamic or it withers and dies. The problem in the sixties and seventies was that it didn't keep up. But people are keener on living here now. The Young Upwardly Mobiles are moving back into the city, modernising the centre, the Docklands. It's the place where people set their first foot on the ladder. For all London's problems, no other city has absorbed so much or so well. Nor can I think of any other city of this size that's so safe.

'Why are there no "I Love London" badges? If you are happy with something, you don't declaim it. It's like people who rush around telling you what a happy marriage they have a week before it breaks up.' It is ironic that in the very next breath he should be singing the praises of the GLC. Talking to politicians can produce the impression of trying to steer a car with a flat tyre: invariably it veers to one side or another.

'Look at this map,' he says, leaping up. The colours of the map represent the way Londoners voted at the last local elections. Red

119

strips spread like spokes from the centre – north, south, east and west. 'The majority of Londoners are for the GLC. That's seventy-four per cent. Not a single ward is anti-GLC. Abolishing it is forcing people to think of the GLC as an entity for the first time since the War.'

And what of the hotel? He looks out through the tall window at his city. 'It's awful,' he says at last, rocking on his moccasins, his hands in his grey trousers.

'But we'll be back.'

CRIME AND PUNISHMENT

In its last year, the GLC put on an exhibition next door in the Royal Festival Hall. On display was a selection of the paintings entered for its competition entitled 'The Spirit of London'. The £1,500 prize-winner was an unexceptional canvas showing a hidden garden overgrown by wishy-washy foliage and over-looked by red walls and a lavatory-blue sky. Other paintings depicted a Victorian terrace seen through lace curtains, a landscape of grey roof-tops broken by an isolated white magnolia tree, and an antique shop.

The single arresting entry was the winner of an anti–racist prize. The scene is the top floor of a tower block. An Indian girl shrinks back from the slanted doorway. Framed there is a dog crouching obscenely in a snarl, its massive red tongue drooping to the lino floor. Its owner ascends the stairs behind. A skinhead in a white T-shirt, he has the same expression as his dog.

In singing London's glory, Ken Livingstone also refers unpoliti-cally and with feeling to the racism, the problems of housing, the crime. 'But it's a myth the area has changed beyond all recog-nition. My grandmother was born in eighteen eighty-eight at about the time the GLC was set up. She had equally horrifying stories to tell of London. It's a mistake to think the attitudes which cause such a furore now are new. The squalor,' he adds darkly, 'has always been with us.'

In 1710 four Mohawk chiefs visited London. Soon after, a gang calling themselves 'Mohocks', and consisting of law students and young men with money, began terrorising the capital. 'Two of the Mohocks caught a maid of old Lady Winchelsea's at the door of their home in the park,' wrote Jonathan Swift on 16 March 1712. 'They cut all her face and beat her without any provocation.' The Mohocks in turn gave rise to a group called the Scourers. On one occasion, scouring for the Mohocks, this group attacked a gambling house, beat the watch, slit the noses of two men, and disabled a woman by cutting her arm with a penknife. They were fined 3s.4d.

In *Soft City*, Jonathan Raban describes the rise in London, in the 1970s, of a group called the Envies. The Envies acted on appearance. According to whether he seemed prosperous, or happy, or blessed for that moment with luck, they would approach a stranger in the street and sever his spinal cord with a penknife. Their methods live on. In 1985 in Piccadilly, this happened to an American banker. He was stabbed not for money, nor as the result of a drugged frenzy. He was stabbed because 'he looked rich and I was jealous'.

Of the 632,341 notifiable crimes committed in London in 1983, the most common was burglary, which occurred once every seven minutes. Between 1981 and 1983 the statistics showed an increase of twenty-one per cent. Today the likelihood is that two in every five homes in inner London have been broken into. In 1985 half the homes in Islington were affected, forty-six per cent more than once.

The steps taken to counter burglary can vary. Gavin Stamp, the architectural historian, keeps six bells on his door so that it resembles the entrance to a busy lodging house. Another tip is to leave some cash on a plate near the door when you go out. If it has disappeared on your return, runs the argument, you will have at least gained the valuable knowledge that someone has entered. One Scotland Yard inspector advises the installation of a cassette which plays the sound of a barking dog when the bell is rung. If you live on your own and the door rings, this inspector adds, it is not a bad idea to say out loud, 'I'll get it, Harry'.

London may be safe compared to most cities, but the violence is escalating. Conducting a survey for *The Standard* in September 1985 on what Londoners really feel, market researcher Maureen Wilson met a man in Pimlico. 'No one gives up an hour of their time for anyone,' he said, and then tried to rape her. In 1985 statistics for rape in London rose by more than half . . .

In Deptford an eighty-year-old woman is raped and buggered by a boy of fifteen, while in Peckham a middle-aged couple have their toes hacked off and stuffed in their mouths – 'and elsewhere'. Rose, a pensioner of Peckham, has not stepped out of her door for five years. She used to walk to the bingo hall, but now she feels there is someone always behind her. A young mother pushing her pram through an underpass near the Aylesbury Estate is mugged by young boys who stub their cigarettes out on her baby's face. They are heroin addicts, animal in their desperation to finance another fix; addicts of violence, mimicking celluloid fantasies. Unloved, unemployed addicts of power. Corrupted by boredom, powerless to control their own lives, at least they can visibly affect the life of someone else.

'I wouldn't like to live in London now,' Reggie Kray said to me in Parkhurst. 'You can't walk down the street without being mugged.'

Mention the word Kray in certain parts of London and, even today, nearly twenty years after the longest, most expensive criminal trial in British history, the name holds a power that borders on the occult. As ever, the expression 'and I used to know the Krays' comes frequently and unsolicited: a mark of pride, a statement demanding of respect, and a safe boast.

In *Soft City*, Jonathan Raban refers to an essay by Robert Warshow, written in 1958.

> For the gangster there is only the city [he quotes]. He must inhabit it in order to personify it: not the real city, but that dangerous and sad city of the imagination which is so much more important, which is the modern world.

In the Bethnal Green area around Vallance Road, 10,000 homes were lost in the Blitz. Brought up in the bombed-out wilderness of the East End, taking refuge in the shelter of the Vallance Road viaduct, the Krays were to construct their own city from the rubble – a city landscaped like gangland Chicago and cemented by intimidation.

It was a city of the imagination in which the twins were king: Reggie, the friend of the famous, the seeker of the good life, the nightclub host in his blue Savile Row dinner jacket and his big American car; Ronnie, the impassive strong man, dreaming of a city in Africa, yet creating a dark continent at home under the influence of drink, Stematol and Churchill's wartime speeches. Like two flat, heavy stones, duck and draking over the water, Reggie and Ronnie turned their cockney fantasies, for a time at least, into miraculous reality.

The surface was broken on 8 March 1966 when Ronnie entered the saloon bar of The Blind Beggar in search of George Cornell. On finding the man who had called him 'a fat poof' behind his back, Ronnie discharged two bullets from his 9mm Mauser into Cornell's head. Inspired by the Leopard Men of Nigeria, where he had hoped to found the city of Enugu, Ronnie now required his twin to be initiated into the act of murder. The taunting went on until Reggie finally sliced the face of Jack 'the Hat' McVitie.

In England, George Orwell once observed, the main motivation for murder is not passion but the desire for respectability. 'The one thing they would really have liked to be,' commented a friend of the twins, 'was a pair of genuine English gentlemen.'

As their dear mother said, 'Both of them was good boys at heart.' In March 1969 the good boys were sentenced to life imprisonment, with a recommendation that they serve a minimum of thirty years. In my view, said Mr Justice Melford Stevenson, passing sentence, society has earned a rest from their activities.

Parkhurst is one of four prisons on the Isle of Wight. Its red brick walls are topped with a pubic tangle of wire. An officer walks by with a black German shepherd dog. Signing in, I walk across a small courtyard to the waiting room. On the wall is a list of items that can be handed to a prisoner. They include a crucifix, a budgerigar, and a radio earpiece. A radio is also allowed – medium and long wave only.

At 6.45 p.m. Bob, the uniformed librarian, comes to collect me. He has a radio receiver in his top pocket, and a bunch of keys that open one gate onto a wet, larger courtyard, a second gate into a building, yet another gate into a corridor, and two more doors into a small canary-coloured room.

In the room are half a dozen inmates. It is furnished with a table, several chairs – one of which breaks when the youngest prisoner sits down – and a thin electric fire, against which the others warm their backs. By 7.00 p.m. most of the ten or so members of the Parkhurst Drama Group are assembled, voluntarily, to hear me give a talk on the subject of royalty in exile.

They include Fred who, before murdering a policeman, was head page at Claridge's. (He wears a shirt, given to him by his valet, that belonged to Prince Bernhardt of the Netherlands.) Also, a small Maltese, who tells me he spent his first three months in London living in a telephone box in Gerrard Street; and, arriving a little later than the others, Reginald Kray.

After talking for an hour on the fortunes of dispossessed kings and queens, we turn to the more interesting topic of Londoners.

'A Londoner is one of the best all-round survivors,' Reggie begins softly. He wears a light blue T-shirt with 'Nike' on the chest, and a gold chain round his neck. His hair is groomed back and flecked with grey. With his large nose, and his sad, blank, open eyes, he looks like an elderly pierrot. 'The good thing about Londoners is they still hold their chin up, no matter how bad they're off.' The others agree, deferentially.

'London, it's good for everything. You can't beat the entertainments,' he resumes, courteously accepting a cigarette. I had been warned to bring plenty of tobacco. It was sobering to think that this diminutive man had once specialised in a 'cigarette punch', involving the offer of a cigarette with the right hand and a punch on the jaw with the left.

'You can't beat Mayfair. There's not anything in this world that can beat Mayfair for class. Every night I would drive from the East End to a club I had in Knightsbridge called Esmeralda's. I used to drive down The Mall. I liked The Mall. I like its wide red road. I used to have casinos in different areas. Each area was different. In Knightsbridge, when they played a game of cards, they played it quietly. In the East End the gambling was much noisier. Yet there were more knockers – bounced cheques' he explains – 'in Knightsbridge. People wouldn't bounce you in the East End.'

He talks of music. 'I went to Milan once and saw *Madame Butterfly* at La Scala. When I came back, I went to the pub and listened to the music there. It was very different,' he says obviously.

Fred complains about the changes. 'Pubs are like cocktail bars now. You used to call it a café. Now it's a restaurant.' Reggie laments the passing of games. 'You wouldn't see shove ha'penny now, would you? Now, everyone watches television. Television's a bad thing. It's wrong not to participate. If you're the audience, you're not taking part in life.'

Gradually the others are drawn into conversation. 'You can move three miles down the road in London, and you're lost,' said a young man whose front tooth was missing. He had a white towel around his neck, and poured glass after glass of water from a jug on the table.

'Yea, I lived in walking distance of the Tower of London and never visited it once,' said another.

'I was locked up in the Tower once,' laughed Reggie. 'I deserted or whatever I did do from the Royal Fusiliers, and ended up there two weeks. They put me in the local guardhouse.' In March 1952, as a new recruit in a dark blue suit, Reggie had punched a corporal on the jaw with the words, 'We don't care for it here.' The brothers were locked in the Waterloo Building, where they slept on bare boards and lived on army tea. 'I used to watch the tourists below where Charlie [his other brother] would come and wave at me.'

Fred claims he would still be working at Claridge's if it hadn't been for National Service. 'I had a fancy uniform. Everyone put a shilling in my hand. The food was good and I met Spencer Tracy.'

I ask Reggie Kray what he misses. 'I miss the sound of traffic, of trains shunting, and buses. Here you've only got the seagulls. The first thing I'd do on getting out, I'd go to an exclusive restaurant.'

'I'd get a plane ticket to Rio,' chirps the Maltese, who wears a gold medallion on the outside of his red shirt. After the Gerrard Street kiosk, he had spent eight years in Soho. He could not read or write, so during the group's play readings he would be called upon for sound effects.

On release, they might find the city changed a little. The presence of punks, for instance. 'A punk rocker's no threat,' says Reggie. 'He's lazy. He's looking for a way out. He's just representing his own identity.' Fred nudges Reggie. 'You're in love with one, aren't you, Reg?' he says, alluding to a girl who comes on visits. Reggie raises his brown eyes, but he cannot raise a guffaw. 'No, what's changed is all this mugging,' he says eventually. 'It's not a safe place to live any more. When I was a kid, we used to sit on chairs outside our house. We sat talking on the asphalt road. We did boxing and roller skating. We'd make our own amusements.' He stubs out the cigarette. 'We'd never dream of stealing a penny.' Fred nods. 'If you snatched a bag, everyone was on to yer.'

As the Parkhurst Drama Group starts chatting amongst itself, remembering those years ago, Reggie leans forward. He talks of his paintings, the book on slang he has written – 'Steve, go and get the book,' he says to the young man next to him – the keep-fit book he plans to write, and a party he's throwing in the spring. It's in Mayfair, apparently. 'George Best will be there, Mike Reid the comedian. I'll make sure you get a ticket.'

The ticket never came, but the book did – a thin paperback with a dictionary of East End slang and several pages of photographs. They show him with Shirley Bassey on his knee; in black tie at a table of drinks with Barbara Windsor; at his club with Sonny Liston and Victor Spinetti. In few does he look at the camera. When he does so, he raises his chin, cockily, exuding an inarticulate power. In none of the photographs is it possible to see whether, under his short black hair, his eyes are sad, cruel or smiling.

The pages of the dictionary are divided in half. Down one side runs a list of expressions like 'Had the manor sewn up', down the other runs their translations – 'Had the area under control'. 'Drop of parnie' is rain. A 'saucepan lid' is a Jew. To 'read and write', aptly, is to have a fight.

Aptly, because at the front is printed Reggie Kray's ambition: to be recognised as a writer and live in the country. Between this proclamation and the slang comes an introduction.

> I do blame the use of drugs for the increasing crime rate [he writes]. Especially in the juvenile age group, who are not aware of the consequences. I have also found in prison many of these young offenders talk from the top of their heads and lack tact and diplomacy which can lead them into trouble especially amongst themselves.
>
> They would have been in serious trouble had they lived in an area like the East End of London in the 1960s.

In 1986 Reggie Kray was moved from Parkhurst back to London, and the meridional confines of Wandsworth Prison.

One of Reggie Kray's rackets in the 1960s was the peddling of purple hearts from an address in Soho. Little John worked as one of the peddlers. He has just returned from Holland where he had beaten up his wife – 'A gorgeous little girl,' he tells me. He is upset that since this incident she has not answered his letter-cassettes.

'I've disliked London since the seventies. I saw more future on the Continent,' begins this Artful Dodger.

'I was born in Simla and came to England in November nineteen fifty-one, aged four. My father was working for the Pakistani High Commission as a clerk. Pakistan had just been, what do you call it, liberated. From what I remember vaguely, he had an offer to go to America – it must have been Washington – or London, and he chose London.

'My parents were very, very religious and I suppose even now I'm retaliating against their beliefs. They believe in whatever they believe in. Their attitude is, if you want to be a member of the family, you must abide by our rules – which means living like a priest. No smoking, no drinking, no going out. They pray twenty-five hours a day. What's the time now? Yes, nine o'clock. They do it right now, at this very minute.

'Who do they pray to? I know it sounds absolutely incredible – you've really got someone this time – they pray to my father, because my father claimed officially in nineteen fifty-nine to be the prophet. How was it taken? Very badly, in Pakistan. People got murdered. I know this for a fact. I've seen photos and letters and newspaper cuttings. His name is still very well known there. What is it? It doesn't matter. He's dead anyway, God bless him. It's a well-respected name.

'Until the age of fifteen I was a typical juvenile delinquent. I didn't realise what I was doing. I went in and out of nick. The first time, I'll never forget it. I was at Spencer Park School and I was, I think, in my second year or my third year, I'm not quite sure. I was fourteen, anyway, and the next thing I knew I was arrested. Breaking and entering. It was a put-up job. You know the sort of thing – two months rent under a cushion. Well, that was really the start of a very bad career up until nineteen sixty-seven, when I decided to change my ways.

'I was sent to Approved School, a terrible experience from my point of view because I was still, funnily enough, Pakistani. I remember my deputy headmaster – a very nice chap, maybe you've heard of him – who was in fact a wicket-keeper for the MCC in the fifties. He taught me to become a very good cricketer, which I kept up until, as I say, I got this West End nightlife business into me. That completely destroyed what could have been one of the best careers any human being could have asked for at that time. What? To be a professional cricketer, of course. That's what the deputy headmaster said to me. He said, I will train you in every aspect because you've got the go in you. I was an all-rounder. We played against Woking Police Station, and we won. Thanks to me. I was supposed to be the man with the gift. I'll never forget, I was batting against . . . I'm trying to remember his name. He was the British under-twenty-one bowler. They put me in front of him and I knocked him for sixes. He came up at the end and said, "If you go on like that you're going to go a long way." I wish I'd been a cricketer now. I'd be a millionaire, respected, seen the world.

'Then I got into borstal, but that was for carrying a gun. Again I know it sounds totally ridiculous – I was put up, although it was partly my fault, obviously. It was nineteen sixty-six and I bumped into So-and-so in the West End, and he said, "Do you want to make some easy money?" Ha, I said, Why not? It's better than a hard day's work. Funnily enough, he still exists round the corner. He's a bouncer now.

'It was selling pep pills – purple hearts, they were called – which were very popular at the time. The guy who was supplying us with them was working for the Krays. They were the power. I bumped into Ronnie once, he was very pleasant. I had a nice long chat with him in Soho, which is where I worked – the discotheque, the Flamingo. I used to stand in the door and people would come up and say, Got any pills? Everyone knew me as the top boy. I used to keep them in me girlfriend's bra – do like I was kissing her. Ten for a quid. I know it's incredible, but I was selling a thousand a night . . . Stabbings, I've seen the lot. I could write a book and a half about it . . . Well, it all ended because of the competition. Some guy called King came up one night. Some guys are after you. They're going to shoot you, he tells me, and he gives me this gun. You see what I mean by a put-up job? I think I did eighteen months. I spent my twenty-first birthday in borstal, in Reading. I'll never forget it. It was the twenty-first of July, nineteen sixty-six or -seven. It was really bad, but the story leaked out that I was a tough guy. You know how stories do go, they get very highly exaggerated. I only hit a policeman across the face, but the story was I killed two men and knew the Kray brothers.

'Then in nineteen seventy I went into the music business. I started a career as a DJ in what is now Boots on High Street

Kensington, but used to be Pontings. I had this close-circuit PA system and girls every night. Then, one night, I was coming back from auditioning some go-go dancers, and I had this idiot driver, and I didn't check his credentials, because apparently he didn't have a driving licence. Well, we were coming back down the Greyhound Road and it's the same old story of "Look before you cross". An old lady is crossing the road and I see her face in the window. Bang! Immediate death. But the driver accelerated instead of braking, and I took my father's advice and left for Holland.

'I saw more future on the Continent.'

Tom is one of London's 27,626 police officers. He is thirty, rosy-cheeked and balding. A top scholar at his public school, and a scholar at Oxford, he decided to join the police force 'to get my edges knocked off'. His middle-class education had made him afraid of taxi drivers, petrol pump attendants, waiters. He wanted not to be; he wanted to develop the policeman's impressive habit of command. What also appealed to him was the bohemian opportunity to walk on the streets, to meet people, and see the colourful side of life. Admitting to a strong streak of social responsibility, he wanted to preserve the fabric of the society he saw there.

'The main motivation of a policeman is not service to the public,' he says, after seven years in the force. 'It is the cops and robbers aspect – the sociability, the money. A policeman doesn't come into contact with respectable people very often. The only middle-class people he tends to meet are those he stops for a driving offence.'

After fifteen weeks' training at Hendon, he was posted to Heathrow, where there are no streets and no residential population. His first two years, which were his first two in London, were spent making sure cab drivers picked up American tourists who only wanted to travel the short trip to the Penta Hotel. At peak time, after an hour and a half of queueing in the taxi pool, the cabbies tended to refuse such trips. Legally, they were not allowed to do so.

After a time in Clapton, Tom was next posted to London's W District. The Metropolitan Police divide the city alphabetically into twenty-four areas. C, for instance, is Soho, H is Bethnal Green, W is Wandsworth, Battersea and Tooting. 'Most officers want to go to the semi-inners where there is urban decay and more crime. L is the most popular.' L incorporates Brixton, Kennington and Clapham.

Tom works three different shifts. For four weeks, his hours will be from 7 a.m to 3 p.m.; then 3 p.m. to 11 p.m.; then 11 p.m. to 7 a.m. At present he is working the first shift. Coming by car, he arrives at his station in W shortly before six in the morning. One of the sergeants on his relief will take over the prisoners in custody. Another will look at any messages which have come in.

'I see the outgoing inspector, who tells me if anybody has been reported missing, if there's any prisoner in custody who hasn't been charged, if there's been any recent trend – a spate of handbag snatching, for instance.'

At 5.55 a.m. there is a parade of the twelve or so constables, at which they are posted to their beats for the day.

'I go through and chat to the station collator – the crime intelligence officer – who tells me that John Stokes, a local villain, has been seen driving a beige car with another bloke, outside a club where there are drugs. If he's seen, he ought to be stopped. Such-and-such a premise has been broken into. An alarm is not working . . . '

An hour is then put aside for correspondence: someone has applied for a billiard hall licence; the council has suggested a new bus lane, a new right-turn sign.

At 8 a.m. Tom gets into the duty officer's unmarked car. In the quiet back streets of Clapham he looks out for youngish white boys with bags who might have stolen a car radio. At Clapham Junction he is alert for handbag snatchers, watching the bus stops to see if there are any groups congregating there who are not catching buses.

Every couple of hours he will return to the station, where there is a canteen. A few bring in boxes for lunch. When on duty, many make do with a kebab. Except for medicinal purposes, drink is not allowed.

Most of the arrests take place at night. Prostitutes account for a good many. 'Hearts leap if someone has to be arrested,' Tom admits, 'because this means overtime. On night duty, a van driver will make for an area where there are lots of tarts, pick up ten, and hand one out to each relief. They have quite a good working relationship with the police because they're often beaten up. Some are arrested so often they could do the paperwork themselves.'

'Underground car parks are a sure place to find prostitutes,' he says. The men congregate in a scrub of bushes on Clapham Common known as 'Gobbler's Gulch'. One trick played by the officers of London's W District is to nuzzle slowly up in the dark and suddenly turn their head lights full on. 'You can guarantee every time that twenty people will scatter. All blokes.'

The oldest police station in the world is at Wapping, the head-quarters today of London's River Police. Founded in 1798 with supplementary help from the West India Company – who were losing £150,000 a year in pilfering – the Marine Police Force originally consisted of 200 armed men. Given that there were some 8,000 vessels in the six miles of river patrolled by the force, this meant one man to every forty ships.

Today, on that same stretch, you would be hard put to find forty ships.

It is Trafalgar Day. Wearing a blue blazer, and sitting with his back to the river, Inspector Patchett talks on the telephone. Fixing his eye on a solitary ski propped against the wall, he discusses arrangements for a forthcoming seminar on the identification of decomposing bodies. 'In my twenty-one years of service, we've had fifteen hundred,' he is saying. 'We're up to fifty-nine this year already.'

The nature of the Thames, and the uses to which it is put, may have changed, but Inspector Patchett reckons the same number of bodies – about seventy – are discovered in its classic stream each year. 'I never really know how many are murders, how many aren't. There's a disproportionate number of blacks, and the average black is not a water-lover. There's a disproportionate number of businessmen who don't carry wallets. Suicides strip their gear for starters, and, if you do have a wallet in your jacket, it is invariably lost in rubbing up and down the river bottom.'

An analysis of the last fifty bodies shows that ten per cent have not yet been identified. In this once-great thoroughfare – the busiest suburb in London, Henry James called it – all identity is washed away.

'The bodies are totally unrecognisable. Pre-mortem injuries usually involve severe bruising, caused by jumping off a bridge and hitting the water from twenty feet. If you hit a buttress on the way down, or you fall on wood, it's far worse. And,' said Inspector Patchett, pursing his lips, 'there's any amount of wood in the Thames.'

He twists round to look at the river. The water is dark from the window but the afternoon light creates a web of yellow reflections on the ceiling. 'Once you've lost buoyancy, you sink. Basically, you stay at the bottom until you decompose and the gas lifts. If you've had a good night on curry and beer, you come up a lot quicker. But there are many variables – temperature, weight, whether you hit something on the way up, what the tide's doing. When the *Princess Alice* went down at Woolwich with six hundred and seventy-two people, bodies were found as high up as Fulham, as low down as Southend.'

Depending on where the body came ashore, there used to be a different tariff. 'At the turn of the century the local authority on the Essex bank would pay one shilling more than for a body washed up on the Kent side. Westminster was a real winner at half a crown.' Today there is a blanket fee of £3.50. 'We used to get another twenty-five pence for washing down the dead body and the sheets and ropes used in its recovery. A review in nineteen eighty-four discovered this gratuity wasn't official, and suggested we use outside launderers instead. Their cheapest quote is twenty-five pounds. Ridiculous, isn't it?'

I walk down the gangway to a launch. Above the shingle, the tarred head of the seventeenth-century British pirate Captain Kidd hung in a cage for five years. On the waterfront, a treasure hunter – the modern equivalent of Henry Mayhew's mudlark – is digging with his dog. In seven months, the pilot tells me casting off, he has combed a hundred yards.

Writing of the Thames in his *Londinopolis* of 1657, Charles II's historiographer royal, James Howell, mentions various foreign ambassadors who affirm: 'the most glorious sight in the world, take water and land together, was to come up upon a high tide from Gravesend and shoot the bridge to Westminster'. Crossing Westminster Bridge in 1802 on the coach from Dover, and looking down from its roof, William Wordsworth also agreed earth had not anything to show more fair. Centuries on, standing smartly at the bow of his police chief's launch, Norman dismisses the view downstream with a sniff and says, 'The river's still the bloody same, but there's so little to see and do. I would hate to be a young man coming on to it now.'

We putter out and head for the tidal barrier. 'It's a lot cleaner, of course. One time, if you polished the brass it would be black in two hours.' The Thames was such a cesspool that to keep out its smell Parliament used to fix curtains soaked in chloride of lime over the windows. If you fell in, it was said, you were given a stomach pump before artificial respiration. Now there are fish. In 1965 a school of porpoises reached Greenwich, in 1977 a salmon. Recently two sea horses were discovered wiggling upstream. Norman can even remember a whale. 'It was dead, mind you. Bigger than this boat. I stuck my boat hook in to get hold and the skipper said, Don't! But I did and, Oh Christ, the smell!'

Everything has been ruined by the containers, he complains. 'You don't need warehouses if you got containers, and if you got containers you don't need docks because the ships are unloaded in ninety minutes onto lorries.' He nods sourly at the warehouses, prettified with red and green pipes, like false lashes on an old woman. 'All luxury accommodation now. See that yellow brick? David Lean's house. Six-and-a-half million. See the place next to The Grapes? That's David Owen.'

In place of cargoes, it is developers who now come to the wharfs. Their brash, cheerful signs hang incongruously on the old buildings. Barratt, Wates, Taylor Woodrow, McAlpine. In 1981 the last of the docks – the Royal Docks – closed. The same year saw the creation of the Docklands Development Corporation, set up to regenerate the derelict area of the Upper Thames Docks, with the result that by 1985 property prices there had risen to £150,000 an acre. Today Docklands may be a centre for the newspaper, television and SDP industries, but the aspect from the river is still what Henry James described as a damp-looking, dirty, universal blackness. 'Few European cities have a finer river than the Thames,' he wrote, 'but none certainly has expended more ingenuity in producing a sordid river front.'

Norman points out where Sir Francis Drake was knighted, and the wall behind which his ship the *Golden Hind* is sunk. 'When I started there were always about four ships unloading here – liquid lard, wood from Finland,' he says. 'We used to watch out for the blokes on those timber ships, to prove collusion. They'd kick the timber in the water, then a mate in a rowboat would take it off to the Receiver of Wrecks.'

Opposite, cranes rise silhouetted against the sky like graffiti. 'Dunbar wharf,' says Norman, indicating the open scrap sites. 'We caught a gang nicking copper there once. And over there, at that mooring, I remember a boat with illegal tortoises from North Africa – a cargo of them in wicker baskets. The bottom half were dead.'

A rubbish tug goes by, one of four a day that steam to the Coldharbour pit. Norman continues his litany. 'There used to be twenty-seven lighterage companies once. Now there are two.'

We turn at the Thames Flood Barrier. One of the supports is chipped where a German freighter rammed it the week before. 'All bridges get hit occasionally,' says Norman. 'You got to look at the river as a road that goes five miles per hour, with a rise and fall every day of twenty-four feet. It's a nasty river. If you fall in, it turns you over and over and takes you away. Unless you're an old lady with a ballooning tweed skirt. You'll float all the way to Southend, then. It's the gent who dives in after you who doesn't come up.'

When I ask about such gents, Norman leads me astern to the bridge. 'Chat about that with Peter. He's the best body catcher on the river. They seem to throw themselves up at him.'

Peter is the bluff, untroubled pilot. He has a coal-black moustache and a watery smile. His record is three bodies in as many hours. 'There's a certain romance about ending it all in the river,' he supposes. He talks about the little peaks, just after Christmas and during the hot summer of 1976. 'They mostly come off Waterloo and Tower Bridge and Charing Cross. They're the favourites. If they jump off Blackfriars they hit the buttresses. Some jump off into the road below, some into six inches of water, some into six inches of mud. One chap landed in the bottom of an empty rubbish barge. But it was the third time he'd jumped that morning.'

We pass under Tower Bridge, once opened twenty times a day, now only three times a week. Ahead, one bridge after another spans the gloomy water. Green brass lions line the Embankment. At high tide they can be seen drinking. If the Thames rises to their eyebrows, the Underground has to be closed.

Peter continues to describe the bodies he picks up. It's funny, he says, but there are very few bare women – at most, twelve a year.

'The biggest change was the coming of the Abortion Act. Before that we used to get babies – dozens and dozens of them – in holdalls or shopping bags, especially round Waterloo Bridge. It was not very pleasant.'

Peter is hardened to adult corpses, however. He describes how a body turns red after the lungs burst, then bright green when it has been in the air for five hours. Finally it turns black, unless it was born black, in which case it turns white. It is known, Peter tells me, as the 'Gobstopper Effect'.

Not everyone visits the river in a state of suicidal despair – the floating leisure business is increasing. Sheppey, with berths for 2,500 yachts, is the biggest marina in Europe. On the main stretch of the Thames, the watermen and lightermen have taken to running pleasure boats and disco barges. After bodies, these cause the main headache for the River Police. 'As soon as they leave the shore, just like a train leaving the station, they cease to have any liquor licensing laws. I reckon out of fifteen boats on a summer's weekend, there'll be trouble on five. Sometimes passengers bring home-made rum for a twelve-hour party and the owners try and charge corkage. One skipper was held at knifepoint and told to go up-river until the party was over. Another Sunday there was a pub outing and two hundred people ended up throwing chairs and smashing the boat up, egged on by the DJ over the mike. You've got to bluff your way on board if that happens, though they can't run away. But the number of times you go into the toilet and its full of blood . . . All you can do is wait for the body to come up – if ever.'

Towards the end of the seventeenth century, at The Prospect of Whitby in Wapping, that brutal judge George Jeffreys used to sit drinking beer and watching the rising tide cover the men he had hanged. It took, he calculated, three tides to wash them. (Public houses go hand in hand with capital punishment. 'No Hanging Round This Bar' was the sign put up by England's last official executioner, Albert Pierrepoint, when he opened a pub in Lancashire.)

Although his father advised against entering the law, Jeffreys rose to become Lord Chancellor and Recorder of London. 'The terrors of that man's face,' breathed a Wapping scrivener who came before him. It was this same scrivener who later spotted Jeffreys disguised as a sailor in another Wapping pub, after his patron, James II, had fled.

Until 1965 hanging was one of the great English traditions, of which only driving on the left seems destined to survive. In 1832 there were over 200 crimes for which the penalty was death. These included causing damage to Westminster Bridge, and associating with gypsies. It was a grim fate. If the hangman had not learnt his ropes, the matter could easily be bungled. The noose broke twice on Captain Kidd in 1701. A film was made about John Lee, the man they could not hang, who braved three attempts. 'What do you take me for, a bloody yo-yo?' is reputedly another victim's reaction. Some, like Robert Goodale, were less fortunate: his head was jerked right off.

Although drawing and quartering was not removed from the statute book in Scotland until 1950, throughout the UK the criminal law today is practised with more leniency. Those who wield the power in court are the judges and barristers. It has been said that those who wield power outside the court are the barristers' clerks.

Bob is a clerk in Lincoln's Inn, on the western outskirts of the City, at the heart of legal London. A solid-looking man with a butcher's moustache, he smokes a pipe from which condensation drips onto a large, empty legal desk. The chambers he looks after contain a dozen barristers. Like an actor's agent, only more powerful, Bob receives the work, allocates it, sets the fee for it, and takes a percentage. Despite the fact that he has no legal training, still less a degree, Bob reckons to earn up to £100,000 a year from the chambers' income of £1.5 million. There are about 200 senior clerks like Bob. One is a woman. One drives to work in a brown Rolls Royce. And several earn more than their top QCs.

Born on Lundy Island, the son of a sailor, Bob wanted to be an accountant, but being good at history and fascinated by legal trials, he caught the eye of a clerk who lived locally. In August 1959 he was duly taken on as a junior in this man's chambers.

'It was still a gentleman's profession. There were eight members of chambers, two or three of whom I never met. Now you must be fully practising. We never had typists. The fee notes were all handwritten.' He laughs drily. 'The law's always about a hundred years behind everyone else.'

Bob's job is largely administrative: 'To bring work into the chambers and to fix up trial dates. Solicitors ring up and say they've got so much to spend and who do I recommend. If I think they've got a particular flair for something, I suggest someone.' There is no set scale for a fee, although it is unlikely Bob would accept under £1,000 a day for a QC. 'The bottom drawer for anyone is thirty pounds an hour – the court day being only five hours, from ten-thirty to four-fifteen, with an hour for lunch. But we don't overcharge. We're great believers that you can't get blood out of everyone,' he stresses unconvincingly.

Bob coyly admits he has the power to make or break a barrister. 'I could dry someone up in a week,' he says. 'There may be members of chambers I think are a pain in the bum, but I tell them so. You can't get on with someone all the time.' Barristers make sure, however, that they butter their bread with the only man who knows what each earns. 'Everyone's in total competition. There's a lot of jealousy, a lot of rivalry. There's no share and share alike. The only common denominator is me, and if I'm making ten per cent off someone, all I want to do is make him successful.'

Occasionally, when a member of chambers is shopping in Peter Jones, having forgotten he is meant to be in court, Bob's duties rise to sweetening the judge: 'A water pipe has burst, you know the sort of thing,' he says. But his duties are never so strenuous that he has to take his work home. 'If you can't do it in a day,' he thinks, 'you shouldn't be doing it at all.' It is the kind of remark he makes to his fellow clerks in the Lonsdale Club, a convenient bolt-hole nearby, where everyone is on first-name terms and no one knows a surname.

Bob sits on the committee which interviews young barristers applying to join the chambers. It is his way of maintaining a stake in the future, even if he knows little about the minutiae of the law. 'I have a working knowledge as to its procedure,' he says pompously, his pipe dripping, 'but barristers often talk to me as if I know it all . . .'

Traditionally, the job of a barrister's clerk was one passed from father to son. Recently graduates have seen the pickings to be made. Bob is not so keen on this development. 'I don't feel it is suitable for graduates. But don't get me wrong, I'm not anti change,' he says hurriedly. 'It's just that a good clerk appreciates traditions.'

Walk out of Lincoln's Inn and through a narrow passage, and you come to Chancery Lane, and the premises of Ede & Ravenscroft, robe-makers to the Royal Family and tailors since the reign of William and Mary. Founded in 1689, the year of Judge Jeffreys' death, Ede & Ravenscroft also supply wigs and gowns to our barristers and judges. From their network of small rooms, they dress a city that likes to stand on ceremony.

Mr Batteson is in charge of the legal, academic and ceremonial regalia. He has a red Dickensian face, and fiddles nervously with a rubber band. When he speaks, a speck of white spittle transfers from his top lip to his bottom lip. On the mahogany desk of his cluttered back room is a brown sandwich.

He was born, he says, in Judge Street, St Pancras, the son of a man who worked for Lambert & Butler, and who only took his wife out for a meal once – one March, when the firm paid a bonus. He was one of twelve children. They slept two or three to a bed. 'Everyone was poor, but we were too rich to have charity.'

The staple of Mr Batteson's work is academic. Each year, when London University graduates collect their degrees from the Albert Hall, approximately 1,800 students hire gowns made at a factory in Stockport. Although only one per cent will buy them, the wearing of gowns has increased. Polytechnics are just as jealous of their new-found traditions.

'I'm more interested in the ceremonial robes,' Mr Batteson says, referring to a collection downstairs of 300 parliamentary regalia. 'It rubs off. They're such lovely people to deal with. You meet them on a personal basis, not like they were coming in to buy a pound of potatoes. They depend on you for advice. I feel they're doing a job, we're doing a job. I always robe the Duke of Norfolk, put his robes on at the House of Lords, tie his bow tie, help with his garter chain. One of the bonuses of the job is the people you meet. You meet the Princess by robing her, though you got to be a bit more careful with royalty – not talk until you're spoken to. But you don't have to feel servile to do a job like that. It's a privilege, to my mind.'

The price of privilege is steep. 'I'd supply you a garter mantle for one thousand, six hundred pounds,' he says helpfully. Wigs come cheaper. 'They're made of horse hair from Italy and Spain, and sent to a small firm in Suffolk to be bleached and cleaned. I've known old legal wigs made from human hair.'

In 1984 Mr Batteson sold 1,462 wigs: 1,200 barristers' wigs; 73 bench wigs; and 79 full-bottom wigs, such as the one Justice Melford Stevenson wore when he sentenced the Krays. 'Those cost seven hundred pounds. They take a month to make, and they include forty yards of handmade curls. They last anything from eighty to a hundred years.'

We walk up an angled staircase, past black-and-gold wig cases marked with names like Joseph Nkamm. 'We do a lot of our business in Nigeria,' Mr Batteson explains. He sets the scene for the workroom we are about to enter. 'The girls who make the wigs, they're young girls in the main, they come from school. If they leave to have babies they become outworkers.' There are six in-house girls and about 100 outworkers, including Mrs Batteson who makes special robes and barristers' blue bags. The in-house girls are listening to Terry Wogan on the radio. One is mounting horse hair onto an elm block, another is applying curls, a third is dressing and perming. On the shelves behind are tens of bald, faceless wooden heads, each one disfigured by countless pin pricks. When telling people what they do, the girls usually get the reply, 'Will you make me one too?'

I turn to Mr Batteson, in the doorway fiddling with his rubber band, and ask how people respond to him. 'I normally say I'm a robe-maker,' he says. 'They can't grasp that it exists as a job,' he adds, a little crestfallen.

'They expect me to be in asphalt.'

MAYHEW'S LONDON

The greatest of all works on Londoners was written by an ebullient Victorian bankrupt called Henry Mayhew. As a play-wright he achieved only limited success with *A Troublesome Lodger* and *But However*. As a novelist, he is unlikely to enjoy reprints of *The Greatest Plague of Life* or *Whom to Marry* – about a prim young girl in search of a good catch. It is as the journalist responsible for a series of 'letters' in the *Morning Chronicle* that Mayhew is remembered. It is impossible for anyone writing about the city to ignore these brilliant sketches on the plight of the working class, published in four volumes in 1851 under the title *London Labour and the London Poor*.

While scouring the metropolis today, Mayhew might well recognise a few familiar faces, and some less eminent Victorians.

NAVVY

According to the results of a survey published in the London *Standard* on 30 September 1985, the happiest Londoner is a man in his sixties living in a detached house in Dagenham. John fits this bill. He wears braces and a green tweed tie, and keeps his gall stones in a honey jar. He shakes them cheerfully, to prove how fit – and happy – he is.

He came down his street on the Becontree Estate in 1932: 'I came down this street and I never left it,' he beams. His wife Vera, a local girl, remembers back to when Londoners used to come up for the day and picnic in the meadows. 'We were in the country,' she emphasises, with a finger rubbing the stocking that bulges over her leg like a thick sock.

There were two or three 'manors' then, including Eastbury Houses where the Gunpowder Plot was hatched, and rows of market gardens. To be at Covent Garden by the morning, the carts of produce would leave the night before at 7.30 p.m. It was a mile across the fields to Dagenham East railway station, but a little less to school. When she went to school, Vera's mother put a hot potato in each pocket to keep her warm.

John was born in County Mayo, Northern Ireland. He came over in 1926 and worked in a Yorkshire sugar factory. In March 1932, aged twenty-three, he and thousands like him came to London. (The year before, the Ford works had opened in Dagenham and work was in the offing.)

'It was a shattering experience. Some of them walked, some of them cycled, some came by coal boat, and the Irish came by the score because Henry Ford's grandfather had been an Irishman. They got to Paddington and walked. One friend of mine came from Newcastle by bike. He paid four shillings and sixpence for it, and his name was Macbride. Some paid seven shilling to come by coal boat from the Tyne – smuggled down of course.

'I looked for building-site work and wore a good suit, a trilby and the rest of it. I made my way to the county town of Brentwood in Essex, where a seven-mile stretch of railway was being built. It was my hope and intention to get a job. Fifty young Irish boys were digging and laying out track. There were faces in the crowd which I recognised from back in my own County Mayo, and I got shouts of Hello from them. But the foreman looked at my modern gear, and he said, We don't need no kid-glove navvies. There were men in a field close by, sitting on newspapers on the damp grass, and I said, What are these men doing? They were waiting to queue next morning for work.

So I went to Costain, the builders, and they said, We might give you a job in Croydon. I went to Croydon, and I got a job operating the sand and ballast pit machinery, and because we finished late we slept out in the ditches. In the morning the foreman said, You've won your medals. If you could sleep rough and play the game of the hard men, you'd find work.

'To show off their tough image these men would remove their shirts, regardless of weather conditions, and the passers-by got a special treat to see them fry their eggs and bacon on their shovels. "You'll need to see a doctor after eating that," shouted a young man once. With a rich brogue came the reply, "My doctor fits into a pint glass."

'I had a brother who could drink twenty pints. You didn't go to the pub and drink half a pint. If you didn't drink six, the men wouldn't work with you. They said you were mean. The navvies didn't know the streets, they knew the pubs. The centres of information were the pubs. The pub was their life and their listening post where all the jobs were. I wasn't a pub man, but I was a boxer. It was the sport of the job. At dinner time there were competitions to be the best fighter. The biggest navvy soon found out I did some amateur boxing, and I had this hand on my shoulder. "Come on, Jock," he said, "I hear you box." We took off our coats and went outside. I won, but we were friends after that.

'I worked as a navvy for two years on a site outside Romford. The foreman was a special breed of bastard. "If I don't see the effing steam come off your back in half an hour, you go," he'd say. Then I went to Fords. I was feeding furnaces. You had to buy your own overalls. They timed you to go to the toilet. They had spotters who took photos from the balconies to see where everyone was. If you were caught smoking, you were fired immediately. It has happened to me the foreman asked, "Where you been?" The toilet, I said. So he takes me off to the toilet and smells around for a smoke. There was no such thing as being bored with those slave drivers over you.

'I considered myself lucky to get a job at all. Everyone wore a badge. I would loan my badge at night to men sleeping rough so they could get a meal or a beer. If you wore a badge you were something special. You'd go to the pub and someone would buy you a drink either because they too were in work, or because they wanted work. It was survival. I brought people home and they hid under the bed for the night.

'Digs were difficult to get, but the men were difficult. One told me he was changing his digs: "You changing your digs, Paddy?" "Yea, there're too many fucking flowers on the table."

'I shared a bedroom with a builder. Our landlady, Mrs Bennett, was a dream. I'd pay her twenty-five shillings a week out of my wages of four pounds. At three forty-five in the morning I got up and she cooked me eggs and bacon. I cycled to work and began feeding the furnaces at four-thirty. At ten-thirty there was a twenty-minute break. We knocked off at twelve, but the land-ladies didn't like you to go to bed. They wanted you to keep away while they cleaned the house. So you used to go and stand in the doorways. Just stand. That's all.'

A more recent account of a navvy's work was given by Jan, a Dutch academic from Leyton, east London. Tall, with a grey beard, he had the sloping gait of a shepherd.

'I worked on a building site. We'd meet at seven-fifteen at Nick's Italian Café on Cricklewood Broadway, waiting for the cowboy to pick us up. Tramps sat in the café. There was one Irish one who played the fiddle. He'd always play "O Sole Mio" for Nick, who missed Italy so much, and for that he got a cup of tea and a slice of bread. At seven-thirty we started.

'We worked for three hours till ten-fifteen and breakfast, a big hot meal with plenty of tea. The Irish had been drinking fifteen or twenty pints the night before and were pretty thirsty. They drank hard, but they worked hard, and they had a curious punctuality. There were great characters. Some were not crooks, though if anything fell off the back of a van they were near it. Some, like

142

Terry Fingers, were crooks. If we needed paint we'd go to the local shop. We'd buy two cans, and Terry would go off with five through the back. He also had a bent friend on the council who'd put council paint into our tins.

'How you got your material to work – and where you got it from – was your own business. People you worked for were always respected, but that doesn't mean the work was always respectable. There was an English artist in West Hampstead with a lovely French accent and an awful line in portraiture. He asked us to clean the gutter. We put the ladder up against the wall, stood around chatting and smoking till he came back, and said, "That's done." He paid us and we left.

'We'd start again after breakfast at ten thirty-five and work till one when we'd spend an hour in the pub. They'd drink five or six pints at lunch. In the afternoon, if there was work to be done on the roof, everyone would be quite happy to go there. At three we'd have a cup of tea – there would always be a kettle – and work 'till six. Then everyone was expected to go off to the pub. "Who's shopping?" meant, Who was buying the round? After you had bought one you were allowed to go.

'Everything happed in the pub. If you were out of work, you'd go there, and the contractors would come in and say, "You, you and you." If you had anything crooked to sell, you'd sell it in the toilet. It was where you were paid each day in cash. A cheque was "a kite" – you refused it bluntly. You had given concrete work and you wanted concrete money. And one by one the cowboy would call you to the toilet – so no one knew what the other was getting. On Saturdays we worked till twelve and we'd be paid ten or fifteen pounds. At least five would put all their money on one horse.

'If it won, they didn't come back to work till the money was gone.'

DOCKER

Walking along quays pungent with the fumes of rum, tobacco and coffee, Mayhew concluded that, to the superficial observer, the docks of London would appear 'the very focus of metropolitan wealth'. The scenes he was to witness, however, in the struggle

143

for one day's work, resulted in 'a climax of misery and wretchedness that I could not have imagined to exist'.

I went to Pinner, on the northern edge of London, to find out about life on the river.

Alex, who is in his seventies, came to Pinner in the War: to a brown, pebble-dashed house, on a street named after one of Henry VIII's wives. When he came it was all sparrows, hawks and cornfields. He was born in Cable Street, he says, the son of a docker whose family had lived there for 150 years.

He is balding, with blue eyes and sinus trouble.

The house had two lodgers and two kitchens underground. The tallyman used to come round with a catalogue of boots and shoes and jackets. The family would choose what they wanted and pay in weekly instalments. Some families could not afford the tallyman's wares. On Monday mornings at the pawn shop, wives could be seen queuing with their husband's suits, hoping for a few bob to get them through till Friday.

Alex spent his evenings in youth clubs on the Ratcliffe Way, where he played billiards and table tennis, and listened to debates. The governor of Wormwood Scrubs was one speaker. Another was Lord Haw-Haw. 'We gave him a real rollocking,' Alex remembers.

Work was difficult to come by. He briefly counted barrels at a brewery in Whitechapel – 2,500 barrels, counted six times a day for 12s. a week. He thought of banking, but you had to have a relation, to be spoken for. The only work available, he was told, was on the docks. He thought of becoming a cook in the merchant navy, but one night, after a few lessons, he was playing billiards and he spotted a queue of men sitting down. 'They're all waiting to be cooks,' someone explained. So he went to the local library and flicked through *Lloyd's List* to see what ships were coming in. 'Casual labour was all there was, one or two days a week.'

In 1938 he got a job 'in the German trade' on a wharf used by ships from Hamburg. He was part of a regular gang, and he was sure of a good week's wage: £10 for loading copper and lead to supply the German war machine. 'This money is very nice,' Alex said. 'But this lead is going to come back in big lumps.'

After the War he went back to the docks.

'At seven forty-five in the morning you went to a wharf and booked on. You'd line up, trying to catch the foreman's eye – just like in *On the Waterfront*. He'd pick his relations and the skilled men, and hand the tickets out. I used to have two scarves – one green, one white. If I knew the foreman was a Catholic of Irish descent whose ancestors had come over in the potato famine, I'd wear green. If he was other than a Catholic I'd wear white.

'They could be bastards. I remember unloading barges of rubber onto the cobbles. They came in bundles of two hundred and sixty-three pounds, and it would take two to truck them to the warehouse. One morning, one-eyed Jock Gilbert said to me, "Alex, give me a run on this truck. I have to go to the toilet to put my trusses on and push my piles back." You see, many men ruptured themselves lifting weights by hand. About half the gang had hernias and wore trusses. Well, the foreman came up. "What are you doing?" he said. I'm giving Jock a run to the toilet, say I. "I'll give him a run tomorrow," comes back the foreman.

'Next morning at Ratcliffe Cross – the rallying point for local work – he gave tickets out to everyone except Jock, who was a regular. This happened for two days.

'We unloaded everything – jute from Dundee, tin plate from South Wales, Sunlight soap from Liverpool. Worse than the rubber was the lampblack. It went right through your clothes and took weeks to clean. The cement was tricky, too – smooth paper bags which you couldn't get a grip on. Anyone could throw them into a barge, but I took pride in stowing all neat and tidy. You did it properly for your own safety too.

'Lunch was at twelve – a couple of slices dipped in the pan. I'd go to the police courts and watch the pimps and petty thieves – and to the toilet. The toilets were like pig troughs. There were no cubicles except for the foreman. And no paper. You wiped your arse on the *News of the World*. In the evening you'd have a stew or meat pie and pudding, and a chicken or piece of pork at Christmas. You never saw a turkey.

'There weren't many perks to the job, except "waxers". They were illicit drinks, named after the sealing wax which was put around the best wines. We had the feeling that what was good enough for the toffs was good enough for us.' Alex remembers with particular pleasure two casks of sherry that were intended as a gift from the Spanish dictator, Primo de Rivera, to Churchill.

He went back to Cable Street after it was knocked down. 'I got lost. The intimacy had gone. People used to leave their doors on the latch and say, Are you there Mrs So-and-so? Now it's frightening. How are we going to overcome this violence? The kids think it's a way of life to go stabbing. We didn't know anything about that.'

RAG-AND-BONE MAN

You would not chance on the totters' yard under the White City flyover, at the end of a labyrinth of cul-de-sacs; nor, even if you did, would you leave your car unlocked. The caravans at the end house Irish gypsies. One rumour has it that the Brighton bombing was planned there. They shoot each other with shotguns, complain the totters; they leave their rubbish everywhere.

Markie is the son and grandson of a totter. He was born in a house long since destroyed for the flyover, and brought up on this site: a square courtyard of red brick stables, newly but clumsily built. 'Look,' he says, scraping the mortar with a finger and leaving a mark. 'And it's only three years old.'

The council has tried to evict them for years. In nine months, the totters amassed £15,000 to fight it – and won. Now the taxman comes round a little more regularly, to look at the totters' licences and to see their returns. It makes things difficult for Markie, who cannot read or write.

Piled in the middle of the yard are old fridges, a basket of doves – and carts. 'See that one,' he says of a red cart on its side, 'it came over from Hungary last week.' Among the six totters are two Hungarians. They drive back and forth to their country in trucks crammed with Shetland ponies.

Inside his own stable, Markie directs water from a tap into a kettle and makes tea. Under a cloth cap, he wears a grey overall with the initials DP – 'from the dairies,' he explains – and brown trousers over leather boots. In the corner is a bin full of crushed cereal from High Wycombe. 'That's three forty-five a sack,' he says, running the grains through his fingers. He eats it himself, but it is really meant for his horses – and his dog. The fridge is full of chicken bits for Mitzi, the white bull terrier. He doesn't fight her, he insists. His father also had bull terriers. When the council forced him out, the old man moped and died of a stroke. He couldn't do without the courtyard. During the War he had sat there with a crate of Guinness. Bricks and mortar won't fall on us, he had said. Now it is the shadow of the A40 to Oxford which falls on the cluttered yard.

Markie chews liquorice, because he has given up smoking, and admits it pains him that his children have not followed in his trade. An honest man, he is pained by a lot today. 'There was no need for this locking of yourself in,' he spits, 'when I was young. Now, if you've got a bob more than someone, everyone's after you.' He looks at the harnesses above him. 'People used to say, Can I come and borrow them? Now they just nick them.' Like many people, he blames 'the blacks' for the drugs and the mugging. Like many who cannot afford to, he takes a taxi home from the pub.

Later in the day, Markie will go out with a van of dung from the heap steaming by the entrance. He might get £10 a load for it. He won't take a cart – not because of the smell, but because the dung rots the wood.

But first he will tot as he does each day, seven days a week.

Dolly the horse is scrubbed down and backed into a cart. Markie is an expert with horses. He buys them from the Welsh hills and breaks them in a sandpit under the flyover. One woman wouldn't buy from him till he had proved the pony could go round Marble Arch. He proved it by taking the horse round twice – the wrong way. He used to break horses for a rich landowner who cheated him. Whenever it is mentioned that he ought to train horses for a living, he says indignantly, 'What, and go and be like X?'

We clop off into the cold north London Saturday morning. 'We'll learn you,' he says, sitting on a stool, with me behind on a pink blanket.

'Where there's chimneys, there's money,' his father used to say. On Mondays Markie makes for the chimneys of Ealing; on Tuesdays, Kilburn; and on Wednesdays, Hayes, sixteen miles away. Today we ride past Wormwood Scrubs and up through Willesden.

'In the old days people used to take their hats off before a horse. Now they try and run it over.' He has been warned twice for going through red traffic lights, but he has not been 'had up' for drunken driving. 'My dad got nicked once,' he roars, 'for being drunk in charge of a donkey and barrow. But it's something I never indulge in. When I'm at work, I'm at work. When I'm drinking, I'm drinking.'

Markie laments the passing of his trade. 'People collect scrap now in vans with bells. They collect from skips – "skip-diving" it's called. When I'm out in the cart, at least people know what I'm out for. But if there was twenty totters in London, there'd be a lot. It's a dying game now. It's finished. People take their stuff to jumble sales or War on Want and all that rubbish. A lot of rot to me. I used to get a bit of antique, a few paintings and pedestal desks. No longer.'

The last bit of decent antique was five years back, when he was given two statues from the Catholic church in Kilburn. As he rode with them down Kilburn High Street, he claims, everyone went down on their hands and knees.

We turn into North Acton. On the corner is a fresh heap of horse dung. Markie says it must have come from Mr Bartlett. He doesn't mind, it won't spoil his beat. 'So far as I'm concerned, nobody's got any regulars.' But he admits that totters tend to make for different areas. He prefers the middle-class patches. 'We don't get much call round the posh lands like Kensington. That's more for the likes of Harry Bridges or Elsie French.'

We go up a street of cladded houses with Capital Radio stickers on their windows and a skirt of red tiles between each floor. When Markie lets out his shout, groups of coloured children pull back the lace curtains of the upstairs windows and wave.

His loud cry varies from 'Olwrappan!' to 'Ennyoleragann-bow!'. Once, someone actually gave him a bone. 'Nothing you can do with it. It's just a saying.' Two black men walk past, drinking beer. They raise their cans. 'What do you want, beer?'

Markie shakes his head. 'I don't drink.'

'Why you say you want iron, then?'

Markie swears. 'Not a lot of good, this street.'

As we enter Buchanan Gardens, a man opens an upper window and asks if we could use a car battery. It is our first scrap of the day. A boy comes up with a television. 'That's no good, boy,' says Markie. Television sets are the one thing he cannot get rid of: 'If you took them, you'd take four hundred a day.' Later, rather more grandly, he refuses a set of three chairs on the basis that people only wanted four.

The cart fills up slowly. 'Do you mind old radiators?' asks a man in a white shirt. We tether the horse by a chain to a lamppost, and follow him through his garage to the garden. Against the fence are three old cream-painted radiators. 'How much do you want for them?' the man asks. I leave Markie to barter. He returns empty-handed, wiping his cold nose. 'Mean sod. Wanted a quid each for them. They don't give nothing away, do they? And he was a rich bugger. Well, he can have his flicking money. I've had a better life than he's ever had.'

As the morning progresses we amass a foot-operated sewing machine, two basins, an iron box of rusty nuts and bolts, a lawnmower and a cushion.

There's a lot more stuff in the summer, Markie explains, with people watering their gardens and washing their cars. 'The dream I dream every night is that an old boy says, "Clean this house out, mate." I forget the last house clearance I did. It's all car-boot sales now. Everything's plastic – the guttering, the piping. That's why totting won't last.' Popping another piece of liquorice into his mouth, he lets the reins out and heads for home.

Leaving Buchanan Gardens, Markie gives one last 'Olwrappan!' for good measure.

He has never been curious about what goes on behind the doors, he says. 'They're probably saying, What a noise is going on out here.' As Dolly breaks into a trot, a man runs over to say there's a fridge in Liddell Gardens. He gives the address, then a telephone number. Markie nods, and says he'll collect it Monday. Does it annoy him he can't read? 'No, it hasn't worried me. I made a living, ain't I? I'm too old to learn all that palaver.'

How much of a living has he made today? He twists to survey the creaking tangle behind. 'That lot? I'll probably get about forty quid at the scrap merchants.' When all is said and done, not such a bad morning's work.

That night I meet a former colleague at a party. He tells me he was woken up by a horrible noise from the street. Looking down, he saw the totter's cart. 'I thought,' he says, 'He's gone down in the world since he left the BBC.'

FLOWER GIRL

In Amy's chubby face, Mayhew would recognise a descendant of the little Irish flower girl who bought her mignonette and violets each morning from Covent Garden.

Amy is reached – early on Thursdays, Fridays and Saturdays – across the Maida Vale courtyard of what used to be the Express Dairies. In the gap between two buildings, a narrow door swings out onto a cast-iron landing. Steps, freshly painted black, lead down into a patio stacked with cardboard boxes containing lilies from Tunfield Nurseries. Drainpipes and air vents grow frailly into the air. It is dark down in the patio, but even darker in the vault under the stairs where Amy wraps and sells her flowers.

Under the feeble light, a tea-cosy hat pulled tightly over her head gives the impression of neatly plaited hair. A shiny gold crucifix slaps against her large chest. A small can of Guinness and a bottle of scent stand on a shelf nearby.

'My mother was here before the First World War,' she says, her voice like the crackle of polythene. 'We used this as a bomb shelter in the Blitz, but we still sold flowers during the War. We'd sell anything – and people would buy – flowers that I'd turn me nose at now. Daisies,' she sniffs. 'They used them for barter. We used to get meat from the butcher's by giving them flowers.

'I used to have a barrow, but at seventy-six I'm too old. I collect from Covent Garden, mornings, and any unsold I give to my friend for her place in Twickenham. Lilies and such like have gone up in price, but anemones are still the same. I have a lot of gents come to buy, a lot of gents. I never ask who they're for . . .

'I used to be missing flowers from up top, and I got the dairy to look out, and they found a woman with an armful of gladies. But that was the last time someone pinched any.

'Now, if you'll excuse me, I've got a lot of work to do – with those chrysanths. If you hammer the bottom, they'll last you a fortnight.'

COVENT GARDEN PORTER

Austen owns a pub on the lower slopes of a fashionable district in north London. He has run it for ten years – ever since he left Covent Garden where he worked as a porter. Now, at the age of fifty, Austen is a Lloyds underwriter and the owner of sixteen properties, which include a flat in Hans Crescent, a place in Antibes, and a boat. When Austen took his wife out to The Ritz on Christmas Eve, the bill came to £125. They drank Tattinger Rosé, which they enjoyed because it happened to be a good vintage and 'not so acidy'. He has stopped hunting with the

Enfield Chase, but has made sure his grandson will have the opportunity to do so. Aged three, the boy is already down for Harrow – 'if they're still good enough for him'. As Austen says, 'to appreciate life today, you have to have education'.

Austen admits he did not have this. He sits in the saloon bar of his pub, examining the tattoo on his fist and shaking his gold bracelet. He has tight grey curls, like scrubland, and the face of a Roman Emperor who has been worsted in a fight.

His father and six uncles were plumbers, his mother a cook at a factory in Paddington. Aged fifteen, Austen decided to follow in his grandfather's footsteps and work in the fruit and vegetable market at Covent Garden. He recalls the first morning at 4.30 a.m. when he stood in front of the gas oven as his mother made him porridge. He took the 5.10 a.m. train, and at 6 a.m. began looking for work as an 'empty boy'.

Each morning for a month he stood on the stones of the piazza looking up at the union office. Up there, firms were putting through their orders by telephone for the help they needed. He waited to be called.

The job of an 'empty boy' was to stack wooden boxes. It also involved taking them, when full, from the wholesaler to the trader and collecting a deposit. 'I'd give the trader five boxes and he'd write out a ticket for twenty and we'd split the difference.' The difference meant that his wages of £5 to £6 a week were incremented substantially: 'It was nothing to get fifty to sixty pounds.' With the money he brought ten overcoats, 'so that when it rained, by the time I got to the end the first one would be dry'.

It was a good life. He would see celebrities – 'like the Duke of Bedford'. Once, he nods impressively, he saw Julie Andrews, at the Italian café where every morning at 9 a.m. he ate a breakfast of roast beef, roast potatoes and a sweet. Less famous people – those who slept out all night for opera tickets – would be bombarded, as they curled in their bags, with rotten melons.

After a short stint in the Grenadiers, Austen returned as a 'staff man', which meant lumping fruit to the warehouses. Sadly for him, 'You couldn't fiddle so much'. Then came the 1955 General Strike. Austen entered into the spirit of things by slashing tyres and pouring sugar into petrol tanks, after which he was promoted to porter – on £47 a week.

'I'd leave home Friday night and not be seen till Monday,' he recollects lovingly. 'There were these Turkish baths in Russell

Square – always packed – which would massage you, wheel you upstairs, wrap you in a sheet, and wake you in the morning with breakfast, a pot of tea, toast and a kipper – all for three pounds fifty. Sundays I'd spend at the pictures, and in the night go to the Lyceum. There'd be dice schools and cards in the toilets. Sometimes I'd pick up a girl, get in a cab, give a quid to the driver, and tell him to drive round the park while we screwed in the back. The West End's no good is it, now? By pushing it underground, you've created – what is it? – perversity. Before, it was just a laugh.' He looks round to see if his wife is hovering. 'The tarts would come to the market after work and there'd be orgies in the empty warehouses. We'd play with vegetables. It was a bit of a laugh,' he repeats.

'The police were not very efficient, though there was lots of money about – a lot of money. Today it's bank robberies. Then it was cigarettes and whisky, stolen stuff – from the Krays,' he explains helpfully. 'Long firms.'

1962 was the Krays' most successful year for long firms. Over £100,000 was cleared by this fraudulent system of renting a warehouse, and filling it with merchandise until enough confidence was established to enjoy a month's credit with suppliers. Whereupon, the full warehouse and its contents would evaporate, to rematerialise in places like Covent Garden. 'At three o'clock everyone was fixed to the television and Shaw Taylor on *Police Five*. It made a difference to the price. If it didn't come on *Police Five* that a truck of whisky had just been stolen, the 'phones would start ringing and people would say, "We'll buy it." '

When Austen left in 1975 he did so feeling that only poor Londoners remained in the centre: 'The ones who can't leave, the real Bill Sykeses. Anyone with any go would move out.'

As a landlord, playing squash with the middle classes, he initially found the process of being polite to customers a little confusing. 'Someone said anything to you in the market, it was crash with the right hand. Here, the hippies would rabbit you with words, insulting you, and you couldn't hit them in public. So I'd go round the back and catch them by their long hair on the way to the toilet.

'To have to do what I did to get a living – I'm not proud of it,' Austen finishes, unclenching his fist. 'Today I'd never do a thing wrong.'

RATCATCHER

I met William Howard at his club in St James's, having found his name in the *Yellow Pages*.

He is the last of a family of ratcatchers who have been in operation since 1750: ten years, he tells me, after the last wolf was caught in Britain. In that time, their many clients have included Harrods, Lyons and the Bank of England.

William has a sharp nose, sharper brown eyes and silver hair. He has just come back from stalking in Scotland where he shot three stags. As chairman of Great Britain's St Hubert Club – named after St Hubert of the Ardennes, the patron saint of hunting – he is responsible for training stalkers and deer management. He is aware of the paradox. 'Once you study deer, you end up shooting them,' he says ordering a Bell's from Debby behind the copper-sheeted bar.

The original William Howard was a lamplighter who did a bit of pest control in the Dalston area in his spare time. 'He was very much a dog-and-ferret man. It comes natural to a ferret. We used ferrets extensively 'till 1939.' The family was connected through marriage to silk weavers from Spitalfields. They also had an ass farm in Hackney. 'There were no fridges then, and my grandfather used to walk over to Buckingham Palace and deliver milk on the hoof.' In the Commoners Gallery, there is a photograph of him entitled *The Ass Boy*.

From Dalston, east London, the family moved north to premises in Stamford Hill with a good half acre at the back for terrier kennels and purpose-built ferret hutches. Before the War they supplied ferrets to King's Hospital for experiments in predetermining the sex of unborn children – much as rats are used now. Rats were also kept at the back – for poison trials.

On the same premises, the family ran a business on the side, loading 12-bore cartridges and .25 Velodog pellets. 'Velocipede was the first name for a bicycle,' William explains. 'The first bicycle owners were always chased by dogs. Hence Velodogs. You would buy a pistol from Gamages department store, and if you were chased, you were entitled to shoot. This was before the Firearms Certification of nineteen twelve. If you shot a dog now . . .'

But the bulk of the family's work was catching rats.

In 1924 it was calculated that the rat population in Britain matched the human population, and that one rat cost £1 to keep. Pestologists like William Howard & Sons were in some demand. An article in the *Town and Country News* of May 1930 devoted more attention to William's father Thomas than to the rise of the Luftwaffe.

'There are two kinds of rat in London,' William explains. 'The large brown rat – or *Mus norvegicus* and *Mus rattus* – the ship's rat, which is small, black, gregarious, and comes from Asia.' The gregarious *Mus rattus* is also primary host to a flea which carries the bubonic plague, septic pneumonia and endemic jaundice.

'There were a lot of black rats during the War. The bombed-out warehouses and buildings made a good habitat. It's much more of a climbing animal, you understand,' says William.

Rat catching was usually done on contract – 'to food establishments, hotels like The Cumberland and Strand, chains of public houses, sweet manufacturers, horse slaughterers like Smith & Spalding . . . I've stood with my cousin and driven up to three hundred a night down the blood gulleys, and into nets that would take two men to lift and dump into a forty-gallon tub of water.'

From his briefcase William produces some old photographs of the equipment. In one, his grandfather holds a mahogany brass-bound ferret box on which are engraved the words 'Ratcatchers to the Bank of England'. In another, dressed for the fray, he wears an airman's uniform and goggles, while around lie gas cylinders, torches, guns, pistols and a *sjambok* – a South African bullock whip made out of rhino hide, and a particular favourite from the Howard family arsenal.

'I was very much brainwashed into a tradition that father should follow son. I killed my first rat when I was less than six. What with? My hands. It was at a restaurant in Holborn, in a gents' toilet at the foot of the stairs. I was whipping it with a *sjambok*, and it chose to whizz up my trousers. The blood ran down my leg. I wouldn't wash it, I was so pleased. Mother called me all sorts of horrible names.'

He shows a picture of himself with a ferret called George. 'After one lunch George smelt food around my mouth. He grabbed my lip and hung on for half an hour. His teeth, which were like a cat's, just punctured the lip – not like a rat's which of course are like chisels. They slash and tear. At weekends, the family would sit in chairs on the Seven Sisters Road and stitch up the wounds they'd given the dogs and ferrets. The ferrets would also suffer from foot rot. Their urine was extremely powerful stuff, and their feet would have to be dipped into pig's lard and medical creosote. We'd perform surgeries for local pets as well.' He orders another Bell's from Debby. 'I've still got my grandfather's castration knife.'

In 1904 William Howard & Sons received the ultimate accolade of a contract with Harrods. For £1 in town, £2 in the country, and the reimbursement of third-class travel expenses incurred, customers of Harrods could also purchase their services.

'Harrods was built on the site of an old property. When it was demolished nothing was done to the drains, so in periods of rain rats would come in from the sewers through holes made by plumbers and electricians. They would then follow the pipework. Rats can't move without leaving tell-tale signs like droppings and bite-marks. Also, their smear leaves a black grease mark. If a pipe was clean and free of dust, it would mean it was being used a lot. Paradoxically the rat is a clean animal, constantly grooming itself.

'Until the late nineteen forties Harrods insisted we didn't use poison, because a dead rat would smell. We therefore had to resort to more sophisticated techniques, like traps. It was a question of knowing the building, building up an intelligence network, and using your eyes. Being creatures of habit, the rats would move from the food halls in the early part of the night, and work their way up through to the staff restaurant at the top. Given a choice, which of course they had at Harrods, they liked to eat the very best – kippers, tomatoes, cheese, cereals, melon seeds. But we've had them in china and ladies' lingerie. A rat likes its creature comforts like we do.'

William would set the traps, crouch waiting, and suddenly snap the lights on. 'You could be looking at as many as two or three dozen.' These would be shot with automatic pistols, care being taken not to damage the walls and fittings, while at the same time terriers and ferrets would be unleashed.

William's father once wrote:

> Even if the rat is facing and has all the advantage, the ferret will crouch with his nose just outside the hole, just staring the rat down until its courage falters; we know when that moment arrives, the ferret's tail wags, and he is inside the hole like a flash. Very soon the rat will be heard to scream and that will be the end of its life.

A rat in a corner, sensing it is to be killed, will bite badly – hence the necessity for catchers to carry antiseptic silks and needles. It will also scamper over rather than round you. 'It has an incredible ability to see the safest way out of a situation. Invariably this is by running up and over your body,' William elucidates.

The rat problem that existed until the 1950s is no longer with us, he says confidently. With the demise of dockland, the source of their import – and sustenance – is gone. His job now is preventative. 'Good housekeeping,' he calls it. And he carries out his duties, largely to do with other forms of pest control, in some extremely good houses.

'People feel it's a stigma if they have pests, they feel they're dirty. That's not necessarily so. We've carried out pest control in some of the finest houses you can imagine – the Sitwells, the Guinnesses . . . Lady Evelyn Guinness gave me a silk hand-kerchief . . . Michael Redgrave, Vivien Leigh. We used to do a lot of moth work for Lady Cadogan – she had some valuable tapestries.'

Since the War, mice have become a bigger problem than rats: 'They are more fastidious feeders. They don't succumb to anti-coagulant poisons, and people don't take so much notice of them.' Other pests include squirrels, especially in the roofs of Hampstead and Barnet, German cockroaches – 'We've dealt with cockroaches since the last century, and use the same ground pyrethrum flower [cultivated chrysanthemum] that the Egyptians used – and bed-bugs.

'Bedbugs have made a come back with the Asian immigrants. A lot of illegal immigrants are exploited by their own people. They are given three pounds a week to work in a restaurant, and sleep on mattresses at the back. You also get bugs in big houses in Chelsea. Invariably, it's a cook or maid who's got a boyfriend in Chelsea barracks who's just back from India.'

William estimates the average cost to treat a three-bedroom house is between £48 and £60. When anxious mothers say, 'You won't poison my children?' he has a habit of replying, 'Not for the money you're paying me.'

He is a widower with one daughter. 'I am the last of the generation; the tradition will die with me,' he says nostalgically.

He has enjoyed his job because the hours are flexible and there is no one breathing down his neck. The only time his whiskers bristle is when someone queries his profession. 'I have to say I'm a "consultant pestologist". If you tell someone you're a ratcatcher, they don't believe you. Tell them you design lavatory seats for royalty and they do.'

RAT RACE

The first time I met my bank manager was when I went to interview him. He sat behind a desk on which, neatly uncreased, lay my letter. Beside it, disturbingly – and I thought irrelevantly – was my personal file.

The office was small and bare and immune to the high street's roar. The only thing on the wall was a white-framed and garish reproduction, of the type to be purchased from Boots, of the River Thames. To the right of the desk, in the same shiny veneer, was a sideboard; on the other side, a cupboard. At one point, when he opened this to get out a black plastic folder, I saw a tube of anti-perspirant. Apart from this – and the folder – the cupboard was bare.

'I've seen people shake in front of me, where you're sitting,' my bank manager said.

His forehead was crinkled, his suit synthetic, his tie silent. 'But, more often than not, they say it wasn't so bad.'

He begins promisingly with the admission that he doesn't actually know what attracted him to the job. 'I wasn't really arty, so when I left school at sixteen with "O" levels I thought of becoming a trainee accountant. But it only offered four pounds fifty a week at the same salary for five years. I was living in West Kensington at the time, and cutting the lawn of a neighbour one day, when she said, "Why don't you become a bank manager?" '

So the boy who caught tiddlers in the Serpentine and took them home in a powdered-milk tin, duly opted for a job with a progressive salary scale. It is a decision he sometimes regrets when he sees the accounts of his 9,000 or so private customers. Not mine, however.

How does he cope with the public perception of the bank manager? 'It's an occupational hazard,' he agrees. 'When I'm in the pub and someone finds out what I do, they say, "Oh, you don't look like a bank manager." ' I wonder idly what he wears in pubs. 'They seem to think we have a stiff collar and go on about profits and charges. They don't realise there's a business side. They think they should get more than they do – for nothing. But we're ordinary people, too, you know. We're changing away from the popular image of the bank manager. We're gradually letting the person out there know what services we offer. We've produced brochures – ' he goes to the cupboard ' – which show how we're giving a better and better service. We're in mortgages in a big way, and we're cheaper than building societies. Then, I don't know if you've heard,' he says, indicating my file for the first time, 'there's things like "Save As You Earn".'

Before joining his present central London branch, he worked in Richmond, Thames Ditton and Twickenham, where he knew most people in the community. In his present job, he deals with bigger accounts, but there are too many customers for him to know everyone. He gets a roughish idea from their cheques: 'If someone makes five hundred pounds out to William Hill, for instance.' Approximately ninety-five per cent of his accounts are private rather than business. The loans requested by the half-dozen customers he sees each day tend to be for domestic items like cars, washing machines and holidays. 'I see all sorts of characters from behind this desk. I'm good at weighing them up. It's something intuitive gained over the years. I know the trouble-some accounts.'

He talks about these, reducing them to safe stereotypes – jokes from a cracker. There was the woman who, when told she was overdrawn, sent in one of her own useless cheques to cover the amount. And a man who, also reminded of his overdraft, angrily replied that he put the names of his creditors into a hat each month and drew out whichever he would pay. (If he continued to receive such reminders, he wrote, he wouldn't bother to include the bank.) A girl cashier in Richmond, confronted by two men with sawn-off shotguns, was reported to have slumped in a faint. My bank manager laughs. 'Apparently, one said to the other, "What do we do now, Harry?" '

Contrary again to popular mythology, Harry is not the real problem. What worries banks far more is fraud. Each year they lose £26 million because of this, much of it through stolen cheque books. And what a criminal does with a stolen cheque book is trot off to Marks & Spencer.

★

'If you want money,' says an Old Etonian who works for Marks & Spencer, 'you come in with your cheque book and card, and you buy a suit for one hundred pounds. You then go straight to the refund counter, say your wife doesn't like it, and get a hundred pounds in cash.'

He is sanguine about his company's reputation among thieves. His own worry is shoplifters. 'I had to arrest a chum of mine's father – for nicking a pair of boxer shorts.' Also, a man who walked out wearing Marks & Sparks shoes and a two-piece suit under his trousers and shirt. It was for his wedding, he explained.

'The first time I dealt with a shoplifter was in a north London branch. I had only been with the company two weeks, and I really didn't know how to handle it. I saw this lady with about five M & S bags. "She looks a bit suspicious," said the sales assistant. When the lady saw me talking to her she came up and said, "I'm from head office. Would you keep an eye on those?" She then walked out of the shop into the bakery next door. Inside the bags she had dropped were thirty garments, all unpaid for. When I went into the bakery, she said, "You can't do anything to me, I've got no bags." She then set off down the street. I decided I ought to follow her, whereupon she started shouting, "This man, he's following me. I think he's trying to rape me!" So, there I was, walking five yards behind her in a pin-stripe, with all this shouting, and all the women in the street looking at me. I just prayed for the police to turn up. They did, finally, but only after I'd followed her on a bus all the way to Marble Arch.'

All high streets lead to the tight square mile of the City. There, where God met Mammon and lost – with the result that the many churches close on Sundays – are found the headquarters of banks and department stores, and other cathedrals of commerce.

Ironically, London's first lottery was held in 1569 at the west door of St Paul's. Thereafter the cathedral doubled as a thorough-fare for mules and porters carrying ale, bread and fish. 'For usurye and popereye' a contemporary witness recommended the south aisle. 'The north for simony and the horse fair.' Dung-hills accumulated in the north aisle.

At £35 per square foot, office space in the City of London is more expensive than a chunk of Southfork (which, complete with a title deed to Ewing oil, is a snip at $25). The whole place resembles an office, almost exclusively male-dominated, occupied during the day by 360,000 crisp, etiolated figures in suits, and at night by a population of 4,850 – comprising caretakers, publicans, and a Dutch vicar who lives in the church of Austen Friars.

'It's a ghost town at night,' he says, making doughnuts in the crypt where London's Dutch community have worshipped since 1550. 'You could shoot a gun and no one would bother you. When the bell rings at seven in the morning you know it's a tramp.' In his isolation, he wipes his hands and shows off a coloured slide of himself, in the same overalls, when he owned a chocolate factory near Ludlow. Then he goes back to stirring the white mixture.

'There is nothing here except for work.'

Most City workers walk to their offices from the tube or the railway station. Ken Livingstone was astonished to find that when he offered free Underground passes to British Rail season ticket holders, only one in ten took him up – 'Something like ninety per cent walked to work from Liverpool Street Station.'

With so many cars descending on London each day, and parking space for only one in every 100, driving to work in the City is particularly impossible – unless, that is, you are particularly important. The head office of the National Westminster Bank has an underground car park for such people.

Each space is allocated, but Tom sits in his little cabin and alertly watches the car park entrance through his gold-rimmed glasses. Born in Bow with ambitions to be a carpenter, he worked instead for thirty-two years in a printing firm making commercial stationery. 'When I was young, I tried to speak better,' he says, scratching his big red nose. 'But who was I going to impress? I realised, just myself.' He has sat, smartly uniformed, in this same cabin for twenty years. He refuses the distractions of a radio or a book, waiting all the while to stand up when he sees a familiar face, wave at it, and press the barrier button. 'I'm one of the old-fashioned sort,' he says proudly after a BMW has sped out. 'It may not seem like it to you, but if I do a job, I do it properly.' In twenty years, he says, very few people have tried to park here when they shouldn't have.

Up at street level, in an oatmeal building a hundred yards away, is the headquarters of one of London's top merchant banks. In a small room to the left of the grand entrance, I meet one of the bank's twenty-eight messengers, a man with a black moustache called Vic.

Vic is dressed in a kipper tie and a crisply ironed grey suit with flaring trousers, which he fills. He was born in Hackney Wick and lives in Pitsea. He is proud, of course, to have known the Krays.

It is fortunate that he has withheld this information from his employers, for his job – one he has held for sixteen years – entails taking cheques each day to the clearing banks. 'My biggest cheque,' he says impressively, stretching his leg a fraction, 'was a hundred and fifty-nine million pounds.'

Vic starts delivering at 10.30 a.m. and works through to when the banks close, which is at 3.00 p.m. in the City. 'You're like a postman, except you're dealing in millions of pounds. It's okay if you do it by three-five, three-fifteen. If it's any later, it's a three-man job to the Bank of England. I once delivered three million on a Friday, and the bank said they didn't receive it.' Evidently I do not register the implication. Vic leans forward significantly. 'The interest over that weekend was twelve hundred pounds.'

The bank paid. Had there been a stronger wind, the bank would probably have paid again the day when a cheque Vic was carrying – for a mere £2 million – blew off into a building site. He spent twenty minutes scrabbling to retrieve it. On blustery days he now carries his cheques in a leather case.

The bank is a good employer. Suits, overcoats, socks and shirts are all provided, and once a year, the messengers are given £13 a head to go to the dogs. Nor is their salary, at £14,000 a year, to be sniffed at. The biggest perk, however, is the five per cent mortgage.

Vic is eager to dispel the myth that the City at his level is full of East Enders like him. 'The messengers here are as common as mud, and from all over London. We have steelworkers, bus conductors, marines, furniture makers. Ken in the postroom has serviced cash tills all over the world. If you called them East Enders, they wouldn't mind.'

Does he envy the bankers whose cheques he carries? 'Whenever I play Monopoly with the kids and I see Park Lane etcetera, it reminds me of those people. Even the chairman's chauffeur is too smart to put his hand under the bonnet. It's nothing unusual for three of them to go out to a restaurant and have a bill for one hundred and thirty-five pounds. Then they tell me to cut some bloke's overtime by five quid. Their world revolves around money. So does ours, but when I go from here I try to switch off. I go to organise a football team, they go to meetings. I have pressure when there are thirteen or fourteen footballers and I worry who I am going to pick. That's enough for me. But they take their work home with them to those great houses they live in. If that's the pressure they're under, good luck to them. Their topic of conversation would bore me to fucking tears.'

'I don't know what they do,' says Michael, a director in the same organisation, and one of the most successful merchant bankers in the City. He is talking of the messengers. 'I suppose we use guys on motor bikes.' But, he points out, things have changed in the time he has worked there. Until twenty years ago, the secretaries were male. Legend has it that directors used to pop their heads around the door with the announcement, 'Perkins, I'm going to have my lunch now. You may go and have dinner.' When Michael first arrived a story was circulating about a clerk who wanted to leave. The man realised he could make more money delivering papers. A senior director heard this and called the clerk in to ask if it was true. It was. 'I can't believe it,' frothed the director. 'Can't you have a word with your trustees?'

We meet for a drink at Michael's club on Carlton House Terrace, SW1. It is six o'clock. With one hand he holds a glass of champagne, with the other he spears three cocktail sausages onto a toothpick. On the bar lies a copy of the London *Standard*, its front-page headline devoted to news of the Channel Tunnel go-ahead. Michael is quite pleased. His bank happens to be funding the venture.

We go through to a room hung with enormous paintings of horses. Sitting down on a squeaky leather chair, he confesses to having been caught up in a membership drive ten years ago. 'It's useful for a drink on the way home, but lunch is a bore.'

At thirty-three, but looking forty, Michael is one of the bank's youngest directors. He arrived there via the well-mapped route of Eton and Trinity College, Cambridge. 'The only thing I left out was the Guards,' he says, tipping his head back and swallowing a handful of peanuts. His silver cuff links are shaped like aircraft hangars.

His profession may have changed in the thirteen years since he joined, but not its traditions. 'Anyone can apply, but we still only send our directors to Oxford and Cambridge on a recruiting drive.' He pulls up a long black sock. 'When I joined, there were six places for two hundred applicants. Now there are ten for a thousand. If you don't have three As at "A" Level, you've had it.' Michael did not have three As, but 'Two Cs and a D and a degree in French Literature'. He also failed elementary mathematics 'O' Level, 'but got it second-time round'.

Michael decided not to apply to Warburg's merchant bank because they analysed applicants' handwriting. When he applied to Baring's, he was asked in the application form to describe himself. On the full page allowed for this, he simply attached a photograph. He was not offered a job. Nor was he offered a job by the other five banks he approached. Finally, Vic's sleepy, aristocratic bank – 'definitely not my number-one choice' – came up trumps.

After he had accepted the offer, he rang the personnel officer to ask what he should do before joining. 'Just read the *FT*,' came the reply. ' "Fine," I said, not having a clue what he was on about. I had absolutely no idea what I was letting myself in for.'

Having finished the peanuts, he rummages in his pocket. 'I opted for investment,' he says, producing and replacing a 2p. coin. 'I was given a desk and a bunch of files on the UK engineering sector, and told to get on with it. It was a pretty dud sector. I was told my best achievement would be to sell everything in the forty or fifty holdings. The job meant going round factories and having lunch with stockbrokers of fifty-five. The sort of people whose daughters I knew. And I was only twenty-one. I'd come in at nine and report on the companies, having read the *FT* first, telling how they were doing, which areas were good. The secret was to be confident of what you were saying. It was common sense predominantly, and I suppose you needed drive.'

At twenty-five Michael was moved to manage the portfolios of private clients. Then, for three years, he was posted to America. He is now in charge of business worth $8 billion. He manages clients and investments all over the world, and has sixty executives working under him.

'I'm no longer in touch with the markets, I'm thinking about new areas and how to manage people. Investment people have big egos and they're all rather aggressive.' Not that he is intimidated. 'I wouldn't hesitate to sack someone. Their cost to the company is two-and-a-half times their salary. And it's very much my arse that's on the line.' Recently he flew to Paris to sack a girl whose work apparently threatened to realign his bottom. 'She had no idea what was coming. She thought she was taking me out to lunch.'

For a banker, Michael is a late riser. 'I'm no good in the mornings,' he confesses. 'I drive the half hour from Chelsea and get in about nine-thirty. I leave the car outside the entrance and a guy drives it into the car park. He once spotted me in a traffic jam two hundred yards from the bank, so I just got out.

'There are ten people in my office. Much of the time is spent in meetings and reading papers for meetings. There's a hell of a lot of meetings. About twenty internal a week and five board meetings a month – three of which I chair. There's a business lunch every day, usually in the bank, and I'll stay till about seven or eight. Very occasionally I'll work weekends,' he says, tweaking his ear and ordering another drink. 'And can we have some more peanuts,' he asks the waiter.

Michael earns £150,000 a year. 'I could double it,' he adds swiftly. 'My salary, good as it is, is modest by comparison with some stockbrokers.'

He invests some of this money, but not in a way to inspire confidence in his clients: 'Badly, very badly. Pathetically, in fact. I've never been successful. I don't have time to follow investments. I joined Lloyd's last year as an underwriter. I joined because I thought it was a good wheeze. I must be mad. I've already paid out six hundred pounds to insure against all risks up to one hundred and ten thousand pounds.'

Michael's salary is reflected more in his clothes. His shirts cost £65 each, and he has ten suits each costing up to £800. He has, he says, 'finally made it to Savile Row'. Apart from restaurants and 'a bit of antique', the rest of the £150,000 goes on a house he rents in the country, and a house he owns in Chelsea – on which, like Vic, he has a five per cent mortgage.

By putting the firm first, Michael has everything he wants except a wife. 'Marriage is high on my agenda. Within two years I'd like to be married. I've had endless chances . . . Endless chances. But going to New York was a perfect way to stay single.

London's a massive gossip factory, quite unlike New York. Here, everyone else usually knows about something before you've even done it. New York functions more around work. You have to have a good job and, having it, you play hard. There's no time or desire to sit around saying, "Who's he or she seeing?" like so many women here with nonsense jobs.

'Read? Do I read? No. I read so much at Cambridge – an unbelievable amount. Though I was driving down to Gloucestershire the other day when the gear box smashed, and luckily there was a biography of Mountbatten in the back – and a case of champagne. I say, shall we get the bill?'

From next door comes the sound of male voices. 'Eurobond dealers,' says Michael, dismissively. 'They come here to discuss their failures and successes with tiresome regularity.' He waits for the waiter to bring change. Does he ever eat here, I ask. 'You can do, but I haven't. Not for years.' Can one sleep here? 'Yes, I think so,' he says, fiddling with his cuff links.

He pauses. 'I'm thinking of resigning, actually.'

Part Four
AT PLAY

'*People are funny,*' *she mused.* '*In London, they don't seem to object to anything.*'

BERYL BAINBRIDGE, SWEET WILLIAM, 1975

'*London is on the whole the most possible form of life.*'

HENRY JAMES, ENGLISH HOURS, 1905

'*There is a London for every man in London.*'

J.C. SQUIRE, A LONDON REVERIE, 1928

People can do anything they like in London, went Mrs Patrick Campbell's celebrated warning, so long as they don't do it in the street and frighten the horses.

Londoners do not like to do much in the street. In London, said Henry James, you must give up the idea of sitting in the open air, to eat an ice and listen to music. There is no culture of the *grande place*, a town square where the young girls stroll. Where on earth, then, do Londoners meet? V.S. Pritchett puts the answer in one of his nutshells.

> Londoners do not meet, do not gather and reject the peculiar notion that people like 'running across each other' in public places. They emphatically do not. We are full of clubs, pubs, cliques, côteries, sets . . .

The image of the club is a strong one: a place off the street, where membership confers an identity, a fraternity, a thread through the Minotaur's tunnel. It was through their billiard halls and gambling dens, like The Double R and Esmeralda's, that the Krays came to master the city. And Charles Dickens considered 'the best club in London' to be the Palace of Westminster, which attempts to control roughly the same area. Swinging in through such doors, you can wear a different uniform to that worn at home or at work; a different face.

This image of the club may be excluding, but it is not exclusive. About thirty-seven per cent of Londoners belong to some kind of club or association. And it is doubtful that the rest feel left out, for the notion of the club embraces and explains everything practised by Londoners in their free time: from the local pub to the Anglo-Argentine Society; from visits to the opera to evening

169

classes in Kurdish or corn-dolly making.

Some Londoners, however, make better use of their spare time than others. In 1973 a survey conducted by sociologists Michael Young and Peter Willmott included an interview with Mr Campbell, an assembly worker from Dagenham. He was asked what he had done the previous evening.

Mr Campbell: 'What did I do? I can't remember.'

Mrs Campbell: 'You fell asleep, that's what you did. You went to sleep at half-past six after your tea and at ten you got up off the settee and went to bed.'

Today, Mr Campbell is probably still henpecked by his wife, but he is also likely to be found slumped in front of a colour TV. The single most popular leisure activity among British men is sitting at home watching television. So concluded a survey undertaken in 1985 by the advertising agency McCormick-Publicis. Television – and video (now owned by forty per cent of Londoners) – is an important reason why the home has become a significant centre of what is known as leisure activity. Vic the messenger may expostulate that 'television's a load of shit. Frankly, if I had a licence, I'd complain,' but he still watches. On average, about twenty-four hours a week.

Dave is the young, quietly spoken editor of BBC Television's *London Plus*, a programme aimed at the London area and transmitted each night after the six o'clock news. It is a characteristic both of the BBC and of London that Dave has been recruited from Liverpool.

'I don't think I've ever met a Londoner since I've been here,' he says from an office looking over the roofs of Shepherd's Bush. 'Most people are just living here, having come from somewhere else. They have no great interest in local stories. If a rapist is loose on your patch, you're interested. If it's not your patch, forget it.' His audience sits everywhere from the wine bars of the British Film Institute to the 'modern poverty' of places like Southwark.

'There's an awful lot of grot out there. Inevitably, the inner-city boroughs dominate the news. It's where the politicians are more active. There's not so many stories from Kensington, New Malden, Putney. You don't very often hear those genteel words on *London Plus*. But on the "streets of gold" principle – bigger expectations, bigger disappointments – a big city's bound to have a great concentration of unsavoury things. Sometimes, looking down the schedule, it reads like a crime bulletin and I think, Oh, my God. We can't have any more of these Oh-what-sort-of-society-do-we-live-in stories. But if you wanted to fill a programme with just good news, what would you have?' he asks realistically. 'Royalty, I suppose. Animals. A junior genius – we'd find some three-year-old violinist. A big contract. And how Farmer Giles has found a new formula for treating wheat.' He continues to look out of the window. 'You wouldn't get twenty-three minutes out of that.'

Shortly after taking over *London Plus*, Dave decided to visit a Chiswick pub on the way home and watch Londoners watching his programme. His aim was to discover which items interested people most. He ordered a drink, and looked around the bar as the important lead story began on a television screen above the pool table. No one, however, looked up at the news of a twenty-four-hour bus strike, of a GLC lorry ban, of a call by the Bishop of Southwark for new homes to be built in London.

'Only three things stopped the pool players and made people pause over their pints,' says Dave. 'One was a story about the danger of VDU screens. There was new evidence which showed they could cause a variety of illnesses. Those with home computers or with wives who had them at work were interested.

'The next was a sports story on the boxer Charlie Magri.

'And the final item, which had them all watching, was a report on how a toucan with a broken beak had to go to the dentist.'

Angela is the duty officer at Thames Television. Each night, she sits beside a telephone in the empty staff room and answers all the calls from the London region. They concern not just the programmes for which Thames is responsible, but the whole Independent Television network. One woman for fifteen million viewers.

She has just begun her shift. She sits munching a sandwich and sipping coffee from a white polystyrene cup. Her shiny bright blue dress contrasts sharply with her dyed blonde hair and pearly necklace. Beside her flickers the screen. She used to be in the theatre, she tells me. It was good training.

'My worst night was my first night. I thought, if that's the job, they can stuff it. A man rang up to complain about the disgusting language. Even his dogs were upset, he said. In the background you could hear his wife saying, "Come off the phone, you effing bastard." ' She takes another sip. 'It's the stupidity I can't stand. A woman comes home and finds her husband and son going coo'er in front of some girls, and they can't bear it. Especially beauty competitions . . .'

The telephone rings. 'Duty officer, Good Evening. Yes, there's a lot tonight. The Rock Hudson movie . . . Yes, I know it wasn't in the *TV Times*, but it's a special. He's just died, you see . . .' She replaces the receiver. 'And so jealous. If it's a beauty show, they ring up and say, "My daughter's just as pretty." On *Sportsnight* it's the men, and how they're as strong as the wrestlers or what have you.'

Through her job, Angela is now on first-name terms with Ian Paisley and Mary Whitehouse – 'But you get all sorts. People threaten to throw themselves off bridges because they've lost their husbands. I try not to pass the buck, but why should I be responsible? They just don't want to know. The majority are complaints. Some demand to know my name because they think I'm off-hand.

'I've cried. I've cried a lot. Not very often, but I have. I had to go home one night. They think I run the programmes. They shout, "You bitch, we don't pay our licence money for . . ." Hello,' she puts her hand over the mouthpiece. 'It's my little regular. Yes, we're putting on a film about a gentleman who died yesterday. Rock Hudson. How are you keeping? Alright? Oh, really?' She starts stroking her shiny hair. 'Well, that's saved a few bob.'

After the Royal Wedding lots of people asked her out, but she declined. She prefers to keep them at the end of the telephone. 'I have a regular in a wheelchair. I give him a nice little ten minutes. I have a nutter member of the National Front. She really gets up my nose. Whenever I see a black man together with a white girl, I know she'll ring. Another little boy rings from a loony bin. He wants *Skippy the Dog*, and he's asked for it every night for a year.'

Another call. 'If you give me your number, I can phone you back. Let me get this right. You can't find *Thames Evening News* on your Oracle. And your name?'

She puts the telephone down. 'Bloody Oracle. It's nothing to do with us. It hasn't been working for nights.'

★

172

When the first telephone exchange opened in Lombard Street in 1879, there were ten subscribers. Today there are 8.5 million telephones in London. Each one of us has come to rely on the perforated mouthpiece to organise our work and play.

In London the number to dial for Directory Enquiries is 142.

'I've got the prettiest girls in this exchange,' the superintendent tells me of the Bloomsbury office. Overlooking Churchill's wartime bunker off Tottenham Court Road, the 104 pretty girls have the nastiest view.

What is more, they used to be prettier.

'You can usually tell how long people have been here,' said one. 'Your bum spreads. Six and a half hours sitting down answering four hundred calls is mentally exhausting. I never had a weight problem till I came here. I've just put on a stone.'

During the day the exchange receives 12,000 calls, all answered within fifteen seconds, the superintendent says proudly. The number of enquiries drops dramatically at night, when only forty-two staff are required to poke their plugs into the switchboard. 'It used to be all men at night – out-of-work actors. International Enquiries particularly attracted them. More glamorous, I suppose.'

There is a regular cycle of calls: 'Everyone makes them during commercials, for one thing.' On Mondays, the most popularly sought numbers are those for doctors and health centres. On Thursdays, less busy due to early closing in many areas, more people want the number of benefit offices. On Fridays, with the weekend coming up, they want railway stations. On Saturdays they want their money back. 'Saturday callers are mostly shoppers who ring from public booths to say they've lost ten or fifty p. in the slot. We call it "cowboy traffic", but the majority are incredibly honest. They usually *have* lost their money.'

More and more telephone boxes are becoming card- rather than coin-operated – to counter vandalism resulting in 5,000 smashed boxes a month.

'To begin with, I was shocked how people spoke to operators – as if they knew them,' said one girl. 'They think we can press a button and give them fifty p. Or they think you're theirs, someone just sitting in an empty office waiting for them to ring. I was also amazed at how they expected us to know what they wanted. "He's just around the corner, dear. You know, opposite the pub," they say. Or you get calls from America, for a Mr

173

George Smith – "he lives in Liverpool". The names can be quite difficult too, what with there being so many foreigners. I remember one lady rang me up to ask how to spell a Greek name. I looked it up and told her and she said, "Are you sure that's right?" Yes, I said. Why? "Well," she said, "I must know exactly because I'm about to have it tattooed on my arm." '

Emergency calls occur more often late at night, from regular locations like Soho. ('There was a man shot dead in the street yesterday, outside a shoe shop. Red lights flashed and buzzed. We thought they were testing or had gone berserk.') In the summer many 999 calls are from American tourists, who dial 9 for the operator, like at home, and then when there is no answer, dial again. On their third attempt, they find themselves put through to the emergency services.

'I once had a baby dial nine-nine-nine. Do you want the fire brigade, ambulance or police, I asked. The baby giggled. Then its mother said, "Ask the nice lady what the time is." But you still have to trace it, just to be sure.' Then she laughs. 'Once I had this normal one-four-two call, and I'm finding a number for this chap, and suddenly he's shouting desperately, "Quick, quick! Oh, no. It's just got run over!" I was so worried, I thought it was a child. In fact, it was a hedge.'

A black-haired girl from Streatham talks about some of her callers. 'I had a man who would ring up to ask me words. "What does sodomy mean," he'd say. I don't know, what does sodomy mean, I'd say. And then he'd tell me. Another chap used to ring emergency services. When you snatched up the phone he'd wait a minute, and then say, "Guess what I'm doing now." But you can usually tell if it's an obscene call because the whole section listens in. There used to be a special number people would want. We knew it as "Sally". It was a recording of a girl talking dirty. When they asked for it we'd lead them along. Who is it you're trying to ring? "Oh," they'd say, "it's my granny from King's Cross," and then you'd hear them try and talk to this recorded message.

'Sometimes you listen in, and hear blokes obviously ringing up their mistresses, and saying, "I rang this morning, but *He* answered, so I put it down." Sometimes you get regular enquiries. There's a man – Tom – who works on a building site, and rings up every lunchtime from Piccadilly tube station, and has five phones going, each with a different voice. Each one gets on your nerves. Maybe he once went out with an operator. Then there's a transvestite called Shirley. First call I ever took. "Oh, operator, I'm going to a party, and I wonder if you can tell me of any nice boutiques." He'd want to know where to buy underwear, moisturising cream and coloured eye shadow to go with his dress.'

She shakes her head disbelievingly. 'It's amazing the queries you get. Only this morning I had this bloke who wanted to speak to the Queen. "I've written to her ten times," he said, "and she hasn't replied once."

'I said she was away.'

I make an appointment by telephone with the editor of *Time Out*. Started as a so-called alternative magazine in 1968 – the year of Ronan Point and the Krays' arrest – *Time Out* provided for the children of the Sixties a guide to London's cultural underground. While its original devotees have changed their kaftans and politics for muesli and mortgages, *Time Out*, now in its eighteenth year, has become as much an institution as *Private Eye*.

For 76,000 readers every week, its contents are synonymous with London at play. Thumb through the news and features, and there are items telling you, inimitably, sometimes raucously, what to think about the latest trends. Thumb through the listings, and you are told where and when you can enjoy these trends – in worlds partitioned into Art, Books and Poetry, Cabaret, Children, Dance, Film, Food, Gay, Music, Nightlife, Radio, Sport, Television and Theatre.

The magazine offices are the fifth floor of a building situated halfway between Covent Garden and The Savoy. They are open-plan and green and hung with lights and pot plants. In the middle, at a reception desk, sits a lavishly made up girl called Geraldine. When I tell Geraldine I have an appointment with the editor, a strange expression crosses her face. I decipher this in retrospect as one of disbelief.

It is difficult to see Don Atyeo, the 35-year-old Australian who edits *Time Out*. At this, our first appointment, he materialised sheepishly from behind a pot plant in the corner, shambled across the room, and smiled charmingly. 'I'm going to have to tell you,' he said, rubbing his chubby face and scratching his mop of fair hair, 'to piss off.'

Another time was fixed, which he entered in a blank diary. Turning up again, I was sweetly told by Geraldine that he had just gone to a film. One more time was arranged. As I left home to make it, the telephone rang. It was his secretary – to cancel. 'Imagine how his wife feels,' she quipped consolingly.

Finally, an hour later than planned, we meet. He apologises for the delay. It had been a bad week. The whole magazine has been redesigned, to fit even more listings. 'We could double the size even then,' he says, trying to find a free room. 'There's just far too much going on.'

He cannot find a room, so we saunter into Covent Garden to Boswell's Coffee House. That, too, is full. We settle for a coffee in an empty café opposite.

Don is the son of the Mayor of Colac, a small town in western Victoria. After working as a cadet reporter on the *Melbourne Age*, doing the shipping round in his three-piece suit, he came to England, where he edited *IT* and appeared naked on the last issue of *Oz*. Since then he has written a book on violence in sport, and an unpublished work on success. He also stands to inherit from an uncle in Vence: a Marxist rose farmer who left Australia for the Spanish Civil War.

'When I arrived in nineteen seventy-two, *Time Out* was *The Daily Telegraph* of the underground press. It had started because newspapers ignored the whole of London at play. The rest of Fleet Street was still trundling around the Mecca ballrooms. You just couldn't imagine Milton Shulman schlepping off to the Tricycle.'

Without *Time Out*, he argues, there wouldn't be fringe theatre, cabaret, one-night clubs. 'When the magazine went on strike for a year, fringe theatre collapsed. Now the underground has gone overground. *Time Out* journalists have joined Fleet Street, and Fleet Street covers events that were unthinkable even five years ago.'

While admitting that he is not a user of the magazine – 'at thirty-five I don't need to pay seventy-five p. to be told what to do with my life' – Don stresses that it reflects only a percentage of what is happening in London. 'London has the best entertainment in the world. There's more going on here than anywhere else. *Village Voice* in New York carries a tenth of what we carry. *Pariscope* in Paris just has films and television.'

He isolates the centres of entertainment. 'The West End is really where everything happens – the theatres, the films, the clubs, the restaurants. Covent Garden is less fashionable, in that it's very commercial, and deals more with style and designer clothes. There are pockets in the East End – mainly galleries. But then again, no one reads *Time Out* in the East End. We never sell copies there. South of the river's dead too. There's no spill–over of business into restaurants.'

He flicks through the latest edition of his magazine to see what has changed in eighteen years. 'Agitprop,' he says. 'That section's a bit of a hangover. It's the demonstration of the week. Politics and entertainment are no longer linked. Rock is less political, record sales have dropped off, and there are a smaller number of Gigs. Wembley used to be packed week after week with The Stones, The Who, Bruce Springsteen. Today, Bruce Springsteen comes once every two years. Now it's issue politics like Greenpeace or local radio, not party politics . . . Cabaret. Well, as I say,' he says, loitering over Fiasco Job Job and their show *Seven Kilos of Wisdom,* 'we invented cabaret and fringe theatre . . . Children. We're still investigating children. The average age of the readership is dropping all the time. It used to be twenty-seven, now it's twenty-three. At my end there's a loyal plateau of thirty-two-year-olds, but it falls off dramatically after thirty-five . . .

'Food. That's an extraordinary change. When I first came, *Time Out* was worried that restaurants smacked too much of consumerism. Journalists might have meals on expenses, but could anyone else afford to go out? When we ran a survey asking what we should cover more, the top desire was restaurants. Our restaurant guide, which comes out twice a year, sells out its forty-five thousand immediately. Eating has become more important than going to films. The idea of a night out to eat has really caught on. The young have become junior gourmets. Before, they would wolf down a hamburger after the cinema. Now you see kids in sneakers drinking American beer, and sitting for hours at a table.'

Don returns to the contents page. 'Nightlife. That section describes the discos and clubs. Everywhere you look the club scene is booming. It changes so quickly, like a mirage. And you have everything from the Camden Palace, to an illegal one-night club in a derelict garage – with bin-liners hung from the rafters, a ghetto-blaster on the table, and beer with a fifty per cent surcharge. Boy George came up through the club scene, but often the pop groups are an accident. They *become* pop stars, they are not

177

manufactured as such. Pink Floyd grew out of the hippies. Punk was an afterthought, too.'

He points at the photograph on the contents page. It shows a man in a green velvet dress, with hair plaited into green worms that trickle down his forehead. He wears black lipstick on his top lip and heavy rouge. He looks like a balding, androgynous Medusa. On catching sight of this creature, however, it is probably Medusa who would turn to stone.

'George,' Don says. 'He does look extraordinary, but that's the great thing about London – anything is accepted, whether you're punk, Mohican or bald. You look at this guy,' he taps George below the knee. 'You meet him at a party,' he threatens, 'and you think you can't relate. Let's face it, you're not going to ask what he thinks about the weather, are you?' I try to nod but whimper. 'Then you listen to his conversation with four girls who look like *that*.' He indicates another photograph. 'Invariably they're saying, "An' then 'e saw me . . ." or "Didn't 'e 'ave a nice pullover!" or "What d'ya think of me beehive?" ' Don leans back and folds his arms. 'You could be in the Mecca ballroom,' he says. 'People haven't changed at all. What's more, no one gives a damn. When other cities try to imitate this, it looks plastic and self-conscious because it's not rooted. That's the reason what happens here is transplanted all over the world. There's London's influence all over the fucking world.'

Don's belief in the Londoner as gourmet would bring many a belch of disbelief from beyond the grave. Charles Moritz on his travels in 1782 spoke for generations of foreign visitors: 'An English dinner is half-boiled or half-roasted meat and a few cabbage leaves boiled in plain water on which they pour a sauce made of flour and butter.' Squire Bramble in Tobias Smollett's *The Expedition of Humphry Clinker* (1771) was even more indignant:

> The bread I eat in London is a deleterious paste, mixed up with chalk, alum and bone-ashes; insipid to the taste and destructive to the constitution . . . Perhaps you will hardly believe they can be so mad as to boil their greens with brass halfpence, in order to improve their colour; and yet nothing is more true.

As for the fish, it was enough to turn a Dutchman's stomach.

At Play

The advent of the package tour, and with it the discovery of Moritz's infinitely better kitchen, has created a palate for foreign foods – as well as a willingness to exploit stores already catering for expatriate communities. With the Poles, for instance, came the delicatessens. (Unable to stomach English bread and sausages, disbanded soldiers got together after the War to make their own bread and salami, which they then dispensed from mobile vans.) With the Italians came espresso coffee.

For twenty-one years, Alvaro has worked as a waiter at Sweetings restaurant in the City, a lunchtime bolt-hole for merchant bankers like Michael. It has sawdust on the mosaic floor, a fan on the ceiling, and a lot of men in three-piece suits who sit guffawing on stools over glasses of chablis.

'I come from southern Italy. There were very little jobs. The only job was building and carrying heavy things. I was not tough enough. I wrote three letters and went to Jersey as a waiter. Then in 'sixty-two to Park Lane Hotel. The others were mostly Greeks. They didn't like me very much. Maybe I was better than they. Then I went to Bracknell near Windsor in 'sixty-four. I like much better. The Etonians, you know. They like me because I used to be funny with them. And they have followed me here, too, some of them.

'I get here at eight. I send away the dirty tablecloths to the laundry and I order the wine. At eleven-thirty, when the restaurant opens, I open the wine. Last week one customer spent two hundred pounds – just on drink. Some people drink chablis, one of the strongest wines, a bottle each, and before that a beer. After that, three or four large ports and I ask them if they going to take the day off, and they say, No, they go back to work. They talk about millions, millions, millions. I just work away at forty-eight pounds a week and tips. It's not very nice listening to them. Then they say, Get the bill only for the food. This bill, they get their boss to pay.

'The kitchen closes at three and I stay till seven or eight o'clock because they have a drink, and I have a drink, and I go home late. And then the wife shouts at me and I go to bed. My boss, he not drink. Maybe he have no problems with his wife . . .

'When I need a pair of shoes or to buy glasses, then I go to work weekends. I used to go to the football till a tin split my face, but now we only go out to dinner. There are no restaurants in Fulham where I live. Do I go south of the river? No, I never been there.

179

Maybe once, I can't remember. I once went to France, but I didn't like the food. The veal chops were tough. When I eat out I never eat in an Italian place because all the staff are Portuguese, and they talk to me, and I speak Italian and they don't know what I mean. They give pork instead of veal, smashed down and cooked with breadcrumbs – or the dish of the day. They go and change the name every day until they sell it. Very rarely must you believe when it say "recommended". And steak – if it say fillet, they give rump. If rump, they give entrecote. And if the fish start going off, they wash with water and fresh lemon. They never fry because it smell. They cook it in lemon sauce, which takes all the smell away.

'Italians is spilled everywhere, but people they got a few bob, they go back to Italy. If someone asks me if I'm British or Italian, I say I'm a Londoner. I'm a Londoner more than anybody else. Everything's beautiful here, and who make the city nice is the people.'

'I feel a Londoner,' echoes an Indian restaurant owner called Bill. He comes from south India via Guyana, and runs a curry house off the Earl's Court Road. He is the youngest of a large family and has a fat belly belted with gold, a golder watch, and a loud laugh.

'My parents died so I have no roots, though you feel lonely when you first come here. I read the *Mirror* then, now I read the *Express*. Tell me, is it true it's owned by the communists? I go for holidays to north Italy, and every year I like going to the Derby because my family used to own racehorses in Guyana. I only have Mondays off, then I sleep in and have a big cooked breakfast, go to the movies, drink a bottle of ten-years-old claret. I like eating out in Spanish and Italian restaurants. When I shop for my restaurant I have to learn the swearwords. How much is that cauliflower, I ask. "You've just stepped off a banana boat, you bugger. It's two hundred pounds." "No, it's not, you bastard, and I've done no such thing. I'll give you one-fifty." ' He laughs. 'When people tease me about my colour, I shout, You pay money to go like this!'

From colour to creed.

Zelik's is a small Jewish restaurant off Golders Green. Every man in the small, full room has thick glasses and a skull cap: blue, red or black. One old man even wears a cap under his trilby. The women, with short black curly hair, are prettier. Beneath their eyes they have thin, bright strips of make-up; on their ears, loud metal jewellery. A brass fan whirls unsteadily over blue table-cloths. On the wall is a map of Israel.

Rising with the steam from the cups of mint tea is the sense of a shared secret, exposing anyone not Jewish. For a moment it is a surprise to hear anyone speak English. A man in a grey suit peers at me, rises from his table and comes near. 'Haven't I seen you somewhere before? With X, my election manager in Winchester?'

I have never set eyes on the man. But how typical of London that one perfect stranger should approach another, make such a mistake, and from it salvage a shared acquaintance: 'X' had been the bursar at my school, where I had been a contemporary of his son. This man, a Euro-MP, was merely plying his politician's patter. He returned to his table and his large wife and began waving at other people eating around him.

Doubtless he recognised them as well.

It has been said that to be a member of The Beefsteak, you need to be a relative of God – 'and a damned close relative at that'. This exclusive dining club has premises in a single room above a shop off Leicester Square. Its members comprise aristocrats, politicians, actors and writers; its steward and waiters are all known as Charles. At the long table, stretching under the timbers of a mock-Elizabethan hall, the members have to take their places in the order of their arrival. On occasions, this custom has led to the bizarre sight of groups perambulating aimlessly outside, having spotted a notorious bore ascend the stairs before them. Once at table, it is left to each member's discretion to account to Charles for the wine he consumes. Honesty prevails. Once, when some-one claimed an unlikely amount, a stage whisper came from the queue behind: 'A man who cheats his club cheats at life.'

Tonight the writer and broadcaster Ludovic Kennedy sits at the head of the table. Discussion ranges from the proposed title of his autobiography – he is keen on 'A Warm Pair of Hands', while the member to his left suggests 'Knock Twice and Ask for Susie' – to the short lifespan of game birds. The Duke of Atholl laments there are no grouse this year. Someone wonders why parrots live so much longer. 'I once shot a parrot,' says Ludovic Kennedy. The jaw drops on the Duke of Atholl, owner of the only private army in Britain. 'It was getting dark,' Kennedy continues, 'and this little thing came over which I thought was a wood pigeon. I was so proud. It turned out to be the pet of some old girl in the village which had escaped the week before. Apparently,' he pours himself some more club claret, 'they're very good to eat.'

The best-known London clubs run off the streets around St James's. In each of their lobbies, under the marble busts of long-haired noblemen, a telex machine chatters, printing out the latest news of the world and its financial markets. Rarely will you see anyone take advantage of this information, but it is a way of making members of these twenty or so clubs feel they have a finger on the pulse of the twentieth century – rather than a hand in the crotch of the eighteenth.

These grand buildings include Henry James' club, The Reform – where Turgenev, who had such an influence on his life and art, also ate baked beans; The Athenaeum – principally the haunt of eminent clergymen; The Carlton – for Conservatives; and Brooks's, which enjoys a reputation for its backgammon table. According to Horace Walpole, 'a thousand meadows and corn-fields were staked at every throw'. The great, but profligate, eighteenth-century Whig statesman, Charles James Fox, lost so much he had to borrow from the waiters.

Danny is a waiter at Brooks's. 'I used to work at The United Services Club,' he tells me in his fast Irish voice. 'The best club I ever worked in. I came over from Belfast at the end of the War and worked there for twenty-seven years. I was too young for a pension and they gave me one hundred and fifty pounds. One chap was a Colonel Lynch. He had a room in Hammersmith and used to eat a bowl of soup. For second course he'd have a plate of vegetables, and complain if he didn't get enough. I used to catch him putting the packets of Ryvita into a napkin, and then, after I'd gone out of the room, into his pocket. When he died he left two hundred and eighty thousand pounds – none of it to me.'

Danny smiles, and looks around the dining room where some fifteen members are eating. 'It's like a morgue in here now. A lot of people have left or died – not surprising really, considering the food . . . I say to the three waitresses, That's Sir Christopher over there, he's quite nice. Lord Such-and-such, he's okay really, but watch out for that crusty bugger in the corner.'

He helps translate the menu. 'I wouldn't have the hors

d'oeuvres or the grouse unless you want to wait half an hour. And we've had a lot of trouble with the whitebait. *And* the sole. Remember that man who was sitting by himself at the table in the corner? He hates me, and I have no great liking for him. I shouldn't have served him the first course so quick. He asked for sole and it took thirty-five minutes, and I had to wait in the next room in case he saw me. When it finally came, he said, "This is bloody disgusting," and left . . .'

For those who have neither the funds, nor the contacts, nor the desire to join a club like Brooks's, there is always the local pub. 'There is nothing which has yet been contrived by man by which so much happiness is produced as a good tavern or inn,' said Dr Johnson in a famously clumsy mood. He even turned a room at The Essex Head into a club that met three times a week. (Absentees were fined 3d.)

In 1831 there was one London pub to every 168 people. Today the ratio is one to 600. And, since the proliferation of the off-licence and the supermarket, fifty-nine per cent of Londoners do not bother to visit these places at all. Les, the Fulham postman, is symptomatic of this decline: 'A pint of beer in the boozer is one pound eight,' he declares. 'The same pint from the shop is bloody sixty-seven p. Why should I pay fifty pence just to stand next to you? No, squire, I'm a home-pigeon now.'

As more and more Londoners become 'home-pigeons', the brewers try to revitalise this great British institution. The barriers dividing class from class, the saloon from the public revellers, are coming down – to be replaced by the trappings and attitudes of the wine bar. Food is now a necessary part of the pub scene. So too is music, which makes many of these premises indistinguishable from clubs.

A full moon in Tooting. It coincides with the feast of Christmas in the old calendar – the exact time for a Black Mass. (At St Pancras Old Church crowbars have been used to remove a tabernacle containing about thirty consecrated wafers from behind the altar. 'We are absolutely convinced this is the work of Satanists,' foams the parish priest.)

In Tooting I go to a pub for the wake of an Irish labourer who died one month before when a ditch collapsed on him. Members of his community have gathered to give a benefit night for his widow, who remains absent. There is a signed picture of a thin boxer – the current world featherweight champion – and several posters of a smiling pop star called Lee Lynch. In a separate room, which requires tickets for entry, is the man himself, singing with a moony unfocused smile into a very loud microphone. He has a red paper napkin in the pocket of his wide blazer, thin black trousers, and a back-up group reminiscent of the Welsh orchestra in Evelyn Waugh's *Decline and Fall*.

'It's now or never,' he sings. A man in a leather jacket with long hair and white shoes slouches up with a plastic bag. This is Lee's manager. Lee snatches a silent but heated conversation with him before returning to the mike.

'Sha-la-la-la, sha-la-la-la,' comes his tremulous chant. It is, out of keeping with the environment and the words, a beautiful voice.

The manager slinks away with his plastic bag, which contains copies of Lee's greatest hits. 'Well, here it is,' proclaims the blurb on the back, 'the best of Lee Lynch. One of the most talented Irish entertainers in Britain.' One who had also, it appears, seen better days:

> Lee's proudest moment was back in 1974 when he was chosen to represent his native Ireland in an international song contest in Bulgaria. 'The old knees were knocking a bit,' he confides . . . 'You never stop learning in this business,' Lee admits, 'and I've been luckier than most and managed to keep going when times got tough.' And times were never tougher than in August 1976 when he collapsed on stage struck down by the rare and fatal illness Addison's Disease. But they make 'em tough in Galway, and three short months later the big fella from Ballinasloe was back singing and writing better songs than ever.

These he sings, in his beautiful voice, with his distant smile, looking over the heads of the packed room. It is a far cry from his Iron Curtain appearance before 50 million people. Many of his audience tonight are psychiatric outpatients from the local hospital.

'The sea, the sea, thank God we're surrounded by water . . .'

A fan circles above the mock panelling and Lee stands down for a waltz. It is the sign for starchy middle-aged women to rise from tables surrounding the floor and stiffly stagger out their dance-steps. One remains resolutely seated. A blonde in an electric red boiler suit, she has a distinguished, proud, scornful air.

When the waltz ends, the space clears. A little figure then takes to the floor. Smiling, she hops alone on the red parquet in gym shoes. She looks like a girl. In fact, she is a woman of forty. A man from Clare, worse for drink, but perhaps out of duty, invites her to dance. She refuses. Alone on the red square, her hands behind her yellow jersey, she hops her solitary, smiling jig.

Rock-and-roll music follows. An ugly woman in black with a gold belt gyrates vigorously. Her dance has a limited number of movements, which she repeats, her cropped head jerking back and forth, her legs moving in a crude stamp. Every now and then, her partner, the drunkard, collapses against her.

'Then spring became summer, who would believe you would come . . .'

Opposite, Lee's manager is dispensing records from his plastic bag. In another corner a man is selling raffle tickets for a packet of cigarettes: 10p. a ticket. He is known as Paddy Two-Strings, after the strings supporting his trousers and belting his coat.

On stage Lee strokes his hand up and down the black microphone lead. The drunkard performs a mime in front of him, convulsing in imitation of the rock-and-roll stars he has seen on television. Lee laughs, points at him, and lowers his smile into the room. 'We went to school together and you wonder how I turned out the way I did.'

He finishes with a 'softy', slipping into a meaningful quaver.

He completes the song. 'When the lights go down in London, Paddy's on the move again. Tonight's my last night in London . . . Come on, everybody on the floor.' He wipes his face and turns to adjust the volume on the amplifier. The hall stirs with dancing figures, among them the woman in the red boiler suit. She has her arms around the drunkard from Clare.

'Ireland,' breathes someone at the next table. 'Where men are men, and sheep are frightened.'

Today, if Dr Johnson were to stalk his old stews, or if Chaucer wandered into the Southwark tavern from where his pilgrims trotted forth, it is more than likely they would find themselves quaffing lager in a gay pub.

Growing up alongside the nightclubs of the twenties and thirties came a network of these bars and pubs. The affinity between gay men and the theatre – even in the 1870s many of the Haymarket's prostitutes were in fact transvestites – led to the best-known being situated in the West End.

Until recently, the most famous of these pubs was The Salisbury in St Martin's Lane. To walk in there was to step back into the world of Joseph Losey's *Victim*, made in 1961. Crowded at the Victorian baroque bar would be a mixture of young and old, Londoners and tourists. At lunchtime, theatre people would congregate, their theatricality of dress and manner matching the red plush and bronze art nouveau of the decor. Those without work to do in the afternoon might meet casually, talk, and disappear together. The slang they used – Parlare – was old Romany, and employed as a safe code of recognition in an age when homosexuals had to survive extreme prejudice.

Until fifteen years ago, gay life in London remained a clearly defined ghetto. Recently, much of the pub's trade has moved across the road to a new bar called The Brief Encounter. The contrast is telling. In essence it is no different from any other cocktail-cum-wine-bar, with food served downstairs and Hockney prints on the pale grey walls. However, the atmosphere is quite different. The men and women who use it are young and indistinguishable in dress and manner from most people of their age in the streets. The tone of voice and manner they use is sometimes revealing, but not always. Clothes, hairstyles and appearances are so flexible and open to interpretation now as to preclude stereotypes. There is also less emphasis on the casual meeting, pick-up or planned assignation. 'The bar is not so much a friendly oasis in a desert as a continuation of Covent Garden.'

The speaker, Steven, is a thirty-year-old gay in the academic world. 'Covent Garden and the King's Road seem to answer some of the questions as to why this change has come about,' he says. 'The sixties changed gay life in Britain. The Wolfenden Report in 1967 and the subsequent legalisation of sex between consenting male adults completely transformed men's lives. Women of course had never been legislated against. It is said because Queen Victoria didn't know about lesbianism, and no one dared to tell her.

'The colour, flamboyance and ambiguous style of many rock musicians derived from gay life and the theatre. In the late sixties the idea of outward masculinity was undermined, and the dilemma of an effeminate homosexual such as Quentin Crisp was eased. He now blended into the fashionable crowd. After the riots in San Francisco, which created the Gay Liberation Movement, politicisation of gay life followed in the seventies. A new seriousness entered the consciousness of being a homosexual. Which brings me to today, and to the process by which gays have become more rather than less like their neighbours in London. Uniforms have become unnecessary, except by choice as an indicator of sexual specialisation, and "straight" clothes have become similar in style to "gay" clothes. The content of the high street shop window, say Next or Woodhouse, is the staple of social dress for all. So you can't spot them in the street.

'Is this, you ask, an international plot, devised by gay marketing men to enable their takeover of London? No, but it does to some extent reflect an awareness of a powerful gay buying force, the so-called Pink Economy which underpins *GQ*, *L'Uomo Vogue*, even *House and Garden*, *Interiors*, etcetera. Two disposable incomes under one roof, and no school fees or toys to buy – an ad agent's dream, in fact. Just consider the average sales pitch in a TV commercial for a new razor. The high-tech styling and dramatic effects appeal to that theatricality which is still inherent in many gay men. The strong-jawed blond who luxuriates in his new razor presents the audience with a jaw to dream of – and not just for the girl who might buy it for her man. That rippling pectoral in the sunset is on target for another consumer as well.

'How does this relate to gay people in London? Well, certainly many gay men have a highly consumerist approach to life. Many gay couples have a need to express their united life through shared possessions, since the conventional bonds of family are impossible. At its worst, these relationships suffer from the cheeseboard-and-table-lamp syndrome, visible every Saturday in Habitat on the King's Road, where you can see laden pairs of men carrying off the durables which will probably outlast the affair they are intended to underpin. A better face of this preoccupation is found among the many gays involved in design – fulfilling themselves by the environment created around them.'

It is in their social lives, argues Steven, that exclusivity still exists. Gays continue to spend more time in single-sex groups – both in bars and, even more popularly, in clubs.

He takes me under the arches of Charing Cross, to the most

successful gay club in London. 'Until the crisis of AIDS,' he says, paying the £3 entry, 'the avowed intent of most people going into a gay club was to pick up someone to sleep with.'

Heaven is an American-style club, initially very Californian. This altered a year or two ago when the tanned beach-boy waiters, in their white vests and blue satin shorts, were replaced by cropped youths in T-shirts and braces.

The first striking thing about Heaven is its atmosphere of restraint, of domesticity almost. Teeming with well-dressed men, who drink a mixture of orangeade and lemonade, or beer, it is devoid of the single quality one expects – predatoriness. Steven leads me to a gallery overlooking the dance floor, over which an elaborate complex of lights, lasers, and revolving silver spheres flickers, flashes and descends.

Below, about a hundred men are dancing, some with each other, others alone. They resemble plants in the water, waving back and forth with the current. In one corner a young man in spectacles awkwardly prances, a jersey over his red lumberjack shirt. Nearby is a Filipino in leather calf-boots and white shorts. There seems no common factor of dress or manner, but practically everyone has a moustache. One, naked to his hairy chest, jerks extravagantly, angling his narrow smile, his dark eyes and his bald head at a diminutive partner. He is the only dancer obviously on display. 'There's only one beautiful child and every mother has it,' says a man in a suit leaning on the rail next to me.

'The herd instinct applies,' Steven explains. 'It's all done by eye contact. The less fortunate the vibrations given off by someone, the more that person will be cold-shouldered – rather as animals shun the sick ones in their group.'

The ceiling lights descend and Steven leans over the rail to describe a few actors lit up fluorescently on the stage below. 'Eddie,' he begins . . .

Eddie is small, attractive and twenty, which means he is in effect illegal as an active homosexual. He was born in Newcastle, which he left at sixteen to find a job in London. In his second week in Earl's Court, he met a hairdresser called Peter. Peter invited him to move in, and they lived together for three years. Peter, like Eddie, was from a working-class background. You would only have recognised him as gay from his profession, and his extravagantly streaked hair. Eddie, with his Geordie accent and unremarkable clothes, you would have difficulty in placing. Until last year they shared a lifestyle of parties, clubs and holidays in Tenerife and Mikonos. Then Peter met another boy, who worked in the record business. Eddie lives now in the YMCA. He has no social life other than that provided by public places like Heaven or the Copa in Earl's Court. His camaraderie with the few close friends he has met here may eventually lead to meeting someone with whom he sets up home. It will be a home much like that with the wife he would have undoubtedly married in Newcastle, had he been born twenty years sooner.

Edward.

Edward is twenty-seven, extremely good-looking, and knows it. He was educated at public school and Oxford. He now works for a Bond Street art dealer. He was previously the PA to a gay business man. Most of his friends know he is gay. The mothers of the girls whose dances he goes to do not. Some of the girls do, and are amused but indifferent. Others suspect, but hope he might be converted. He might be seen occasionally also at The Gardens, above High Street Kensington, where preppy young men feel at home in blazers and khaki trousers. He shares a house in Hammersmith with four other people, none of whom is gay. His holidays are spent in friends' houses abroad. His relationships are infrequent, and since AIDS his casual encounters are nil. His future is uncertain. He might settle for sharing his life with another man from his own social world, but he is less likely than he would have been fifteen years ago to marry. He is extremely popular with older men, and is also useful as an extra man for dinner, or similar occasions. In the final analysis, Edward's life as a single man is preferable.

David.

David is a 45-year-old barrister. He is tall, slightly greying, and has perfect manners. His appearance is smooth and masculine. Many of his friends smile at his conviction that no one can tell he is gay. This is a hangover from the era when to be so was to be a screaming queen. In fact, David has not really registered the changes in society, and he hovers between the old and new worlds of gay life. His flat in South Kensington is decorated in the manner of Colefax and Fowler. It was done by his last boyfriend, ten years his junior, who left him six years ago. David first knew gay life in London in the mid-sixties. Through an actor friend from Oxford he went to some memorable parties, most of which he left early and alone. He then lived for a number of years with an American lawyer twice his age. That ended when the lawyer returned to the States.

David is to be found every Sunday at All Saints, Margaret Street, the High Church centre of Anglican high camp. In his pinstripes and starched collar he is a little seedy. However, nothing is more embarrassing than to meet him in The Queen's Head on a weekday evening in consciously 'casual' clothes, making heavy weather of a conversation with a boy who clearly is not interested in his advances. If he is persuaded to go to a club, he dances with the concentration of one drying his back very thoroughly with a bath towel. His income enables him to live as he chooses. He entertains a great deal, but keeps his gay and straight friends carefully apart. David is lonely, but resigned to this, for he will never lose the basic fear of illegality with which he grew up.

Rupert and Patrick.

Everyone has heard of Rupert. His plays were highly successful in the fifties, and his critical articles are always worth catching in the Sunday papers: both for his wit, which is sharp, and his style, which is highly personal. The years have not been kind to him. He is tall, but bulky now. The strong features which have been on and off the television for twenty years are weakened by late nights and drink. There is seldom a literary party at which he is not found, red-faced and anecdotal in the corner. He is frankly 'queer', a word used by all his set in the fifties and sixties without any sense of prejudice. However, Patrick will not be at his side at these parties, and it suits Rupert to keep it that way.

They met in a pub in 1964. Patrick, twelve years his junior, was slim, fair and camp. Rupert took him home, to the untidy flat he then rented in Bayswater. The physical pleasure Rupert and Patrick both derived from the encounter led, in Patrick's case, to a deep emotional involvement, while Rupert, surprised by the turn of events, was pleased to find someone prepared to tidy up after him. He is a male chauvinist pig at heart. Patrick, conveniently, is one of nature's housewives. Patrick collects Victoriana and art deco – or did when these things could be had for pennies in the Portobello Road. The house they share in Chelsea is cluttered with objects that are beautiful without being valuable. They have a number of gay friends, but Rupert does not enjoy entertaining them on gay terms. A famous theatrical knight, he is welcomed with his lover as a couple – but only when diluted with male and female company. Rupert's attitude to homosexuality remains unchanged since the Wolfenden Report, which he happily alludes to as 'The Bugger's Charter'. Patrick is slightly wistful for what he sees as the modern romance of gay life. This is a generalised wistfulness only, usually emerging when a Bette Davis film is on television, or when he has re-read his favourite Daphne du Maurier.

Paul, or Poodle to his friends.

Poodle is a survivor from the great age of gay life. When Oliver Messel, the stage designer, and his rival, Cecil Beaton, were weaving their social webs in Pelham Crescent, Poodle was there – as well known to a côterie of art historians and socialites as any of his hosts, but less celebrated generally in the media. Since the others are dead, Poodle has now come into his own, and successions of young men queue to extract recollections of those halcyon days. London remains Poodle's oyster, and he wheels himself ruthlessly out to all and any social event, as likely to be found at a Buckingham Palace garden party as the latest gay night spot. His own parties are famous, attended by celebrities as varied as Diana Vreeland and Norman St John Stevas, and liberally scattered with titles. Poodle thinks the whole business of 'liberation' in the seventies was a bore. He loves, however, the new emphasis on *style*. Having withdrawn gracefully from the sexual field, he regards homosexuality as almost socially irrelevant. He is lucky that he is old enough and grand enough to do as he likes.

'From Poodle's point of view,' says Steven, summing up, 'one might conclude that being gay in London is no longer a separate issue. But sexuality, like social cachet, depends on where you are to start with. Sex breaks down social barriers, yet desire is often informed by social standing. As long as gay people fantasize about truck drivers, it is more than likely that they are actually "getting off" on the barriers they claim to transcend.'

Time Out devotes two pages to a gay section, listing the week's events in pubs, clubs and workshops. It devotes much more space, however, to the classified ads at the back, and to the listing of Lonely Hearts.

My conversation with the editor took place in the week he was preparing a Valentine issue. It was to include page after page of personal columns.

'London may be the city with the most going on, but it is also the loneliest city. We reflect that loneliness,' he said. 'We list so much that it seems you couldn't fail to have a good time. Yet it's very difficult to connect in this city – the lousy weather, the English reserve. In New York, you sit at a bar and someone will talk to you. In London, after two years, you may still be sitting alone at the bar, through no fault of your own. Unless you can slot yourself into a way of thinking, rather than a physical circuit into which you can be connected, you will be bitterly disappointed. Everything happens behind closed doors.'

The myth of the closed door is as common as the village myth.

'It's horrid being lonely. Really, really horrid,' said a 65-year-old woman on the telephone. 'You feel lost, you feel inadequate, you feel nobody wants you.' Her husband had died a while ago and she lived alone. She wanted an address for a magazine called *Singles*.

When I asked what she did, she told me she was a London guide.

In 1852 the Russian emigré and revolutionary thinker Alexander Herzen described this sense of purdah in his memoirs:

> There is no town in the world which is more adapted for training one away from people and training into solitude than London. The manner of life, the distances, the climate, the very multitude of the population in which personality vanishes, all this together with the absence of Continental diversions conduces to the same effect.

Everyone enjoys reading a Lonely Hearts column. Almost everyone has an image of it as a refuge for the weird and socially inadequate. Yet, looking at those who advertise, this image is increasingly far from the truth. With a divorce rate that has risen 600 per cent over the last twenty-five years, there are 14.5 million single people in Britain today. More single people, in fact, than trades unionists.

In December 1818, giving as his address the *poste restante* in Paris, Count Sarsfield, Lord Lucan, descendant of the royal families of Lorraine and Capet, placed a notice in the Continental journal *Galignani's Messenger*. In it he announced his wish 'to contract an alliance with a lady capable from her rank and talents of supporting the dignity and titles which an alliance so honourable would confer on her'.

The author of an advertisement in today's personal columns may be less keen to identify himself, but there is no shortage of blue blood behind the box numbers. Each month in *The Tatler*, nuzzling against Missing Pets and Yacht Charter, can be found a selection of company chairmen, upper-class widows and erstwhile Sloanes in search of 'genuine relationships', or, failing that, a 'gentleman with title'. Education is as much a requirement as class.

In America, where such ads are franker, *The New York Review of Books* allows a whole page for people who may not read the paper, but who would like to meet those who do. Abbreviations like SWJF denote a Single White Jewish Female, leaving room for what has been coined 'erotic esperanto'. Sometimes, as in the following ad from *The Village Voice*, it reads more like double dutch: 'You notice me sitting alone, my long dark blonde hair tumbled forward as I pore over Gogol or *The Wall Street Journal* . . . You're curious to know me, but thinking of your herpes, hesitate.'

Lonely Londoners have not yet reached this level of self-mockery. They take the process a lot more seriously, as a readership survey in *Singles* illustrates. Aimed specifically at lonely hearts, *Singles* is a glossily printed monthly magazine which consists of some fifty pages of personal ads. In canvassing its 19,000 readers, the survey concluded that the average female was a confident divorcee with children and her own home, who was looking for a long-term relationship with a 'professional' man. The average man was a shy non-smoker of thirty to thirty-eight who was seeking a physically 'attractive' partner. There were a lot of men under twenty-five and a lot of women over fifty. A quarter of all men and women were graduates.

According to *Singles*' research, by far the loneliest profession for men is engineering. The most gregarious career turns out to be that of a golf professional. Nurses and secretaries top the female scale. At the bottom, oddly enough, comes engineering.

John Patterson, the bashful power behind the scenes, is responsible as well for the computer-dating agency, Dateline. He is also an engineering graduate.

'*Singles* attracts many middle- and upper-middle-class people,' he explains in his Kensington office. From downstairs comes the disconcerting hum of the computer, pairing off Tricia with Rodney, Violet with Harry, but never Dave with Basil. Loneliness is strictly a heterosexual business in Abingdon Road.

'Typically, they've been thrown out of one environment into another. They have been brought up, say, in the country, educated at a public school somewhere else, gone on to university elsewhere, built up a career and lifestyle in yet another place, and then come to London. Consequently, they find it hard to make new friends. Nice girls don't hang around in pubs, do they? What we do is give people an opportunity of meeting. It's all good fun.'

'Good fun' is Patterson's catchword. He repeats it unconvincingly, as if he has not yet found quite the right phrase. Not finding the right phrase, he repeats it again.

I ring up some of the men and women behind the box numbers.

> Dulwich Village Lady. Slim, smart, sincere, 40, loves to laugh. Enjoys home, music, theatre, wining, dining, squash, many other interests. One son at prep school. Busy professional life, but missing friendship of mature gentleman.

Her husband, a successful businessman, has walked off with a 22-year-old blonde. Not looking for a husband now, but for 'a male friend', she has advertised like this because she feels in control. She also feels sick of her Dulwich friends trying to match-make at dinner parties and then bumping into her saying, 'How's it going?' She has received twenty replies, including one from Guernsey and one from Scotland: 'Very dull, very pleasant letters from what I would call professional types.' Five were from university lecturers. 'I don't know what university lecturers get up to,' she says.

Her standards are high. She works as a public relations adviser to an international company. 'And as the former wife of a very successful chartered accountant, I'm not going to live in a garret with an artist.' She met five for a drink in The Hilton or The Ritz. 'The way you meet almost precludes having an instant rapport. You know you're there to see if you are going to get on.' She had not got on. They were as dull as their letters suggested. What would her husband think? 'He'd kill himself laughing,' she says.

I ring a lively but responsible graduate divorcee mother of fifty-four, who wants to share a purposeful life with a thoughtful professional man, preferably Oxbridge. She turns out to be well-off, with two children currently at Oxford, but finding it impossible to come across like-minded men – 'fairly academic with a family'. When her marriage broke up she had just qualified as a marriage guidance counsellor.

Over a hundred men answered her ad. A lot were Old Etonians; a lot more were not. This was reflected in the photocopied paper – 'as if some people make an occupation of this'. Some of the letters sounded promising. 'Then you speak on the 'phone and you can't believe it's the same person.'

She has seen three. One was a psychotherapist she arranged to meet in a car park. They would recognise each other, they agreed, by his clothing and her book. 'The moment he got out of his car, I just wanted to run.' Another came for the weekend to her house in the country – 'a weekend which I cut short'. He went on about his marvellous wife, how in love they had been, even when she left him, and how he still loved her. 'It gradually dawned on me all this had not happened twenty years ago, but three.' The third man was an American. 'He came straight out with, "Shall you and I have sex?" I said I'd rather talk about economics.'

'Still,' she says sanguinely, 'if nothing else, I suppose one's widened one's horizons.'

The mature history graduate with a young child does not want sex either. 'If that was all I was looking for, it's available on the doorstep. It's finding someone you can face afterwards. I think my experience can be summed up in one word – disastrous.' She sieved through her letters and came up with two. She met them in a wine bar. One was a customs and excise man. 'He didn't have a wooden leg, a glass eye or a squint, but almost.' He was shy, self-obsessed, and interested in train-spotting and DIY improvements to his bungalow. The other was a headmaster who bred spaniels. 'Need I say more? His wife had left him. He was bitter about it. That and the spaniels vied for the topic of the hour. He thought I was alright – except that I was female. He obviously needed some kind of therapy.'

This is roughly the experience of a 35-year-old mother with a Lotus sports car, a son at prep school, and a convent education which taught her that 'men did everything'. She thinks it would be nice to have a house in the country and a couple of dogs;

someone also to talk with her son. Among those she heard from were managing directors, farmers and life assurance executives. 'They all seemed to say the same thing – I am terribly successful, I am wonderful, it's not my fault I'm alone. Invariably they modelled what they wanted on a caricature of their last wife. Invariably they were the ones who had been left.'

While such women are fatalistic, the men I speak to are self-conscious and, by their own admission, socially awkward. Most importantly, they do not want anyone to know that they have to 'resort to this'. Finding it impossible to advertise their personality and life history in twenty words, many describe themselves as cars: '1950 reg, sunshine roof (– bald –), mechanically sound, garaged Richmond . . .' Either that, or they over-egg the pudding. 'It's a good thing to aim a bit higher,' says a man whose curriculum vitae would bring a blush to the cheeks of Sylvester Stallone. 'When you want to sell a car, it's better to give an unrealistic price.' Or, as Don Atyeo of *Time Out* said: 'Even if you're a crippled hunchback, you're going to write a glowing ad. You're not going to say you're an ugly bugger and dull as ditchwater.'

A consultant physician at a London teaching hospital suspects some 'dreadful flaw' in those who, like himself, have advertised. 'I just don't believe people with ordinary social skills need do this.' Having worked abroad and lost his old network of friends, he wants to get away from professional contacts. It was his lodger who put him onto *Singles*.

'She's a scruffy little creature, and yet she has these hordes of men ringing up. One day I summoned the courage to ask her how she did it. I was looking for someone to take out to the theatre, to Ascot and Henley. My journalist friends find it difficult to understand how isolated other professions can be. My first ad. brought absolutely no response whatever. "Professional gent seeks buxom brunette", that kind of thing. I got one outraged letter from a feminist.

'The next ad. my lodger composed – she's the publicity director of her company. Most of those who replied to that were teenage mothers from places like Fife. They had written in capital letters on what seemed to be prison block notepaper. "Dear Advertiser, You sound lovely to me . . ." The people I did meet were highly unsuitable. There was this forced intimacy. Unless you like the voyeuristic approach of Professor Higgins, the people you normally choose to meet are from your own class. The groundwork has been done. You know how to behave. In the cases of the four people I met, I had to be franker earlier on than I would be ordinarily. They were very keen to know my intentions. If I was not looking for someone to marry, they did not want their time wasted. One was a terribly guarded lawyer from a city hall who kept forgetting which name she'd used. One was a lady from Cambridge whose main problem in life was her philosopher ex-husband. One was a pedigree Sloane gone very wrong indeed. After dinner, I went back in her Porsche nine-eleven to her house in St John's Wood. Over brandy, while inspecting her black nail varnish, she explained how she had been kept by two men. One had since left. She was offering herself to me for one weekend in three, and two days a week if paid half her outgoings, the rent of her flat and a dress allowance. This was a five-figure sum. Oh, and she wanted me to meet the other fellow.'

My contact with these people was through the channel they would have used to sound each other out. On the telephone it was hard to picture them.

'You say you're attractive,' I challenged the Lotus-owner. 'Doesn't everyone?'

'I'm not beautiful,' she replied reasonably. 'But people chat me up in Waitrose.'

Neither weird nor extraordinary, they were all decent, articulate men and women, starting up again after a broken relationship. At a loss to find others like themselves, they had chosen the personal column because it removed a degree of social pain and probing; people who are available do not care to carry the message on a sandwich board around their neck.

A few had been lucky. One couple decided to marry after two hours on the telephone. But most, like Lord Lucan, were not. He re-advertised seven years later.

'Everybody manages to make themselves sound so wonderful, you find yourself wondering why on earth they are advertising,' one woman confided. 'I think it's better in theory than in practice. Though I'm past believing in Mr Wonderful – he's a bit like Father Christmas – and I am looking for Mr Acceptable, expectations are raised, despite oneself, which are bound to be disappointed.'

It explains the response to John Patterson's cover advertisement on the Christmas 1979 edition of *Singles*: 'Saintly single. Tired of hectic once-yearly journey, would like to settle down. Based

Greenland. Have reindeer, will travel.' Twelve people replied, says Patterson, one worried the reindeer might not get on with her dog.

There are, of course, more time-honoured means of connecting with the opposite sex in this 'great flower that opens but at night', as Richard Le Gallienne describes the London he knew earlier this century in a famous ballad.

'City of Dreadful Night' is the less exuberant title of James Thompson's poem written in 1874. It is more in keeping with the Bond Street nightclub where I met two dreadful flowers.

The evening had begun with a drink at The Chesterfield Hotel. My host was the principal secretary and receiver-general of the Monarchist League – a slightly eccentric institution which enjoys as its war-cry, 'Monarchy is the best policy'. At the hotel bar we had listened to the pianist giving a précis of his second volume of memoirs. 'I remember it well,' he kept saying. As he entered the fifties we left for dinner.

At dinner, the receiver-general told how he had published a slim volume of poetry and a book on faith healing. In the patently republican Sicilian restaurant, and in a very loud voice, he then proposed a toast to the king of Italy. Afterwards, in the street, he decided the night was still too young. Hailing a taxi, he leant against the lowered window and delivered what can only be described as music to a cabby's ears. 'Take me,' said the receiver-general, 'to the best nightclub in London.'

Lawrence, the former dustman, later explained to me what a cabby does with a request like this. Of the thirty or so nightclubs in the West End, about six are known to pay a generous tip. The Hanoverian, for instance, pays Lawrence £18 for a single customer, £16 a head for two, £14 for three, and £12 for a taxi-load of four. These tips may seem generous. They are nothing, though, to what the nightclub makes.

Our destination turned out to be The Kabaret. An entry fee of £6 seemed reasonable. Having paid, we went downstairs through a bead curtain and into a scantily lit room. As our eyes got accustomed to the dark, we realised that not only the lighting was scanty. On a black dance floor, an even blacker stripper spun from her breasts what seemed to be bits of the curtain we had just

At Play

passed through. At tables about her in twos and threes, and
exuding a boredom as blatant, sat groups of topless girls.

As the receiver-general and I ordered a campari, which again at
£2.50 seemed reasonable, two figures emerged from the red
gloom, sat down with flopping breasts, seized our names, and
ordered two bottles of champagne at £65 a bottle.

Somewhat taken aback, we reduced this order very quickly to a
single bottle. The waiter, however, refused to leave the table.
'And would the young ladies like anything to eat,' he told, rather
than asked, them. Oh yes, they would. Caviar. In considerable
accord, my host and I drew a line at caviar.

The whole process cannot have taken five minutes. Pallidly
turning to my companion, who rejoiced in the name of Ariel, I
attempted to engage her in conversation. She lowered her dark,
curly head. 'Are you happy with me?' she asked. I replied that it
was a little difficult to tell, having so far only spoken with the
waiter. 'I'm afraid you have to make up your mind now,' she said.
In the circumstances, circumstances I do not wish to repeat, I told
Ariel that I was happy with her. Then she asked me for a hostess'
fee.

The minimum amount was £20. It would have to be a cheque
then, since I had no cash. She asked me to make it out to a man
with a Greek name. It was the first time I had ever paid for
conversation, I told her. She smiled, tucked the cheque into her
stocking, stretched an arm along the seat behind my back and said,
immortally, 'So what do you do?'

Ariel detonated conversation through the celebrated method of
repeating a customer's last phrase. Given the information that he
came from Lower Slaughter, she would put her hand confes-
sionally on his knee, blow his hair and say, 'So you're from Lower
Slaughter, eh?' With this simple question, the onus was trans-
ferred back to the man who had paid not only for the conversation
but a lot, lot more.

As I chatted with Ariel, the waiter returned. A look of apology
mustered on his face. He was sorry, but the club rules were one
bottle of champagne for each couple. One for a table of four was
not allowed. Another bottle was duly ordered. Ariel explained
that a customer could only take a girl away after two bottles had
been drunk, and how she was meant to order as much as she
could. As the room filled with other men – French bankers,
northern businessmen, Arabs – her attention began to waver.

L-8   199

When the bill came, she disappeared altogether. Gazing dumbly at the total of £342.68, I was not surprised.

Stepping upstairs, the receiver-general muttered how wonderful they had been, and how we must all meet at Wilton's. Sallying into the night and another taxi, he suddenly and unbelievably asked the driver if there was anywhere else in London open at this hour. Fifteen minutes later, we found ourselves in Jermyn Street.

The operation was the same, except the hostesses were fully clothed and we were broke. Our coats were taken at the door by a short-haired woman with bones that protruded from her shoulders, and a smile as hard as a coin.

Sipping a vodka and tonic, the principal secretary and receiver-general of the Monarchist League engaged a girl from Kilburn in conversation. She was new here, she said. So new that she parted with her telephone number, which she wasn't meant to, she whispered, until we had ordered champagne. Since there was no chance of that, we left.

On the steps outside, we were joined by the girl from Kilburn. Mournfully she told us she had been sacked.

I ring up Helen, who owns a nightclub off Regent Street. 'It opens at ten,' she says. 'I get there at ten-thirty, and my customers sometimes never get there at all.'

I arrive at eleven-fifteen. A pink sign juts out into Regent Street, and a brass plaque – an inkling of better times – instructs which entrance should be used for the delivery of goods. I walk along a long red corridor with photographs on the wall.

Helen is about sixty and very thin. Her narrow face is crowned by a wreath of fair hair. From her neck a gold circle dangles airily in the space between her breasts. She wears a black and silver dress and a fragrance called Al Di La.

She leads me to a table overlooking the spacious club. On stage in shiny blue suits, a band is playing musak. Lots of tables, each with a red lampshade, spread out through pillars decorated with palms. Apart from a girl sitting against the opposite wall, the place is empty.

Champagne is ordered and brought to us by a girl in a short red dress. Helen makes an issue of looking at the label. Other clubs, she says, don't show you the label. The waiters turn their backs, cover it with a napkin, and serve a bottle which is – she can barely bring herself to say it – Veuve du Vernay.

She talks about London at night. 'There isn't a night life as it was ten years ago. It has deteriorated. It is dead, with this so-called permissiveness. Now you go to a hotel suite and you ring down to the porter and say, "Can I have a girl who's five-foot-three, who's blonde and doesn't talk." You might as well say, "Can I have twenty fillet steaks." It's the hotel porters who've become the pimps. And the girls come up. "No more than twenty minutes," they say. "Hope you have a Durex, don't try any kissing and, by the way, what's your name?" '

She runs a hand through her hair and then looks at me. 'Are you a queer? It's practically compulsory today.' She does not wait for the reply. Handing me an old brochure, she gets up. 'When the bell rings,' she continues, though no bell has rung, 'I must go to the door.'

The brochure announces that 'in Regent Street, in the centre of the greatest capital in the world, Eve is internationally recognised as London's premier nightclub'. There is a photograph of Helen in a white wig, and the information that she was a starlet of the Bucharest State Opera Company. Her début aged nine had been in their production of *Beauty and the Beast*. Perhaps it was this which prompted her mother, when Helen was small, to say she was made of gold.

She sits down again.

She is Rumanian, from a family who were friends with King Carol. Her mother was an aristocrat, her father a director of a Bucharest insurance company – the Reunione Adriatica de Securidad. 'My mother was lucky. She left six months before the revolution and never went back.'

She does not say what happened to her father.

Following the War, Helen married an English RAF officer stationed as part of the British Mission to Rumania. After a month's marriage, they decided to give a party. They went to tell his batman to arrange things. 'When we knocked at his door there was nothing. "Let's go," my husband said. As we went, a shot happened. I looked around and found myself looking through the door at the barrel of a gun, and the batman, who was drunk. I looked down and saw my husband of one month on the floor. "Come on, get up," I said, shaking him. When I opened my hands, they were full of pieces of liver.'

She reaches out to pluck a Dunhill from a half-filled box of fifty. 'This was a shock to the system, you can imagine. I just disintegrated.'

Then the Rumanians declared her a British subject and therefore undesirable. 'I am, to use the vernacular, an obstinate little mare, so I said, I'll go.' She came by military plane to Northolt in 1949, expecting a city of wider avenues. 'On arriving in London, one's feeling is of disappointment. Yet London has a magnetism that perhaps no other city has. Go away from it, think of all the places in the world where you have been, and all you want to do is return.'

She applied to the BBC, flaunting her Russian, Rumanian, French and Spanish. 'They asked if I could type.' One day, an application for a job led her through the back door of Murrays cabaret club. Did she have any dresses, she was asked. Six, she said. She was offered a job as a hostess. 'Of course,' she says disingenuously, 'I had no idea what it was. I'd never been to a nightclub.'

Below, in the first movement of the night, two embarrassed Oriental men come in and sit at a table. The girl opposite, accompanied now by three others, stays motionless.

Helen first started the Eve Club in 1953. 'How? You want to know how?' She laughs. 'Now that's a story. That is a story.' It is not a story she tells, however, beyond lamenting the viscounts and lords who had sat in the shade of the fronded pillars, watching elegant shows like *The Mind of Goya*. (The mind boggles.) 'And Nicolas Ceauşescu's dear little son came too. I refused to speak to him, he was so paralytically pissed.'

A man comes up and they whisper. 'Any auditions tonight?' he says. 'No, Tuesday,' she replies. He goes off in the direction of the stage, deserted by the blue band.

'I wasn't brought up to work. I am a misfit. I happened into it by accident,' she says despairingly. 'I just do the lights and audition the girls. It's very depressing. I did some beautiful shows. It's never full these days. Never, never full. I need fifteen hundred pounds per night to make a profit. I need a hundred and fifty pounds from each person. And we are not expensive. Just thirty-nine pounds for a bottle of champagne, forty-two for pink champagne. What's more, I refuse to pay commission to taxi drivers like other clubs. The result is I have to fight the Inland Revenue.'

Rummaging in her bag, she produces the copy of a letter she has written to her local MP. Circulated also to the prime minister and the editor of *Private Eye*, it complains about the Revenue's insistence that her girls are employees. 'They are not. I advertise in the *Financial Times* for them. They are artists engaged,' she says proudly.

From a loudspeaker above the stage comes a man's voice. 'Ladies and gentlemen, Miss Adèle Warren.' The floor show has begun, and Adèle, in a gold sequin jacket and top hat, taps her black stick in a mime of *Cabaret*.

The song sends Helen back to pre-war Rumania. 'When I heard on the radio the Russians had invaded, or as they say, *liberated*, I burst into tears. That afternoon I went riding on the estate, to exercise a stallion. We had twelve of our own, but this one, Argenteuil, belonged to King Carol. Suddenly three Russians appeared on horses that would make Don Quixote's mount look like Red Rum. "Where's the nearest bar?" said one of them. "That's a nice horse you've got there," said another. "Get off," said the third. I dug my heels in, Argenteuil took off, and with my bottom in the air and bullets whizzing past me, I galloped home.' She taps another cigarette against the carton top, then adds it to her lips. 'We had a friend. I can't remember his name. Names that are no longer necessary go from the memory. Ah, yes, Colonel C— . . .' Having remembered the name, she forgets the story.

On stage, Adèle has made way for Jane. Clad only in a blue boa and suggestively sucking her thumb, Jane does not look as if she has read the *Financial Times* for some considerable time. 'She's the best,' says Helen. 'I've had her four years. To be exciting you must have girls with class, not scruffy little tarts. Now if you see a sign saying "Nightclub" you run away. They're all clip joints. Last week three Finns were beaten up when they could not pay a bill of five hundred pounds. They did not have that kind of money. And the owners get away with it because foreigners have to be in San Francisco tomorrow. The last thing they want is to get involved with the police about how they've been overcharged. English people don't complain because they don't want to tell their wives they've been conned.

'If waitresses have been in a clip joint too long, they're very difficult to de-programme. They don't know how to laugh, to drink, to give pleasure. All they know is how to make men spend as much money as possible. My girls are here to dance, to joke, to take the mind off the VAT man, or the wife, or whatever is giving men concern. At times, the customers say, "My wife is so intelligent that I want you to bring me the most cheerful, stupid girl there is." It's only right that at the end of the night she should expect him to appreciate her company.'

The hostess fee averages £40, but the club's fifteen girls can sit in the shadows for up to three nights a week without being appreciated. Grandly, like an exiled empress, Helen plucks some of her brighter lights from the shadows.

The first, dressed in black, wears her dark hair in a bun. Sitting down, her mouth spreads into a wide smile. When it reaches its full frame, it remains stretched there uncomfortably. She comes from an upper-middle-class family, in Gloucestershire. She does not give her age, which is about thirty-five; nor does she tell her friends what she does. At weekends she returns home to parents who believe she has worked for the last six years as a secretary. She has coaxed them into a routine whereby they only ring between six and seven at night.

'I do this for the money,' she says. 'It's old hat. The men – mostly businessmen – say I'm mistreated, misunderstood and unhappy. You've got to sit and look pleasant and the moment you're asked for, you must go. Otherwise, who would sit with the horrid people?'

Had she ever fallen in love?

'Yes.'

What happened?

'Nothing.'

It had lasted for a year, says Helen, when the girl has left to eat her breakfast. I spot her in the shadows again, eating it alone.

The next girl, Carmen, is bouncier. She has been entertaining the two Orientals. 'They were frightfully boring. One was Pakistani, the other from Java. Conversation was minimal. Generally you begin by asking their name – that's because you haven't caught it when you've been introduced. Then where they come from, where they live in Britain, where they have lived, what they do. Lots of them lie. One said he was a lion tamer. But you always say, Oh, how interesting. What they get really stroppy about is the bill. The second night I was here the chap fell asleep, then under the table, when the bill came. A rather forceful girl said, "Kick him." Do I ever fancy any? Yes I do. You couldn't do this job without liking men. Oh, it's terrible sometimes. It's absolutely bloody awful.'

Carmen tells only very close friends of her work as a hostess. She tells her parents she is on the dole. They do not understand how their daughter with a degree in biochemistry from London University can have such trouble finding a job.

As Carmen says, sipping her buck's fizz with a petite giggle, 'I was never born to be a biochemist.'

On stage, Jane has ceded to a girl dressed as an odalisque.

Three months later I read in a newspaper how one of Helen's male dancers has died in the frenzied finale of his act. Playing the part of an Egyptian slave, he slipped while spinning Cleopatra high above his head.

In the mid-nineteenth century one London house in sixteen was a brothel. Today, the city of sin which so caught the imagination of Europeans like the peripatetic Hippolyte Taine, and the illustrator and cartoonist Gustave Doré, is fragmented into the felt-tipped pseudonyms which are found in every telephone box and bus shelter throughout the capital. Usually the telephone numbers belong to Ebony and Trudie and have a Maida Vale or Paddington prefix.

An insurance executive, 'as randy as a frog up a pump', tells me of one belonging to an executive masseuse called Michèle. The number leads him to a room overlooking Harrods. At a bar in the middle of this room, she pours a glass of red wine. Many of her clients, she tells him, come from the nearby magistrates court. Then, accompanied by her servant Terry, and in a position overlooking Harrods – a view responsible for some percentage of the stimulation – she begins whipping him. 'She made me feel,' he says of the experiences which follow, 'like corn on the cob.'

'I've never been to a brothel in London,' says Martin, who has written of his experiences in brothels all over the world. 'I imagine, even after the closing of Cynthia Payne's famous establishment in Streatham, that there are some. They wouldn't be in the *Yellow Pages* or on the tobacconist's window – more likely through private introduction, private membership, on the 'phone, coming round to your place. Maybe it's because Londoners don't go out, preferring to sit in their own little houses. It's a secret city, but one thing I learnt about humanity from my book is that there are a lot of strange people out there.'

Stephen used to change the sheets for prostitutes in a Paddington hotel. While working at a boatyard, he answered an advertisement for a night porter in a 120-bedroom hotel near the station. 'I thought it was a legitimate hotel, full of coach-loads of Germans and Dutch. My job was on reception, but effectively, since the manageress was having an affair with the owner, I was running the place by myself. I wore a natty red jacket, answered the switchboard, took the money, gave people their keys, made sure the place was serene.

'One midnight during the first week, a brown girl appeared dragging a drunken businessman. She gave me the wink. "Got a room, love?" Well, I thought, Paddington is Paddington. This is just a one-off, just a bloke with his girlfriend. They signed themselves in as Jones. All the couples that came after that were Jones as well – endless Mr Joneses.

'I didn't realise at that time there were very few hotels where girls could go. This one always had ten to twenty rooms free, usually on the ground floor at the back. The central heating never got that far, nor did the housekeeper, and it was easy to whip in and out. The usual time was twenty minutes.

'I can proudly say I built that business up. Word got round that I was prepared to do business. Girls came in from the clubs, midnight on till about four in the morning. Always on a weekday. There was no business at all at weekends. They mainly came in with businessmen, mainly with Japanese businessmen. They liked the Japanese because they were very quick – in and out in ten minutes.

'Once a person had signed the room for the night and left after half an hour, I would put that money into the hotel bank and pocket the rest. Once they had signed, you see, that room was legitimately theirs till eleven the next morning. After each couple had left, I used to scuttle upstairs to clean the room. Hookers use a hell of a lot of towels. Often the bed hadn't been touched – they'd done it on top – but go into the bathroom and you'd see they'd gone mad with the towels, which were always soaking wet. Since I had no access to new towels, I used to put them on the radiator.

'Sheets could be a problem. Some of the girls had high standards when it came to cleanliness – they'd even 'phone down to say they didn't like the state of the room. Some didn't. A very nice Norwegian man with a young son took me round his room. The chambermaid hadn't changed the sheets, and there had been two blokes and four girls there the night before. I got another room for him, and told the manager next day they hadn't liked it because there was not enough sunlight.

'The girls used to give me a five- to ten-pound tip, and I started up a sideline bringing cheap bottles of Algerian hock and charging them a lot more. They were happy to make thirty pounds, but they were sad things. At the top of the tree you had graduates, at the bottom skimpy little girls from Wales and Scotland. The majority were old pros, old dogs really, who trundled in with their drunk men.

'One of the saddest girls used to fall in love with her blokes. Instead of the usual quickie-do, she would be there all night. I always had to ring her to get her out of bed.

'After three months it got out of hand. There I was, by myself, every few minutes couples coming in, and not enough rooms, rushing round making beds, clearing towels from the bathroom, taking money, worrying about the police, and trying to do off-licence sales. Then, one night I had a queue of taxis outside with fifteen black hookers and a load of drunken Japs. Walking back through Hyde Park in the morning, I thought, that's it.'

On the other side of the park, behind a pillared entrance on the Gloucester Road, Nice Girls are learning a very different allure. At the Lucie Clayton Grooming College, established in 1928, the Young Londoner Finishing Course is 'entirely devoted to vanity and the building of self-confidence'. For £340 a term, for four weeks, mornings only – or six weeks, evenings only – young girls are taught all they ever need to know about make-up, social etiquette, figure correction, epilation, 'professional advice on bras' and above all, deportment. 'That casual and graceful walk for which our graduates have been envied across the world', proclaims the brochure.

'It takes four weeks to acquire and it lasts a lifetime.'

Emma and Penny are Young Londoners who attend this course as part of their year at the Lucie Clayton Secretarial College. They share a flat off the Fulham end of the King's Road with an inflatable birthday cake on the marble mantelpiece and an empty grate. Emma is the pug-nosed daughter of a man who owns some advertising hoardings along the M4 exit to Berkshire, where he lives. She wears a green T-shirt and her chestnut hair swept back from a fat tanned face. She sits on the floor drinking whisky within easy reach of two packets of Marlboro. Penny, wearing a jumper knitted in coloured letters saying 'Benetton', sits with her legs drawn up on a sofabed. She has fair, stringy hair and the face, like claret splashed in milk, of a country girl.

'We had this social etiquette talk,' says Emma. 'So stupid. About what to do when we're invited to Balmoral.'

'Or any of the other royal castles,' reminds Penny.

'It wasn't If, it was When. The woman just took it for granted we'd be personal friends of Prince Edward.'

'If you shut your eyes,' says Penny shutting hers, 'she sounded like a man.'

'The queen,' resumes Emma, lighting another cigarette, 'doesn't like ladies to emerge from their rooms till after . . . was it twelve o'clock? You don't have to request any papers since you get every single one of them. At shooting lunches you're not allowed to drink if you're under twenty-one.'

'No, eighteen,' corrects Penny.

'And if you don't see an ashtray, it's not prudent to smoke. Apparently the Duchess of Kent lights up after a meal and never smokes. It's a subtle way of saying, Everyone can have a fag and it's alright by me.'

'There must have been something else, Emma.'

'Only that Buckingham Palace has the most simple writing paper, which one should emulate at home. Plain white or cream.'

Among the twenty-five on their course who are expected to befriend Prince Edward are two Japanese and a girl from Manchester.

'It's a real mixture,' explains Penny.

Emma nods. 'I don't think we've got a single black.'

Whether she intends by this to confirm or deny the mixture it is difficult to know.

Men are not allowed past the brass plaque on the Gloucester Road, but bubbling within is the secret recipe for getting on with them; the social alchemy that commences with the dark knowledge, handed down in whispers through the generations, of how to step correctly into their MG. For this purpose, Lucie Clayton have constructed a hardboard model of the passenger side of a small sports car. 'It's got a nasty vinyl seat and the door doesn't shut properly,' complains Emma. 'It's tied up with a red ribbon.'

'It was designed in the days before we were emancipated,' adds Penny, without irony. 'But the principle is to swing round with your legs together so you don't show everyone up your skirt.'

Skirts are de rigueur at Lucie Clayton – except for Mondays and Fridays when trousers are allowed – the assumption being that girls have just jumped off their horse, or are about to jump on.

Once driven to the restaurant, the private dinner table, the palace, Emma and Penny are instructed to look at the cutlery and 'work inwards from the outside'.

Flirting with the waiters is out, remembers Emma. 'Because they're not allowed to respond to you. And three things you mustn't talk about are sex, politics and religion.'

'Not sex,' says Penny. 'I don't remember sex. Money, surely.'

'And if there's an argument, you must change the subject to something general and lighter.'

'And, Emma, how you must tactfully powder your nose towards the end of the meal, so the man can deal with the bill.'

Once a term Emma and Penny undergo what is known as a 'Grooming and Grading' with a woman nicknamed 'Chickenlegs'.

'She has a passionate thing about plucking eyebrows and the colour red. Everyone should wear scarlet lipstick. Anyway, you go in and she'll say in a husky voice – they all seem to have husky voices – "Will you do your walk, please?" '

Emma gets to her shoeless feet and struts about the room. 'Bottom in, chest up, head high, shoulder back. It's got to be taken with a pinch of salt. You suddenly think you must have been walking wrong all your life.'

(To help in the acquisition of a lifetime, Lucie Clayton now use video cameras, confident that as soon as the girls see themselves on screen 'jeans loosen and unnecessary fat dissolves more discernibly away'. Emma has not yet seen herself on video.)

'You walk three times across the room. "Lovely. Once more," says Chickenlegs in that husky voice, as if you are a prize thoroughbred. "That's a nice dress," she might add, or "Don't put any more weight on your hips, will you?" '

'Didn't she actually tell Tanya to lose weight?'

'Well, Tanya needs to. She's a marsh monster. Then keeping eye contact with her, you walk over to a chair, look once, feel it with the back of your leg and hopefully sit down. After this you get an end-of-term report which will say at the bottom: She should wear blusher, Her hair needs conditioning, Her deportment needs attention.'

On the sofabed, Penny proudly stirs. 'My last one said I made good use of colour and accessories.'

There are other lectures at Lucie Clayton besides etiquette. In preparing Emma and Penny for the modern world, a junior barrister talks about the law; a flower arranger introduces what might become 'a lifelong hobby', a bearded cook demonstrates his recipes.

'We were going to have a journalist,' says Emma, 'but he was called off to cover some riots.'

Emma and Penny do not see themselves as Sloane Rangers. 'Their whole attitude,' shudders Penny, 'I can't bear it. They're always bumping into people they know in Peter Jones and announcing it to the whole shop. "Oh, Darling, what have you been doing with your life?" "Oh, I saw Caroline in a restaurant the other night." '

In disassociating herself from such creatures, Penny insists she wants a job 'that won't just tide me over till I'm married'. Like orchestral management. 'Of course, if I marry some director who's earning pots of money, I'd chuck it in.'

In explaining why she is at Lucie Clayton, Emma laughs and unnecessarily tears the wrapper on a fresh packet of cigarettes. 'It just sounded quite a dossy thing to do. Next year I'm doing a history of art course. Really I want to write and that sort of thing. My mother writes a lot,' she explains, sweeping her hair back. 'I put down any old thing that I think about. A lot of poetry.'

No doubt her present course will come in handy when she has to type it out.

Sitting in their Fulham flat, anything seems possible. Emma might burgeon into a great novelist, Penny into an orchestral manager. Or they both might suddenly rebel and develop into penniless peeresses like Lady M., singing with the milkman.

Or they might meet Prince Edward at a party and receive an invitation to Balmoral – and come to resemble the conventional grown-up debutantes so indelibly described by Louis Simond.

In *An American in Regency England*, this French emigré to America tells of ladies arriving at St James's Palace on the occasion of the monarch's birthday. They are carried there in sedan chairs.

> To enable them to sit in these chairs, their immense hoops are folded like wings, pointing forward on each side. The preposterous high head-dress would interfere with the top and must be humoured by throwing the head back; the face is therefore turned up, kept motionless in that awkward attitude, as if on purpose to be gazed at . . . The glasses of the vehicles are drawn up, that the winds of Heaven may not visit the powder and paint too roughly; and this piece of natural history, thus cased, does not ill resemble a foetus of a hippopotamus in its brandy bottle.

Secure in his bottle, or behind the door of his chosen club, the Londoner rarely ventures out. When he does, the excuse is more than likely to be a sporting one. Londoners may not do very well at games, but they are conscious of London as the world capital of cricket, football, squash, rugby, tennis and rowing. The only time they notice their river is during the annual Oxford and Cambridge Boat Race: a tedious competition to watch, since the winner is known after the first minute, and always wins for ten years on the trot.

While his bosses at the bank play six-a-side football each Monday night in the Knightsbridge barracks, Vic, the merchant bank messenger, spends his free time organising full-side football teams in Pitsea. At the weekend, up to 2,500 players like him can be seen scampering across Hackney Marshes. On Wednesdays, after delivering his stripey, Steve the milkman plays for Express Dairies against teams from the Post Office, the police, or anyone – like cabbies – with an afternoon to spare. 'The league was ruined when the police had to drop out for the miners' picket lines.' Rarest but most amusing of all to watch, on pitches at Wormwood Scrubs and Chelsea Hospital, are the teams of television sports commentators, unfitly emulating their screen heroes.

Hand in glove with sport, and for those who cannot compete, goes gambling.

White City has been home for the Greyhound Derby since 1927. In 1985 its stadium closed to make way for new housing.

Now, devotees of greyhound racing have to drive south to Wimbledon.

It had been raining heavily the night I went but it did not matter. 'Dogs always run,' said the man at the turnstile. Entry was £2.50 – into a swirl of blondes in furs, gents in sheepskins, flash Harrys in gold necklaces. One or two in the crowd were pensioners, come to place their minimum bets of 20p. The restaurant, past the Gracing Bar, was built on several tiers. You looked through the glass, through the reflected diners, at the dark stadium and the stand opposite. 'There is trouble with the electrician', said an off-the-peg voice on the loudspeaker. It was like watching an enormous television screen.

A set meal for £9 accompanied the ten races, one race every fifteen minutes. Waitresses in black uniforms and hennaed hair brought the staple English menu: watery prawn cocktail, brown slabs of beef marinating in powdered gravy, tinned peaches in syrup.

The tier had its own betting girl, who wore a home-knit white cardigan and black boots, and carried a satchel of money around her middle. Her hair looked as if it had been washed in the gravy. Before each race she took orders on a yellow pad. Then she punched the bets into a computer by the central stairs.

The first race was at 7.45 p.m. – 460 metres flat around the dark course. Six dogs in different coloured coats were led on to the track. 'The one cocking its leg before the race is sure to win,' says the girl. 'It's the most scared.' Wasp-waisted, spindly legged, none of them look scared. Nor do they look doped, their urine having been checked for substances like luminol and chloretone; their toes for elastic bands intended to slow them down.

Having failed to cock their legs, the dogs enter a white box. The lights in the restaurant go down, and a man on the track drops a green flag. From the stand opposite comes the hare. Juddering vulnerably, like a dog-eared teddy on a string, it passes the starting line. The hounds leap – twelve feet with every stride. Forty miles an hour. In less than thirty seconds Number 5, Sinbad's Blonde, has apparently won. The lights go up. The dogs stop suddenly, in the same movement springing back towards their trainers with tails wagging tautly like twists of metal.

As the race is replayed on a blurred television screen below, the man on the loudspeaker tells of the disappointing numbers who have taken advantage of a bus service from Shepherd's Bush to

Wimbledon. His disappointment gives way to Glenn Miller. At the next table, a Catherine Oxenberg lookalike fingers three large rings and laughs at her companion – a man in a tropical yellow shirt. 'Regulars,' says the betting girl. 'But the White City mob has chased a lot of the Wimbledon crowd away.'

What is the sum of her wisdom after fifteen years as a betting girl? 'The sum of my wisdom is that I had to get a job down here because I was no good at punting. The computer has made things easier, though. We used to have to rush up those stairs. But it means my figure's not so trim.'

She tells of a young man who inherited a firm from his uncle. 'He came down here for a month, spent thousands, sometimes three hundred pounds on a race. He lives now in a council house.'

Graciously, she takes a £1 bet for Stepaside Lady at 6-1.

Greyhound racing began in 1909 in Tucson, Arizona, where it was sniffed at by horse owners. 'Animal roulette', they called it. Over here it caught on, in a nation of dog lovers. Mick the Miller, the most famous hound of all, and originally owned by an Irish priest, earned his obituary in *The Times* with sixty-one victories. Today he stands, stuffed, in the Natural History Museum.

That will not be the fate of Stepaside Lady, who bounds in fifth. At the next table Mateus Rosé has given way to champagne, cigarettes to cigars, in celebration of a bet placed elsewhere than on hound Number 3. Above our heads Glenn Miller gives way to the invisible man on the loudspeaker, reminding us about the bus service from Shepherd's Bush. 'While it will definitely run next Tuesday,' he warns, 'whether it continues to do so depends on its use.'

The life of a greyhound lasts anything up to six years. Then, if a home is not found, it is put down. 'Fussy Boots found a home,' says the newsletter dispensed free to each table, 'but having been spayed for it, she became allergic to the catgut in her stitches. In the operation to replace them, her kidney became infected and had to be removed.'

The Londoner's affection for animals has always struck the passing foreigner as curious. Writing in 1725, the Comte de Saussure was astonished at how 'a lady will offer five guineas reward for a little lost dog worth 5d.'. Little has changed. In 1985 a notice in a window in exclusive Motcomb Street, SW1, read:

'We have lost our beige pussy cat. Six months old. £100 reward if you have seen it.'

The most extravagant parade of this British affection can be seen each year at Cruft's where 11,000 canine specimens are displayed in kennels on piddle-proof mats. Many bear an alarming resemblance to their owners in haircut, expression, even walk. Afghans are the most popular, then setters and retrievers. Poodles are also making a comeback, being promoted as active intelligent dogs, which carry themselves very proudly. A black poodle won in 1985, with the long sleek face of a gypsy.

Until 1915, Londoners buried their favourite pets at a cemetery in Hyde Park. Among those resting in peace by Victoria Gate are Puskin, Sweet Baby Quita and Fluff-Fluff.

The parks are London's precious feature. Its lungs, Lord Chatham said. Devised for the 'singular comfort' of the monarch, these former hunting grounds remain the property of the Crown, and the most effective emblem of the royal city. They are also a safety valve for the people – where the anarchist stands on his soap box, the city on its ceremony.

When the Mediterranean lends us its sun from the end of May, clothes come off, beer bellies tumble out, and men walk round ridiculously in brown pants, shoes and socks. In the 5,671 acres a Londoner can be at his loneliest or his most gregarious; withdrawn or hung-out – like the 'impeccably dressed bowler-hatted elderly gent' who exposed himself to Susan Hill, the contemporary novelist, close to the Albert Memorial.

For some Londoners the parks exist as an outdoor sports ground; for others as a place to walk – if not bury – the dog. For the majority they are a private garden, and jealously guarded as such. When asked what it would cost to enclose a section of Hyde Park, Sir Robert Walpole told Queen Caroline, 'Only Three Crowns, Madam – those of England, Ireland and Scotland.'

In his *Letters from England*, published in 1923, Karel Capek tells how, when watching a man amble off the path and across the grass, he could not believe his eyes. Looking nervously about him, Capek decided to follow suit. He put one foot tentatively forward, then another. 'Nothing happened,' he exclaimed. 'Never have I had a feeling of such unrestricted liberty as in that moment.'

214

Much of the Londoner's character and view of the world, he concluded, was explained by his right to walk across a meadow as if he were a combination of wood nymph and landed proprietor.

'Most Londoners are within reach of a park where they can lose themselves,' says Ken Livingstone, a man who cannot walk down the street without being recognised and stopped. 'In all of them, you can get to a point in the centre where you are completely cut off.' Second only to politics is his love of natural history. 'I often take my nephew and his friends and poke around in ponds. Salamanders and Manchurian toads aren't demanding.'

An early winter morning in Kensington Gardens. Gulls swoop on the Round Pond where Percy Bysshe Shelley sailed his paper boats. Dogs chase leaves hopelessly. A man stands unnaturally still, feeding two squirrels. A woman walks briskly to work, crunching down the Broad Walk between the lime trees.

I cross the Serpentine bridge and head towards Jacob Epstein's statue of Rima. It commemorates the bird woman in *Green Mansions*; also the place where the novel's author, the naturalist W.H. Hudson, slept on first coming to London. A little further on are the red brick offices of London's Central Royal Parks.

From an upstairs room in a hidden building, the young superintendent is marshalling her staff as they prepare for the day's planting, pruning and turfing. Over a cup of tea she decides on Ahmed's application for leave, and on other matters relating to her 187-strong team. She then looks at the letters requesting coach permits; permissions to hold a demonstration, a sponsored walk, a school outing, a veteran car rally. Most are run-of-the-mill, but she is alert for anything that challenges the status quo. Due to their central location her parks are always subject to pressure – from those who want to lay cables, build underground car parks, even tunnels. Patrick Abercrombie's 1943 *Plan* envisaged a tunnel all the way to Whitehall.

Her paperwork done, she goes out. She aims to spend half her time in the open. It is why she wanted the job twenty-one years ago, after a childhood spent on an estate in the City, overlooking a window box. From the age of sixteen, and from Regent's Park to Wandsworth Common, she has dug, forked and hoed a path which has led to her present responsibility for the Central Royal Parks, and the gardens of 10 Downing Street, Clarence House and Buckingham Palace.

Because the system has been built up over decades, much of her job consists of caretaking and maintenance. In the spring she plants the garden beds opposite Buckingham Palace with 40,000 tulips. In the summer, with 14,000 geraniums – the red of a Guardsman's tunic. On state occasions, her staff sweep and clean The Mall. Traditionally, the major occasions happen in Hyde Park, where there has been a gun salute to the monarch since the time of Elizabeth I. With fewer trees and more open space, Hyde Park lends itself to both military events and demonstrations. In 1984 the Campaign for Nuclear Disarmament held a rally for 300,000. Then the major general reviewed the Household Cavalry. Since the increase in fast food, rubbish has become a headache. So too has lead pollution, which damages the trees close to the road.

The superintendent lives in a cottage on Hyde Park. One of thirteen such buildings, it is guarded by two ferocious dogs. Previously she lived in Richmond. She saved two hours a day when she moved. It is quiet at night, but if she wants peace on a hot summer's day, she has to leave the parks altogether. At night she can hear the bats, rabbits and cormorants, although the owls seem to have gone. Occasionally, a fox can be seen making its way across the grass. 'It usually gets run over.'

On her walks the superintendent is sometimes asked by tourists if they can tread on the grass. Americans, she says, are surprised it is safe to walk in the parks at all. She talks with affection of the die-hard solitary bird-feeders. Following the same route, they are recognised every morning by the birds and squirrels which come flocking for crumbs.

Recently she has noticed a new trend in the park. It involves young men and women going up to trees. Wrapping their arms around the trunk, they remain there and hug for a few minutes.

Along the south side of Hyde Park are the Knightsbridge barracks, the modern regimental headquarters for the 514 soldiers and 273 horses of the Household Cavalry.

I was ten minutes late for a meeting with a lieutenant called Timothy, and he had gone. Punctuality is everything in the army. Eventually he appeared in a peaked cap, dragged along the courtyard by a black labrador on a silver chain.

That morning, between seven and eight, he had taken some of the horses through the streets on an exercise known as the 'Regimental Watering Order' – 'a hangover from the trough'. Leading his men, one man to two horses, and clasping his *A-Z*, he had trotted noisily down Oxford Street for some mounted window-shopping. 'The *A-Z* is essential if you've had a good time the night before,' he says. Once or twice he has lost his way in the little back streets of Kensington. If his turn for the Watering Order falls on a Saturday, he makes for Soho, where the market traders offer fruit to the horses. He can go anywhere he likes, except the Palace. 'We have to keep clear of the Palace because of the noise.'

Leaning against a rail at the back of the ceremonial courtyard, Timothy talks me through the parade under progress. In a maroon cloak, an officer on foot is inspecting twelve mounted troopers who will shortly form the guard at Buckingham Palace.

'It's a short guard because the Queen's away from London,' he explains. 'A long guard has fourteen, with a trumpeter, and an extra dutyman to escort the Standard. The trumpeter blows a royal salute when he leaves the barracks, and when he passes both Buckingham Palace and Clarence House. So he's quite busy.'

Below, the maroon captain lifts up a tail and squints into the depths of a horse's bottom. He then murmurs something to the man beside him, who scribbles it down on a pad.

'You raise the tail to see if the dock has been sponged out. The inspecting officer has got to establish a priority, since the four cleanest men will do the mounted sentry duty. The rest will be stuck in the boxes. What he's doing there is starting each man off with fifteen points and deducting a quarter for dirty buckskin gauntlets, or eyes that haven't been cleaned. Either you've got the ability to clean kit or you haven't. Warm leather, beeswax, water and polish is best. Not spit. If you've had a Coke and a pork pie, it causes an unhappy chemical reaction. Some soldiers are expert at polishing, others at plumes, so there's a lot of dealing and swapping around. In winter you wear cloaks, which means much less cleaning.

'When I inspect, I usually stand back and look at the individual to see if the proportions are right. Then I get down to the nitty-gritty. The jack boots are the focal point. If a man can do them, he can do everything else.'

The inspection is completed, the officer marches to the front of the parade, and a man in a loud voice calls out the relief: 'Number one, Hanley!'

'Yes, sir!'

'Number two, Osborne!'

And so on, down to the unfortunates Whitfield and Shorter. ('They've got the bum relief – bad times and grotty block jobs.')

The guard leave the yard in a clatter and head into the park. Their relief lasts to 4.00 p.m. when there will be another inspection. It is a legacy from the occasion when Queen Victoria came upon her guards one afternoon and found them drunk. To prevent a recurrence, she declared they would be inspected at 4.00 p.m. for a hundred years. 'When the hundred years lapsed we duly stopped doing it, but the Tourist Board grumbled.'

Timothy takes me to the forge. Farriers in red shirts are hammering shoes onto Caractacus. The letter of a horse's name denotes his year of arrival, he says. 'Kitchener and Kew are untrained remounts.' The drum horse, in a blue polywarm husky, looks on and snorts. 'They have to be shod once a month. Their squadron numbers are burned into the hoof.' This is another legacy. To prevent horse stealing, and claims that a soldier's horse had been shot from under him, the hoof had to be produced to substantiate death.

Outside, a granite memorial provides a sobering reminder that such claims do not belong to the past. Inscribed on the stone is 20 July 1982 – the date of the IRA bomb – and the names of those horses, like Rochester and Zara, which it destroyed.

Ironically, the majority of mounts are bought in Ireland. Four times a year, a purchasing commission goes out to inspect all black horses of sixteen hands or more. Only the trumpeter's horse is grey, and easily spotted on a battlefield when used to convey messages.

Since the bomb attack, a radio transmitter is carried in a flap under an officer's saddle for state occasions. Otherwise, Knightsbridge barracks houses a world of few changes. The red hair of the Blues and Royals used to be yak, now it is treated horse hair. The white on a Lifeguard's helmet is nylon, whereas it used to be whalebone. But the musicians' uniform remains the burgundy gold and blue of Charles II's racing colours.

And fiancés are still not allowed into the mess after eight. 'It is very much run on the principles of a gentleman's club,' says Timothy, indicating on the mess walls some portraits of the club's gentlemen. One in particular strikes the eye: that of Colonel Fred Burnaby who died in the Egyptian campaign. 'He had a party trick, which he once performed before Queen Victoria. Can you imagine what it was? Horses are a clue. No? Well, you won't believe this . . .'

Colonel Fred Burnaby's party trick, apparently, was to pick up a horse under each arm.

A rainy Saturday morning in February. The sky is grey like a heavy-smoker's skin, the wind bitter. On the Serpentine the water puckers into choppy goosepimples. Even the black-necked birds cling to shore.

A morning to stay in bed.

Under the roof of the Serpentine Lido, five members of the swimming club pull on plastic caps, rub hands, kick feet, and wait to race. By the pillars are tin baths of steaming water. Inside, changing for the next race, or drying their pink bodies from the last, are another dozen swimmers. On the blackboard the day's temperature reads 36°F.

Members of the club, totalling about sixty at any one time, have swum every day, all the year round, since 1864. The oldest swimming club in Britain, it was formed to promote the 'healthful habit of bathing in open water all through the winter season'. Subscriptions were originally 10s. per annum, paid quarterly in advance, and dinners were held in The Florence Restaurant, Rupert Street, Soho. A speciality was 'Bombe Serpentine'.

Patrons of the club have included Viscount Camrose, the Duke of Westminster, Lord Howard de Walden, Lord Lonsdale and Sir James Barrie, who initiated the most prestigious cup, competed for each Christmas Day – the Peter Pan Trophy. His spirit keeps them young, the members say, referring to the boy who would not grow up. Past members have included a cross-Channel swimmer, a bus driver, a window cleaner, the author of a play called *Henry of Navarre* and an MP who got himself into trouble with a Guardsman at the time of Profumo. They are just as eclectic today. Under their plastic caps, they take in the whole spread of Londoners from boys in their early teens to men in their late seventies.

'We have a bat expert, a sanitary inspector, and a man who's re-binding *The Domesday Book,*' says Alan, the secretary and treasurer. '. . . A man who works at Highgate Cemetery, a neuropathologist, a silversmith, a dustman – he probably won't be here today because QPR beat Chelsea – a Greek shipping magnate, a lunatic, and an Irishman who plays the bagpipes and looks so like Jimmy Savile that he is always stopped for his autograph. We've also got an antique dealer with long hair and a bit of a hump, who wears an old man's mac. He's sometimes stopped in the park as he does his warm-up. "And where do you think you're going?" the policeman says. "I'm running round the park." "Oh, yes, and how long have you been doing that for?" "Thirty-seven years." '

The president is an American painter who treats the parks as his back garden and the Serpentine as a lucky dip. From its muddy bottom he has brought up a parking meter, an aerial bomb with fins and 1,200 bottles, lugged by the Victorians from their picnic spots. Among them, bottles that once contained Mexican Hair Remover, Batty's Nabob Pickles, Californian Fig Syrup and an unclear substance simply advertised with the words 'Harrods Serves the World, London SW'.

The members compete for about thirty cups. 'Everyone wins one,' says Alan. 'It doesn't matter if you're good or bad. All are handicapped, so that the fastest swimmer in the bridge-to-bridge race may take sixteen minutes but he'll lose to the chap who takes an hour. Nothing's compulsory. No one minds coming last. Points are totted up. It froze over last Sunday, so those who went in got two points. We dug a hole in the ice. There's always a hole in the ice.'

He goes outside, waiting for his heat. Past him hop a shivering gaggle who have survived today's fifty-yard stretch. 'Some swim differently in different temperatures. Cyril, he's good in about thirty-two, when it's freezing. The water's not so dense then, like it is today. It keeps him trim. How old are you, Cyril?' he asks the last dripping figure.

'Seventy-three,' he rattles.

'Spring chicken!' shouts someone from inside.

Tommy, who comes round the corner with his dog, a packet of digestive biscuits and a bag of sweets, is even older. 'Eighty-seven,' he says, handing out his sweets and cocking his trilby. He gave up swimming five years back, but he comes every day in his scarf and hat to watch his successors. He has a cup named after him. He thinks it is being competed for next week . . . The week after, Alan tells him.

He joined the club in 1919, fresh from the North Russian Relief Force. He remembers fishing here as a kid, like the Benedictine monks who sat on the banks of the Westbourne long before Queen Caroline dammed it in 1730 to make the Serpentine. 'If I had been caught, I would have been fined forty shillings.' He looks at old photos of the club with an eyeglass. 'The likes of other days I call them.' There is one of him, fifty years ago, having won the Peter Pan Trophy. When he dies he wants his ashes scattered at the statue's feet. He tells of a duck that used to sit on his back and waddle into the changing rooms afterwards to untie his shoelaces with its beak. 'It must have been the spirit of past members. Once a member, you're a member in spirit for life.'

Alan comes in, having won his heat through 'the champagne water'. (Before approving the first lido, George V examined a sample of the lake through a microscope.) 'Most members I know have died of natural causes,' says Alan. 'We live no longer, no shorter.' Cardiologists remain unenthusiastic about the Christmas swim. Nevertheless, it was the temperature which cured the stammer of a postman called Cliff. His speech impediment, the result of a war wound, disappeared every time he took the plunge. Another survivor, torpedoed at midnight on a troopship to Egypt, remained fourteen hours in the water. He owed his life, he said, to the Serpentine races – in particular the All-clothes Race, for which participants must wear a jacket, waistcoat, trousers, shirt and leather shoes to the total weight of 6lbs.

Alan's most vivid memory is that of a member called Teddy who came for a swim on the day of his marriage. 'During a race he lost his false teeth in the water – complete set, top and bottom. We spent hours diving for them. All you could see were a lot of feet waggling on the surface. Eventually we gave up, and went to a dentist for some provisional dentures. You could hear his teeth chatter throughout the service. The old ones were found six years later by police frogmen diving for a body.'

I go outside onto the diving board and look down the course. Through the chestnut trees comes the traffic's hum. A young swimmer joins me. This morning he had woken the geese up in the dark. He points out the swathe in the trees over the marker flag. Framed in the space, its clock face a distant yellow circle, is Big Ben. Like the torch in Hero's tower at Sestos. 'With the moon behind me, and my eyes on Big Ben . . . You can imagine,' says this Leander.

The scene seems chill for romance. Perhaps it was on this same stretch that Shelley's wife, pregnant and deserted by him, drowned herself in the cold grey water.

And so to the park's edge, overlooking Marble Arch and the old site of Tyburn gallows. When the gallows moved, the hangman's noose was sold. For the old rope, hawkers wanted a shilling an inch. Now gaudy paintings and cheap leather bags litter the railings running west along the Bayswater Road.

But here, men stand on upturned plastic milkcrates and freely bellow things that one day might have hanged them. 'One of the minor wonders of the world,' said Orwell of Speaker's Corner.

On a stepladder over a British Airways bag packed with gospels, a man with a grey moustache, a pea-green shirt, and a look of the lost speaks to a dozen tourists. On the railings behind hangs a notice board. 'Britain Under Judgement', it reads. 'Legalised Abortion' (in red), 'Sodomy' (green), 'No Cure For AIDS Virus'. On the ladder, under his gloved fingers, another notice proclaims the second advent of Christ. It has been proclaiming this every Sunday since 1947.

'When I was in my sins nearly forty years ago,' the man with the moustache shouts urgently, 'I looked alright walking about, but I was a sinner.' Each year, he reckons he introduces 350 people to the gospels in his bag.

Ten yards away, a small man in a brown tweed jacket, from which fluffs a red handkerchief, holds a Bible which has lost its covers. He struts more raucously, in a circle.

'I'm an ex-rapist, robber, thief, alcoholic,' he recites, his eyes focusing on the gaps between his audience. 'Praise the Lord, I'm not drinking. If you're a rapist, if you're a homosexual, you can change your ways. You hear that, lesbians and homosexuals?' he snarls at the much larger gathering next to him, who are listening to a young gay. One or two at the fringe boo him, and he pouts, unsmiling. 'I find a lot of fools in Hyde Park. They think they know all the answers. You may look nice outside, but each single person, each one of you stinks.'

A bearded drunk in a blue wool cap enters the circle, comes up to the speaker, and offers him cider from a yellow plastic bag. The gesture seems more a bribe that a test. 'Talk about yourself a bit more,' urges the drunk.

The man looks through him. 'Are your lives so empty, so lonely and messed up, on a Sunday when it's cold, that all you can do is come here and laugh? I used to come here and laugh. I spent years listening to this. But Jesus can take hold of your life. He can take it and change it. I no longer rob, rape, drink. I work in the poshest club in London . . .'

'Where is it?' asks a black man in a pin-striped suit, suddenly interested.

'If Jesus can change me he can change anybody,' the speaker continues imperviously.

The questioner is not satisfied. 'If you can't tell us where you work, how can we believe you about Jesus?'

Even the policeman, watching, smiles at this. Alert for anything anti-Semitic or treasonable, he monitors from a discreet distance outside the circle. Too close, and the speakers draw him in. It is an offence to break up a meeting, and to hold a meeting within a meeting, which means that a twenty-yard gap is imposed between Americans and communists, Bible-bashers and homosexuals. You never find hecklers speaking, the policeman says. He thinks it is a pity there's so much potential which isn't used. The subjects are much the same, and a lot of his time is spent referring speakers to Bow Street when their swearing gets out of hand. At this moment, he has his eyes on that chap over there, an elderly man in a tightly wrapping dark coat. He commands the biggest crowd of all.

'I do not come to educate,' this man shouts, punching his hands and delivering his practised prejudices. 'I come here to upset as many people as I can, and I believe I'm doing quite a good job.' The crowd laughs, appreciatively. 'As a Londoner, I have never done one day's work in my entire life. You people have got to ask yourself one question and one question only. Is it intelligent to work? Now, any comeback on what I've said so far?'

'Who's your shrink?' an American asks quietly, unheard, at the back.

The black man in the suit, having given up investigating the ex-rapist's club, decides to try his luck here. He puts up his hand. A glimmer comes into the speaker's eye. His finger stabs the air. 'Why don't you go back into the trees and look natural,' he says good-humouredly. The crowd roar. Face alight, he explains how the origin of the Black Power salute lies in a fist clenched around a branch. 'We knew the blacks were coming long before they did. And we prepared ourselves.' He points to the leafless chestnuts. 'We put railings round the trees.'

Nearby, against one of these railings, a young man with twitching eyebrows partially hidden by dark glasses stands on a blue milkcrate. 'What do you think this is?' he rasps at the group closely hemming him in. 'Some sort of entertainment stunt? I come here for intellectual stimulation. Maybe there's someone here who can explain the common cold. Or maybe there's some nuclear physicist amongst you.'

The drunk with the yellow bag forces himself to the front of the crowd. He is joined by a man holding a single banana. The drunk mumbles something. Whatever it is irritates the man in dark glasses.

'I want relevant heckling to what I'm saying.'

'But you're not saying anything,' says the man with the banana. The speaker splutters. 'Is this what six thousand years of human development has come to? Is this what Socrates and Plato bust their brains for?'

The crowd listening to the ex-rapist has dispersed and re-formed about a woman in a grey anorak and mess of blonde hair. Against the short ladder on which she stands is a notice with the words 'Hyde Park Gays And Sapphics'. 'I socialise with people regardless of their sexuality,' she is saying. 'We as gays and lesbians have as much rights as you heterosexuals. I would not strip myself to show off.'

'I wouldn't neither, if I was you,' comes a raised voice from the front.

'I'm a lesbian. I'm a parent. I'm a grandmother,' she continues gamely.

'Who's been fooling who, then?' comes the answering voice. At her feet, below the stepladder, appears the man with the banana. He holds it above his head and under her nose. 'Does this remind you of anything?' he asks.

I wander off as she tells him how disgusting, how *utterly disgusting* that is. Making for Hyde Park's open spaces, I walk past the bigot with the biggest crowd. 'To be a Londoner,' he is shouting, 'you've got to be first intelligent. And second good-looking. When you're a Londoner, you don't have to think. You know the answers. Not only do you know what you know. You even know what you don't know.

Alone, content, I return into the quiet park, knowing that, were Dr Johnson to materialise from behind a bush, adjust his wig and saunter into the city, he would not be tired of life today in London Town.

Selected
Bibliography

There are so many books on London that one even carries the title *Blimey! Another Book on London*. Invaluable among them are *The London Encyclopaedia*, edited by Ben Weinreb and Christopher Hibbert, and *Soft City* by Jonathan Raban.

Allen, Robert, and Guirdham, Quentin, ed., *The London Spy*, Anthony Blond, 1972

Ash, M., *A Guide to the Structure of London*, Adams & Dart, 1972

Ash, Russell, comp., *The Londoner's Almanac*, Century, 1985

Bainbridge, Beryl, *Sweet William*, Gerald Duckworth, 1975

Boswell, James, *Life of Samuel Johnson*, OUP, 4 volumes, 1934-50

Bourne, Richard, *Londoners*, J.M. Dent & Sons, 1981

Capek, Karel, *Letters from England*, Geoffrey Bles, 1925

Carvel, John, *Citizen Ken*, Chatto & Windus, 1984

Clayton, Robert, *Portrait of London*, Robert Hale, 1980

Coleman, Alice, *Utopia on Trial*, Hilary Shipman, 1985

Conrad, Peter, *Art of the City*, OUP, 1984

Le Corbusier, *Towards a New Architecture*, tr. F. Etchells, The Architectural Press, 1946

Crosby, Theo, *How to Play the Environment Game*, Penguin Books, 1973

Davies, Hunter, ed., *The New London Spy*, Anthony Blond, 1966

Len Deighton's London Dossier, Jonathan Cape, 1967

Duff, Charles, *A Handbook on Hanging,* The Journeyman Press, 1981

Egan, Pierce, *Life in London*, 1821

Eliot, T.S., *Collected Poems*, Faber & Faber, 1963

Engels, Friedrich, *The Condition of the Working Classes in England*, 1845

Escher, Lionel, *A Broken Wave*, Allen Lane, 1981

Esquinos, Alphonse, *The English at Home*, Chapman & Hall, 1861

Ford, Ford Madox, *Return to Yesterday*, Victor Gollancz, 1931

Ford, Ford Madox, *The Soul of London*, Gerald Duckworth, 1905

Le Gallienne, Richard, *Ballad of London*, The Society of Authors

GLC, *A Social Review of Greater London*, 1980

Goddard, David, *Blimey! Another Book on London*, Johnston & Bacon, 1974

Green, Benny, comp., *London*, OUP, 1984

Grosley, M., *A Tour of London*, 1765

Alexander Herzen: My Past and Thoughts. The Memoirs, tr. C. Garnett, Chatto & Windus, 1968

Hibbert, Christopher, *London*, Longman, 1969

Howell, James, *Londinopolis*, 1657

James, Henry, *English Hours*, William Heinemann, 1905

Jenkins, Simon, *Landlords to London*, Constable & Co., 1975

Knevitt, Charles, *Space on Earth*, Channel Four, 1986

Kray, Reggie, *Slang*, Wheel & Deal Publications, 1985

Lessing, Doris, *The Diaries of Jane Somers*, Michael Joseph, 1984

Massingham, Hugh and Paulene, *The London Anthology*, Spring Books

Mayhew, Henry, *London Labour and the London Poor*, Penguin Books, 1985

Milton, John, *The Poems of John Milton*, Longman Group, 1968

Moritz, Charles Philip, *Journeys of a German in England*, Eland Books, 1983

Morris, Jan, *Destinations*, OUP, 1980

Nelson, Walter Henry, *The Londoners*, Hutchinson & Co., 1975

Orwell, George, *Down and Out in Paris and London*, Victor Gollancz, 1933

Pearson, John, *The Profession of Violence*, George Weidenfeld & Nicolson, 1972

Powell, C.G., *An Economic History of the British Building Industry*, The Architectural Press, 1980

Pritchett, V.S., *A Cab at the Door*, Chatto & Windus, 1968

Pritchett, V.S., *London Perceived*, Chatto & Windus, 1962

Raban, Jonathan, *Soft City*, Hamish Hamilton, 1974

Roberts, Glenys, *Metropolitan Myths*, Victor Gollancz, 1982

Ross, Alan, ed., *Living in London*, London Magazine Editions, 1974

Rudofsky, Bernard, *The Prodigious Builders*, Martin Secker &

Warburg, 1977

Saussure, Comte de, *A Foreign View of England in the Reigns of George I and George II*, John Murray, 1902

Simond, Louis, *An American in Regency England*, History Book Club, 1968

Simon Sykes, Christopher, *Private Palaces*, Chatto & Windus, 1985

Smollett, Tobias, *The Expedition of Humphry Clinker*, 1771

Squire, J.C., *A London Reverie*, Macmillan, 1928

Stow, John, *A Survey of London*, 1598

Swift, Jonathan, *Journal to Stella*, 1712

Symons, Arthur, *London, A Book of Aspects*, William Collins, 1918

Taine, Hippolyte, *Taine's Notes on England*, Thames & Hudson, 1957

Tennant, Emma, *The Adventures of Robina*, Faber & Faber, 1986

Thompson, James, *City of Dreadful Night*, Reeves & Thompson, 1880

Torre, Paolo Filo della, *Viva Britannia*, Sidgwick & Jackson, 1985

Flora Tristan's London Journal, 1840, George Prior, 1980

Voltaire, *Letters Concerning the English Nation*, Peter Davies, 1926

Weightman, Gavin, and Humphries, Steve, *The Making of Modern London, 1815–1914*, Sidgwick & Jackson, 1983

Weinreb, Ben, and Hibbert, Christopher, ed., *The London Encyclopaedia*, Macmillan London, 1983

Weymouth, Anthony, *Of London and Londoners*, Methuen London, 1933

Wilde, Oscar, *Intentions*, 1891

Wordsworth, William, *Poetry and Prose*, OUP, 1973

Young, Michael, and Willmott, Peter, *The Symmetrical Family*, Routledge & Kegan Paul, 1973

Young, Michael, and Willmott, Peter, *Family and Class in a London Suburb*, Routledge & Kegan Paul, 1973

Magazine Article
Petit, Christopher, 'City of Dreams', *Time Out*, 1985